PERCHANCE TO IRELAND

Patrick H. Hughes

MINERVA PRESS
LONDON
MONTREUX   LOS ANGELES   SYDNEY

PERCHANCE TO IRELAND
Copyright © Patrick H. Hughes 1998

ISBN 1 86106 684 8

First Published 1998 by
MINERVA PRESS
195 Knightsbridge
London SW7 1RE

Printed in Great Britain for Minerva Press

PERCHANCE TO IRELAND

Contents

Avant-Propos

The Travels of Professor Pictet, 1801

In June 1801, or as he would have it *l'an IX*, Marc-Auguste Pictet, Professor of General and Analytical Physics at the Calvin Academy of Geneva, journeyed from Geneva to London with the ostensible purpose of meeting scientists and friends in England and Scotland. He also nursed a hope that he might be enabled to extend his tour to include Ireland where he was anxious to visit the Giant's Causeway and the Edgeworths, Richard Lovell and his daughter Maria, especially. Pictet, his brother, Charles, and another partner were the proprietors and editors of a journal published in Geneva with the significant title *La bibliothèque britannique*; significant because most people in Geneva thought that after Geneva most good things came from England. He hoped to use his journey *inter alia* as 'copy' for that journal. A chance meeting in London with an Irish scientist of Huguenot origin, Richard Chenevix, whose sister resided some ten or eleven miles from Edgeworthstown gave him the needed resolution to make the Irish journey also.

Professor Pictet and his partners did, in the event, publish an account of the entire journey but in book form under the title *Voyage de trois mois en Angleterre, en Ecosse et en Irlande*. Its contents were twelve letters he wrote back to Geneva as he travelled, plus two letters written on the basalts of Antrim by Dr William Richardson, Rector of Clonfecle, Moy, Co. Tyrone, who spent most of every summer in Portrush, then a small village, not even a parish.

Though England and France were at war in 1801 the scientists of both countries regarded the war as having nothing to do with them, at least as scientists. Pictet, therefore, though a French citizen, encountered no obstacle in his wish to meet scientists anywhere on his journey; if they were to be contacted, they were available to be met. Indeed he did meet an array of the top scientists in the three countries:

Sir Joseph Banks; Humphry Davy; William Wollaston; Count Von Rumford, with whom he stopped in London; Charles Greville; Sir James Hall; Richard Kirwan; not to mention the inventor, the 3rd Earl of Stanhope; the great agriculturalist, the 5th Duke of Bedford; and the politician/scientist/agriculturalist squire, Sir John Sebright, friend of Sydney Smith and Maria Edgeworth. He met with no reserve, indeed a modern reader may have cause to raise the eyebrows to find Pictet, the citizen of an enemy country, detailing in his book the locations of a couple of military strongposts and describing the manufacture and the qualities of a special kind of naval gun, the carronade, at a foundry outside of Glasgow.

Primarily this book concerns itself with the translation and annotation of the letters dealing with the Irish part of the journey, but that part cannot be lifted neatly out of the whole without doing less than justice to the part itself, for several reasons:

(i)   The scientists of the British Isles were a strangely integrated, interconnected lot as will be seen from notes and annotations. The Irish scientist (perhaps more correctly the French scientist) Richard Chenevix for example, was the rival of Wollaston in science, the mentor of Davy in science and his rival in the matrimonial stakes.

(ii) Perhaps the most important reason for including extracts and summaries from the English and Scottish letters is the perceptible change of atmosphere between Britain and Ireland which comes from reading the letters concerning Ireland side by side with those concerning Britain. Nowhere is the contrast between the two islands more in evidence than in transport. In both England and Scotland the major revolution brought about by the mail coach is fairly established so that the two travellers, Pictet and Chenevix, use the mail coach for most of their English and Scottish journey; Pictet indeed savouring the first part of the journey from London to York like a boy on his first train ride. In Ireland they depend entirely on dilapidated post-chaises. Canals in England are vital; in Ireland they are a picture in still life.

(iii) There are several good reasons why the Scottish outings with Sir James Hall should be, as they are, included. Not the least of these reasons are Professor Pictet's descriptions of the geological trip to the east coast of Scotland near St Abb's Head.

(iii) It would be a pity, for the sake of being over observant of the rubrics, to omit for example, the unconsciously amusing accounts of groups of scientists setting precedent for glue-sniffing by their inhalation of a certain type of gas in sessions at the Royal Institution of London; or, at a more serious level, of Professor Pictet's genuine delight and appreciation of the singing and organ playing at the Foundling Hospital, London, the institution founded by the seventeenth-century ex-sailor and colonialist Thomas Coran and patronised so well by Handel. Everybody who was anybody attended the services in the chapel of the Foundling Hospital. Only the best preachers were given the pulpit. The choir, composed only of inmates, produced some outstanding singers who were, at times, rented out for public performances, unfortunately to contract some undesirable habits in the process. Two of the blind orphans were organists of great talent.

One of the most interesting English visits was that to Charles, 3rd Earl of Stanhope, at Chevening during which Professor Pictet was shown a working model of an inclined plane to be used in canal navigation. The account of this visit was given in LETTER XI of Pictet's book. Included here is an extract from the letter dealing with that model in view of remarks that the Professor makes in his LETTER VIII on a canal he saw near the Phoenix Park in Dublin and further, of the understanding it brings to an attempt to adopt an inclined plane for a canal in Tyrone.

Finally, the two letters written by Dr Richardson and published in *Voyage de trois mois* are not here included since they are mostly given over to a sterile controversy.

On his journey through the United Kingdom Professor Pictet stopped with or made a longish visit to: Count Von Rumford, Sir Joseph Banks, Dr William Belcombe, Sir James Hall, Dr William Richardson, The Tuites of Sonna, the Edgeworths, the 3rd Earl of Stanhope, the 5th Duke of Bedford and Sir John Sebright and, as stated, he was accompanied on his journey from London to Edinburgh, to Portrush, to Sonna, Edgeworthstown and Dublin by the scientist Richard Chenevix. Fairly detailed biographical notes are given of all these people with the exceptions of Sir Joseph Banks, Stanhope and Bedford, these being excluded because it is considered that the lengthy notes required for them, would shift the emphasis unduly from the Irish part of the Professor's account of his journey. The note on Sir John Sebright is included for, among other rather obvious reasons, the relationship of Sir John with Richard Chenevix and Maria Edgeworth.

The order of the book is accordingly:

(i)   a biographical note on Professor Marc-Auguste Pictet (Part One);

(ii)   the translation of selected letters, parts of letters, summaries of letters or parts of letters with appropriate footnotes and notes, the twelve letters, that is, which compose Professor Pictet's book *Voyage de trois mois en Angleterre, en Ecosse et en Irlande* (Part Two);

(iii) the biographical notes referred to (Part Three);

(iv)   bibliography.

PART ONE

The Author

The Author – Marc-Auguste Pictet

The title page of the book here translated, *A Three Month Journey in England, Scotland and Ireland*, describes its author, Marc-Auguste Pictet, as Professor of Philosophy and Experimental Physics, Associate of the National Institute, Member of the Royal Societies of London and Edinburgh, of the Athenaeum of Lyons, and of several other literary bodies, Member of the Society of Physics and Natural History of Geneva and president of the Society established in the same City for the advancement of the Arts.

The name is said to be of Pictish origin, but in any case, two branches of the family settled in Geneva in the fifteenth century. One branch was known as Pictet de Rochement and the other as Pictet de Sergy; Marc-Auguste was a Pictet de Rochement, a family with its origins in la Haute Savoie.

Marc-Auguste was born in 1752. His father, in the Swiss mercenary tradition, had been an officer first in the pay of Sardinia and later in Holland. In 1762, when Marc-Auguste was ten, his father came under the displeasure of the Council in Geneva for dissenting from its condemnation of *Du contrat social, l'Emile* an incident which does not seem to have had any serious consequences: he did not find it necessary to go into voluntary exile in England as did those of his Genevese compatriots who found they could not endure the stultifying atmosphere of a hyper-conservative Government. Accepting the inevitable (not always to his disadvantage) was to be a characteristic of his son the scientist.

The Genevese School of Scientists

The boy's early education was directed by his father, a man of learning. Marc's first avocation was for the law and after the requisite study in that discipline he became an advocate, but drawn to science, which he considered his proper vocation, he forsook the law to become a student, at the Geneva Academy, of the great naturalist, de

14

Saussure (1740–1799). He accompanied de Saussure in his pioneering work in the Alps and contributed one of the maps which appeared in de Saussure's classic *Voyage dans les Alpes*. He did not follow his master in his work in petrology but he retained a keen interest in rock structure (an interest which at times, in its manifestation in his account of his Irish journey, non-geological readers might wish he had curtailed somewhat if they forget that it was this interest which took him to the Giant's Causeway). It was whilst working with De Saussure that Pictet developed the interest in meteorology that was to stay with him all his life. As indicated, his main contribution to science was to be in another field, that of heat. It may have been their mutual interest in the subject of heat which at length drew him and Von Rumford together; at any rate Von Rumford was the first to query the existing theory of heat, the caloric.

In the mid-seventies, Pictet became a professor at the Calvin Academy of Geneva and eventually, when De Saussure retired in 1786, Pictet, on his master's recommendation, succeeded him in his post but as Professor of General and Analytical Physics, becoming one of the chief scientists of a school which numbered such men as De Luc[1] and Prevost.[2]

Enthusiasm for science was second to that for religion at the Calvin Academy of Geneva and Professor Pictet became a knight errant in the cause of science, prepared to go anywhere, any time to meet men of science to share with them and increase his own knowledge. His account of his visit to England, Scotland and Ireland is, in a way, an expression of his dedication to science.

Napoleon too had an interest in science. As First Consul he visited Geneva and at a reception in his honour he came on a copy of the *Journal bibliothèque britannique* of which Pictet was a joint editor. A glance at the journal started Napoleon off in an animated conversation about geology, chemistry, mathematics with Pictet and other members of the staff of the Academy. By the time Napoleon could be induced to take his place at the table the meal had long since been served and the assembly had to be content with it cold.

It was the so-called Age of Enlightenment. Modern chemistry had begun in France with Antoine Laurent Lavoisier (1743–1794) who, with other Frenchmen such as Louis Vauqueline (1763–1829), made

---

[1]   De Luc, Jean André (1727–1817). Swiss pioneering physicist.
[2]   Prévost, Pierre (1751–1839). Outstanding physicist and man of letters.

very great developments in its study. In Scotland, Joseph Black (1728–1799) discovered magnesium and in the field of physics latent heat, a discovery which was to advance the perfecting of the steam engine. Professor Pictet himself, in an account entitled *Essai sur le feu*, published in 1792, may be said to have discovered radiant heat.

In his journey to England Pictet was to meet men who were uncovering the mysteries of electricity such as H. Davy (1778–1829), and W.H. Wollaston (1766–1828), who also discovered palladium (see the biographical note on Richard Chenevix).

In England the Hanoverian-born William Herschel (1738–1822) had discovered the planet Uranus in 1781, and two satellites of Saturn in 1789.

Geologists such as Dolomieu and Hutton were distressing religious fundamentalists with their new thinking on the origins of rocks.

Education

Several times in his account of his travels in the United Kingdom Professor Pictet shows himself critical of the type of education available there; he thought more highly of what was available in Scotland than in England with one exception. This was what was then proposed at the Royal Institution, established by Von Rumford and others, where the education was to be theoretical, practical and useful applying the discoveries and advances being made in science to industry. As can be seen in the biographical note on Von Rumford, the reactionaries were to prevent the Institution from developing as he had intended. In Scotland, though Pictet was impressed by what was being done in Glasgow, (as will be seen from his eulogy of the education of one the Edgeworth boys in the letter describing the visit to Edgeworthstown) he was far from impressed by a lecture he attended in Edinburgh where the lecturer, a Dr Allen, read his notes to the audience in a monotonous voice. Much of his strictures could be levelled at a good deal of the lecturing in universities in the United Kingdom today. For Pictet a lecture should first of all find a starting point in previous knowledge of the audience, it should establish rapport with the audience. Whilst the lecture should be prepared, the lecturer should be able to lecture and not just read, keeping his notes for reference. The lecture should come out of the lecturer's interest in and knowledge of his subject. With rapport established there should be community of interest between lecturer and audience which should lift the teaching out of the notes even to the extent that points not made therein would be made and developed. Professor Pictet develops the theme of his disappointment with his Edinburgh experience in the account of his travels in Scotland, much to the annoyance of a reviewer in the *Edinburgh Review*. Nevertheless, the lecturing Professor Pictet experienced in Edinburgh compared badly with the standard practice in the Calvin Academy of Geneva where he taught and was a very important influence.

He was a member of *La société economique* and *Le jury d'instruction* of the Academy, the former concerned with the finances and running of the institution, the latter with appointments, curricula, liaison with teachers and the whole area of what today would be called communication. He himself was regarded as a master of exposition. His inaugural lecture was said to be a brilliant performance, lucid and exact. The brilliancy did not end with the inaugural lecture. In the scholastic year 1811–1812, the German geographer Karl Ritter (1778–1859) was in Geneva accompanied by his students. He attended all Pictet's lectures in that year and later he asserted that for 'nothing in the world' would he have missed them.

> His exposition is magistral. Instead of the usual textbook approach of general theories and hypotheses he bases his exposition on an appropriate experiment correctly done under our eyes, going on by the analytical method to the study of the subject. He avoids the lack of order which this method risks for the course by general recapitulation, by tables and by clarification, giving a faithful résumé of the chapters and developing afresh the main theme of study.

For Ritter Pictet had an irresistible verve in his lecturing and recorded 'I have taken down the entire course in French and the notebook containing it is the most valuable thing I take with me from Geneva.'

It speaks a great deal of Maria Edgeworth, and her father, Richard Lovell Edgeworth, that such an accomplished educationalist as Professor Pictet should make the long journey to Co. Longford to visit them, that he should invite them to Paris and treat them with great favour and hospitality when there.

Marc-Auguste Pictet's was the guiding hand which in the difficult years, from the annexation of Geneva by France until the fall of Napoleon in 1815, steered the Academy of Geneva through risky waters. Napoleon, who disliked the Genevese, also had an exaggerated notion of the wealth of the Academy and had a fixation that it had hefty investments in England. To disillusion him Pictet, with a mixture of courage and flattery, wrote to him beginning with the address, 'Citizen First Consul, you love the truth'. Pictet pointed out that it would not be possible for the Academy to have funds invested in England derived from a considerable revenue because the Protestant population of Geneva amounted only to 73,000 souls. The adult money-earning members of this body had to finance, not only the Geneva Academy, but primary schools, a school of drawing, two other schools, as well as the upkeep of their temples and pastors: he asserted 'I have been a member of *La société economique* since its creation until last year... it has never had any funds invested with any foreign power whatsoever'.

In the year of 1801 Napoleon, as First Consul, concerned with the image of the Consular Government set up the Tribunat, a body composed of men of the highest standing and abilities, a sort of opposition whose function was to search out weaknesses in proposed legislation. Pictet became not only a member of the Tribunat but its Secretary.

When, in 1808, Napoleon established the Imperial University, the Academy of Geneva became a constituent, in fact one of the front-ranking constituent colleges of that University, Professor Pictet becoming an inspector thereof, a post he was to hold until 1814.

The Academy now had a friend at court, a much-needed one indeed, at the time of the birth of Napoleon's son whom he nominated King of Rome.

Te Deums were de rigueur in all state institutions including the Geneva Academy. Even though the good Protestants of Geneva were privileged to give their own version of the Romish *Te Deum* a member of the staff had qualms of conscience about attending the Academy's thanksgiving for the birth of the King of Rome and with his students stayed away from the ceremony. The Academy did not suffer for the want of respect to His Infant Majesty.

Genevese Politics

A good deal of what has been said under the heading of 'Education' has, of course, a political dimension, hardly to be wondered at considering the times and the fact that the Pictets were something of a dynasty in Geneva. At the time of the French Revolution Geneva was puritanical and very conservative although she was the oldest republic in Europe. Shock waves came from a France in turmoil, and there were those who wished to make Geneva a more liberal place. Trouble seemed almost a certainty, and as one of the leading citizens, Marc-Auguste, advocated peace and compromise but to no avail. In the commotion which followed he took the side of the Government. Order was eventually re-established but by then Pictet had lost a considerable amount of his worldly possessions and consequently he had to devote himself even more assiduously to his work and writings.

Then in 1798 the French annexed Geneva. Professor Pictet was one of a group of fourteen who met the French and negotiated terms. He seems to have adopted the new regime completely. For example he gave primacy to the Revolutionary calendar in his account of his journey in the United Kingdom giving it the title *Voyage de trois mois en Angleterre, en Ecosse, et en Irlande pendant l'été de l'an IX, (1801 v. st.)*[3] and as shown he took office under the French. It must be admitted, though, that there was an element of the 'if you can't beat them join them' approach in what he did. He looked after the interests of the Calvinists and their Academy in Geneva well.

More than this, he gained concessions for the Reformed Church in France, concessions indeed denied to the Catholic Church there until the signing of the Concordat in 1801. As Secretary of a Biblical Society in Geneva he promoted kindred societies all over Europe.

He was never a man to forsake his friends. Following his invitation to the Edgeworths when he met them in Ireland in 1801 to visit him in Paris Richard Lovell Edgeworth purchased a roomy coach and set out for Paris in the autumn of 1802 travelling via Brussels. He was accompanied by Mrs Edgeworth, Maria and Charlotte. Pictet, 'grown so fat and looking so well, more friendly no man can be', met them on their arrival in Paris.

But the name Edgeworth was not a pleasant one for the ears of the First Consul. The Abbé Edgeworth, who had ministered to Louis XVI

---

[3] *Vieux style* – old style.

at the scaffold and whose courage had won him the respect of the blood-thirsty mob howling at the King, was a second cousin of Richard Lovell. Whatever respect the Abbé had earned at the scaffold of Louis was more than cancelled out by his later ministering to royalist troops in exile, in fact he lost his life from a fever caught in doing so.

Napoleon, thinking that Richard Lovell was a brother of the offending Abbé, had him expelled from Paris. The family removed to a village outside the city whilst Pictet interceded with Napoleon on their behalf, pointing out the true relationship of the Abbé and Richard Lovell. When Napoleon had relented Pictet, accompanied by a M. le Breton, went at once to inform them that they were free to return to Paris. But Richard Lovell was not prepared to take any slight to the memory of the Abbé whom, despite his difference in religion, he revered, and if he could return only if the Abbé was not a blood brother, the slight to his memory was too much to take. To return was to accept the slight. Never was Professor Pictet's diplomacy more required. In the end, using a formula which seemed to satisfy all the parties, he succeeded in getting Richard Lovell to accompany him back to Paris.

Though he voted for the establishment of both the Consulate and the Empire as Tribune, Pictet tried to concentrate on the non-political aspects of his position. In this way he set out to emulate for the French the progress, in transport, which had so impressed him in England, and in the roads in Ireland. He became an advocate for canal and road building. He busied himself about Customs and his activities as an inspector of the Imperial University.

Yet, with all his adoption of the Empire, he was quick when Napoleon fell to seize the opportunity with others to re-establish the independence of Geneva and to become one of its chief magistrates.

Further Scientific Pursuits

His travels through Europe under Napoleon gave him plenty of opportunity for scientific observation. He always carried with him logarithm tables and a barometer, constantly using them. He managed to keep up some lecturing at the Academy though normally he had a stand-in there. Whenever his official duties took him to Geneva he never missed the opportunity to address the Society of Arts there, of which he was President.

He never lost interest in meteorology, and in pursuit of a plan of establishing observatories on high mountains throughout Europe, he visited the St Bernard Monastery in the Alps. There he sought and got the co-operation of the monks to record meteorological details using instruments which he supplied. He was very moved when he saw the rigours the monks endured and the austerity of their lives, so much so that he launched an appeal throughout Europe for much-needed repairs to the monastery and heating – no doubt on the principles used by his friend Von Rumford and applied in the Royal Institution of London; Heriot's Hospital Seminary in Edinburgh, and the Dublin Society in Ireland; as well as in his own home in Brompton Row in London.

In 1820 he visited Tuscany to return 'laden with scientific riches', and a wealth of scientific correspondents.

He deposited in the Institute of France an exact English yard which he had had made for the purpose by the Cumberland born genius at the making of astronomical and other instruments, Edward Troughton (1753–1835). He was, it may be stated, an associate correspondent of the Institute.

Always interested in mensuration he attempted on several occasions, apparently without success, to have the observatory at Geneva linked up with the grand triangulation network covering France and other European countries.

Bibliothèque Britannique

In 1798 Marc-Auguste Pictet, together with his brother, Charles and another man, Frederic-Guillaume Maurice, founded the journal *Bibliothèque britannique* (often mentioned in Pictet's account of his travels), an important aim of which was to make known to the French–speaking world British advances in science, industry, agriculture, and even the thinking of the Edgeworth father and daughter in the sphere of education. By Pictet's own claim in his LETTER III, the English had nothing on the Genevese in the matter of education. This journal and its name was to a great extent the product of what has been described as '*l'anglomanie des Genevois*' originating in and sustained by the strong Protestant sympathies between England and Geneva. The *Bibliothèque britannique* appeared throughout the

French occupation of Geneva and we have Maria Edgeworth's word for it that it was to be found in every library in France as she discovered on her French visit 1802–1803. Napoleon disliked it and the Genevese. He referred to Geneva as the most English city on the Continent and later the Genevese historian and economist Sismondi (1773–1842) said that if French was spoken and written in Geneva it was in English that people thought.

But Marc-Auguste Pictet knew how to survive. *Bibliothèque britannique* avoided political comment. The works of Byron, Maria Edgeworth, Dugald Stewart and such thinkers and writers did not merit condemnation and in this event the journal was to have a long life, under different titles. It kept its original name from 1796 until 1815. Catering for literature, science, the arts, and, until 1808 when the subject was dropped, agriculture; it was widely read in intellectual circles, wherever French was read.

In 1816, under the same editorship of the Pictet brothers and Maurice, the name was changed to *Bibliothèque universelle de sciences, belles lettres et arts* – *'faisant suite à La bibliothèque britannique, redigreé par les auteurs de ce dernier recueil'*. In this form it ran until 1835 when it became *Bibliothèque universelle de Genève, nouvelle série*. The *nouvelle série* lasted until 1845 to give way to the *Quatrième série* which ran until 1857. It continued under various mantles until 1924 when it was incorporated with the *Revue de Genève* as the *Bibliothèque universelle et revue de Genève* which became defunct in December 1930. The journal which owed itself to the initiative and breadth of interests of Marc-Auguste Pictet, his brother Charles and Frederic-Guillaume Maurice, thus bridged the long span between the Europe of the French Revolution and the first dictator of modern times, Napoleon, to that of the Nazis and Hitler.

Pictet the Scientist: Pictet the Politician

Making all due allowances for the dictum that, during the Anglo-French conflicts at the end of the eighteenth century and the beginning of the nineteenth, 'the scientists were never at war', it is still open to question whether Pictet disclosed in his account of his travels the entire reason for his journey to the British Isles in 1801. In his book he mentions unspecified motives and the desire to meet Count Von Rumford. He goes on to eulogise science as the one link which, though slender, holds the warring countries in communication whilst all other links have snapped. Thanks to the unsevered link, he would have it, he, though a French citizen, was able to visit England whilst she was at war with France.

His visit was made at a time when virtually all movement between England and France was suspended. He was Genevese but still a French citizen, moreover he was in good, perhaps close relationship with Napoleon. In November of 1801, the year of his visit, he was to become a member of the Tribunat set up by Napoleon and he must have known he was to become a member when he made his journey in the summer of 1801. To undertake the duties of that office he resigned from *La société economique* and *Le jury d'instruction* of the Geneva Academy shortly after his return from England giving as his reasons, 'the state of his health and numerous commitments'; but significantly, he was stated to be having disagreements with some of his colleagues on the Genevese bodies who were less accustomed than he to having problems solved in Paris rather than in Geneva. The 'state of his health' did not prevent him, a week after his resignation from the Academy bodies, joining the Tribunat and undertaking the duties of Secretary to it nor from simultaneously becoming Conseil General de Leman. The assumptions of these offices must be construed as comprising elements of the 'numerous commitments' he gave as part of his reasons for the resignation.

Shortly after Pictet returned from his English, Scottish, Irish journey Napoleon concluded a Concordat with Rome which re-established the right of public worship for the Roman Catholic Church in France. In LETTER IX, of his account of that journey, Pictet, describing his experiences at Holyhead where he had just landed from Dublin, shows himself much moved by the sight of the people of Holyhead attending church. It was a Sunday. He goes on to wonder when if ever the right to public worship would be restored in France. He was too close to the Government in Paris not to know that the Concordat was about to be signed so this piece of writing can only be construed as a piece of flattery to Napoleon. In fact, by the time the book came to be published, the editors were in a position to append a footnote praising the 'peace-making and conciliatory government' for the Concordat.

Mutual scientific interests can on the face of it explain his reception by Von Rumford who, before becoming a Count of the Holy

Roman Empire, had been knighted by George III as Sir Benjamin Thompson. Von Rumford had established himself as a scientist of note; he had also played a leading part in the establishment of the Royal Institution and he had the ear of many important people both in England and the Continent. When it came to the point he was able to get permission for himself and Pictet to sail from Dover to Calais at a time when a complete embargo was being enforced on all sailing to France. Pictet's influence would have facilitated the landing in France however it might have acted against the chances of Pictet and himself getting out of England – had it been known in England.

Then there is the mystery of the unidentified travelling companion with whom Pictet landed in England in June, 1801, a man who could speak no English. Von Rumford put the man up in his home because as Pictet says, he and Pictet set considerable store on being near to each other. He never again figures in Pictet's account of his travels.

Professor Pictet's Irish Timetable

This timetable presents difficulty. To begin at the beginning he dates his arrival in Donaghadee from Portpatrick as *'mardi matin 16e juilliet'* i.e. Tuesday morning 16th July. He did arrive on a Tuesday as his record of journeying and stops will show. He states that he arrived at Sonna on Sunday afternoon, when the family there was at church, and this is perfectly borne out by his record. Tuesday night he and Chenevix spent in the inn at Ahoghill; Wednesday night they spent with Dr Richardson in Portrush; Thursday night they spent in Coleraine; Friday in Armagh and Saturday in Kells, to arrive at Sonna on Sunday afternoon. But his dates are wrong. The Tuesday of the arrival at Donaghadee was the 14th July, 1801, as the interested can discover by referring to a calendar or to a newspaper or journal of the period, July 1801 e.g. *The Freemans Journal*. So Pictet and his travelling companion arrived at Sonna the home of Chenevix's sister, Mrs Tuite, on the Sunday afternoon of 19th July, 1801.

On that very evening, to allow the family to have the company to themselves of the newly returned brother, brother-in-law and uncle (which Richard Chenevix was to Mrs Tuite, her husband and her children, in that order) he retires to his room to write a letter to Geneva but he dates that letter 23rd July, 1801. The correct date should have been 19th July, 1801 and from that point error or mystery takes over in a big way. Reading his account of the sequence of events at Sonna, and indeed his own word for the intended duration of the stay at Sonna he spent three nights there: that of his arrival, that of the evening of the dinner in his honour and that of the evening spent in the intimacy of the family, so that he left for Dublin on Wednesday 22nd July, 1801, arriving there the same day. On his own account he sailed from Dublin on 4th August, 1801 to arrive in Holyhead 5th August, 1801, which he says, was a Sunday – but leave that for the moment to look at the sojourn in Dublin.

It is just not possible to escape the conclusion that Professor Pictet is being deliberately misleading about the length of his sojourn in Dublin. He arrived there on 22nd July. He represents himself as departing 4th August. Giving him the benefit of the two 'lost' days which seem to have dogged him from his arrival at Donaghadee, that would mean that he left Dublin on 2nd August which would have given him eleven clear days in that city. Yet he bemoans the shortness of the time available to him and the record of his activities in Dublin would cover three days at most – visits to the Customs House, to Kirwan, to the Dublin Society, to the Botanic Gardens and the abortive attempt to visit in the country the second highest personage in Ireland. This projected visit was likely to have been to the Chief Secretary, Abbot, but it could have been to the Chancellor, the notorious bigot Fitzgibbon the Earl of Clare.

Pictet's confusion, if that is the correct word, as to dates, might be traceable to the fact that until he arrived in England he had been using the Revolutionary calendar in which Thermidor straddled July and August; but there remains the fact that his account of his stay in Dublin is far from covering all his activities there. Whatever his relations with Abbot or Clare there is no doubt as to those he had with Napoleon and, whether or not he carried communication from France to Dublin, the state of affairs in Dublin in the wake of the Rebellion of 1798 was made known to Napoleon soon after the return of Professor Pictet to France.

There is a further point: he writes two letters under (or above) the date 5th August, 1901, the one on the boat going from Dublin to Holyhead, the other in Holyhead where he was held up for twenty-four hours. Later, writing in London, date 25th August, 1801, he refers to the 5th August, not in so many words, as being a Sunday. The sight of the good people coming from church to enjoy the lovely evening filled him with pity for France where public worship was then forbidden. Now, the 5th August, 1801 was a Wednesday; the preceding Sunday was the 2nd August, 1801; the succeeding one was 9th August; which means that his 5th August was three days from the previous Sunday and four days from that to come. Two questions arise: was he in Holyhead on a Sunday at all? Had he got his dates so very wrong? Elsewhere it has been suggested that the point he makes about the Sunday observance was made as a piece of flattery to Napoleon. Dare one suggest that he invented the Sunday and the Sunday scene to give occasion to the flattery?

Referring only to the English part of his visit, whilst it may be accepted that Professor Pictet was on a mission to gather scientific material, meet scientists and educationalists as well as to collect copy for his journal, *Bibliothèque britannique*, there was also a diplomatic dimension to his visit. Many people were anxious for peace. The Treaty of Amiens was signed in the year following Pictet's visit, fragile though that peace proved to be.

Though Professor Pictet does not say he did so, we can be sure that he renewed his appeal in person to that tireless worker on behalf of scientists, Sir Joseph Banks, for the imprisoned Dolomieu (1750–1801), held under particularly harsh conditions by the Neapolitans, as he had already written to Sir Joseph on the subject in April, 1801. He then had asked Sir Joseph not only to use his own influence on behalf of Dolomieu but to enlist the help of the British Ambassador to Naples, Sir William Hamilton.

Last Years

He spent the last ten years of his life in his native Geneva in literary work and social activity. He lived an unusually active life, sleeping little and at will, a lifelong custom. In the letters he wrote back to Geneva and which form the material of his book, he reveals himself as rising long before his hosts or travelling companion. In this he was true to the spirit of Calvin's Geneva where the only concession to winter was the rise at 6 a.m. instead of the summer 4 a.m.

He gave over a considerable part of his already scarce time to having improvements made in sacred music in Geneva and this included amendments in the versification of the psalms. His visit to the Foundling Hospital in London reveals his great interest in the singing and musical education of young people. He was very active in the affairs of a society, founded in Geneva, for encouraging young people to participate in sacred music believing, as he did, that such participation inspired spirituality and the practice of religion. But his interest in music extended to the secular. In the second decade of the nineteenth century there sprang up in the various Swiss cities and towns musical societies and each year a musical festival was held in some one of the larger towns. The musical society of Geneva was formed by Pictet.

But it was the *Bibliothèque universelle* as the *Bibliothèque britannique* had been renamed, which absorbed the major part of his time and energies. It was work he found compatible and fulfilling. As an editor he is credited with sure judgement in finding out the heart of the matter in a paper submitted to him for publication and for editing it so as to let the writer speak for himself. He himself contributed abundantly, writing on physics, astronomy, and surveying. But the policy of himself and his co-editors was paternal and politely censorious. They would publish views with which they did not agree (and it may be assumed that there were views they would not publish), but they would insert comment or a note saying where they did not agree with the writer. Despite all the political disturbances and the absorption of the editors in public affairs from 1796 to 1814 the *Bibliothèque universelle* was never once late: in fact it was never late in thirty years.

It was not only with the musical society that he was liberal with his time: he devoted a great deal of it to the Society of Arts. The principal purpose of this society, was the advancement of the skills of the craftsmen of Geneva in horology. Pictet made it his business to become acquainted with the craftsmen, hearing their problems and their suggestions for improving the quality of the clocks and watches they turned out and feeding back information he had gathered from his studies and travels. He was generous with his purse in the affairs of the Society and of its members and in other areas. He died a comparatively poor man.

More than once in *A Three Month Journey* Professor Pictet shows himself interested in collections. He himself built up one from the rocks of Switzerland. To these were added a collection of scientific instruments including those brought back from his travels, such as the snuffbox sextant made by Troughton.

Apart from his original work on heat, Pictet was not a pioneer. His mind and inclinations turned to the employment and adoption of useful and labour-saving systems. He displays this trait in his interest in the improvements made by Von Rumford in his home and in the kitchens of various institutions. These included fuel-saving stoves and draught-free rooms.

In our day it would be too easy to regard Pictet as an eighteenth-century Quisling for his co-operation with the French invaders of Geneva. Pictet was Swiss. His family had the mercenary (and the word is not used in any pejorative sense) tradition, with much of the outlook of Shaw's hero in *Arms and the Man*. He believed in accepting a situation as it was and in working on it from the inside to achieve the possible. He gained concessions from the French. In France itself he devoted himself to roads and canals and later to education. It may well be that he was being circumspect in avoiding spheres where fortune could change at the whim of a dictator; if so it is merely a further instance of his good sense.

His interests were wide-ranging, his capabilities outstanding; he learned German late in life. He was then a man of letters, a musician, astronomer, educationalist, mineralogist, physicist, a prolific writer and, be it said, a politician and traveller. His visit to England in 1801, the subject of this book, was his fourth to that country, the Scottish and Irish parts being new.

Being a scientist during the long Revolutionary and Napoleonic Wars meant belonging to an international – perhaps a supranational is the better word – community which existed apart from wars and the politics of war giving him very considerable influence throughout Europe.

In his book Professor Pictet reveals himself as a somewhat pompous man wanting to see a lot but without the time to see all there was to be seen. His pomposity makes him appear slightly silly at times as when he meditates on his crossing the narrow sea between Portpatrick and Donaghadee, or still more so when he describes his serpentine curve for measuring the quality of a day just passing. One wonders what the shrewd Maria Edgeworth, to whom he offered it, thought of this theory. His pomposity can make him forget his manners: he is hardly through the door of a host's house before he is impressing upon him how little time he has to give. His holier-than-thou lectures to Mrs Elizabeth Tuite on her manner of entertaining, his going into the room where the ladies were making tea to critically appraise their conversation, which he no doubt inhibited, were very insensitive. He added insult to injury by making it only too obvious to Mrs Tuite that he was using her home as a base to visit the Edgeworths.

If he appears sentimental over his farewells, it is as well to remember that the world of 1801 was a much bigger place than that of today. London was not just less than an hour or two from Geneva. You saw fewer people and those you saw engaged your attention and your memory more; a farewell had a great element of finality about it.

He became a widower early in life. There were three daughters of his marriage so that in his mature years he was surrounded by numerous grandchildren in whom he took much pleasure, and extremely busy as he was up to the end of his life he always ensured that he had time for his family every day. He kept up all his interests until his death but the affairs of the *Bibliothèque universelle* occupied more and more of his time. His death was sudden: '*il a succombé aux atteintes d'une maladie violente le 19 avril, 1825*'. He was seventy-three. It is somewhat remarkable that he, the last of the three to die, should have died within months of the other two editors of the *Bibliothèque universelle*.

The British Museum Catalogue of Printed Books attributes eight publications to him but in addition his output through the *Bibliothèque* must have been enormous. The long survival of the *Bibliothèque* under its various names and amalgamations is surely a tribute to its founders. They seem to have caught the spirit of the age.

PART TWO
The Letters

Letter I

London, 21 June 1801

My dear friends, when I first had the idea of undertaking the journey which has put such a distance between us, we all accepted that there were good and valid reasons for me to undertake it. Thus, apart from advancing our common interest in literature and science it was felt that it would enrich my knowledge and experience. Besides, there was for me the attraction of friendship in the person of Count Von Rumford residing here in London and whom I was most anxious to meet, a privilege I had never had.

So, it was with a vague feeling of anticipation that I set out. To date the realisation has far exceeded that expectation. There were possible obstacles about which we were apprehensive owing to the war which separates our two nations, two nations which have so much reason for highly mutual respect. Well, these obstacles have proved non-existent. Governments though at war realise the benefit of maintaining certain communications which transcend the dictates of politics and which confer reciprocal benefits. Such a realisation maintains a link which cannot be severed by war.

After a weary crossing dragged out by contrary winds to seventeen hours, I disembarked at Dover eight days ago and, setting out with a friend who had travelled all the way with me from Paris, we reached London the following morning at 8 a.m. It was Sunday and a profound calm reigned in the very populated quarters through which we passed. People, whether on foot or in carriage, were nowhere to be seen: indeed our coach seemed to advance by stealth and my companion for whom this phenomenon was new could not get over his astonishment at it.

Count Von Rumford as you know, had given me a long-standing invitation to an apartment in his house. I have accepted the invitation with pleasure. As I approached the house I experienced a lively sense of anticipation. I recognised it in the distance distinguished from the others in the terrace by its double encasements embellished with flowers at every storey. I enter. Though the Count and I have never met before we recognise each other at once. After the manner of the English we shake hands and here I am as much at home as if we had merely wished each other a happy night's dreams the previous evening.

I was anxious that my travelling companion,[1] who speaks no English, should be accommodated somewhere near me. Noticing my concern the Count at once declared that he would have my companion to stay with him also – and here we are in the same house together.

I shall, perhaps, describe his house for you one day – a house in which genius and good taste seem to have vied with each other in sheer pleasure in its building giving a home which is a charm to live in. But full as I am with the mastering impression made upon me by my visit to that great establishment the Royal Institution, which England owes to Count Von Rumford, I must begin with that and a summary description of it will make up the subject matter of my first letter.

Count Von Rumford accompanied us there the very day we arrived and unfolded in the most agreeable manner a detailed account of the Institution. I should be hard put to it to repeat his account in the same detail were I not to be helped by a report which appeared in

---

[1]   Professor Pictet gives no clue as to the identity of this person, nor does he mention him again. As nowhere else in his letters does Pictet withhold the identity of people mentioned it seems reasonable to suppose that the name is kept back here for some reason known only to Pictet.

the second number of the *Journal of the Institution* and which will serve as my text. The printing of this report was authorised at a meeting of the managers of the Institution on 25th May last [1801].

Description of the Institution with Pictet's laudatory comments omitted.

Letter II

Edinburgh, 18th July, 1801

Since I saw it three years ago I find London much grown. The streets and the grand residential areas called 'squares' are advancing on the countryside to the north in very rapid progression. It is a polyp-like vegetation at work on England. The population, I am told, is not increasing in proportion with this enormous proliferation of houses which is, for the most part, the result of a change in living habits. Hitherto the merchants lived exclusively in the central part of London known as the 'City' but now they regard it as essential to reside elsewhere away from the scene of their business. Possibly they gain in health by the arrangement, but, be that as it may, there can be no doubt that the architects are profiting by it. A small house, three windows wide having the kitchen below ground-level (they are all on this pattern), with ground floor, first storey, second floor and garret – two rooms on each storey, costs finished £1,200; yet, if it be remembered how the value of money has fallen in England, this price is low and, besides, the purchaser has something tangible for his money though of an extremely flimsy construction. Indeed the houses are so flimsy that they are something of a danger to passers-by when the framework only is in position.

On my way to visit Mr Greville's[1] superb collection of minerals at Paddington, one of those villages which

---

[1]   Greville, Charles Francis (1749–1809). Collector and MP with scientific interests. He had a common-law wife, Emma Harte, whom he sent to his uncle, Sir William Hamilton, the British Ambassador to Naples, to plead that she and Charles Francis be

the metropolis in its outward expansion has caught up with, I saw a pleasing stretch of water coming up to a quay over on my left but extending away out of sight in the distance. A large force of workmen were at work and a large brown barge was tied up at one of the wharves. Coming closer I conceived a very healthy respect for that stretch of water on learning that it is the terminal of a canal having already many branches running to every corner of England. By it distant Liverpool communicates with London. It will shortly link up the two seas. It is proposed to bring it right round the city. Is it possible to imagine a plan on a grander scale or one more beneficial? Were it not that supplying London with fuel and grain requires very considerable internal transport these canals might appear something of a luxury in a country where roads are in the highest state of repair.

Canal transport is slow but not costly; and where fast transport is needed the means are so plentiful and in keeping with the call made on them that there is nothing elsewhere to compare with them. Every hour of the day public coaches of all sorts and sizes run to the surrounding districts of the capital and every day vehicles of the same kind depart for the principal towns.

The main roads provide a spectacle of continuous movement. Some coaches have ten seats within and as many on the imperial. These moving mountains, drawn by as few as four horses but at a spanking trot, the

---

allowed to marry and be given support in their marriage. Emma remained in Naples to become Lady Hamilton – with a subsequent place in history as the mistress of Horatio Nelson.

Vaccination against smallpox was engaging the medical and science worlds, which were very much the same thing at that time. Pictet then gives some account of the results being obtained by both British and French doctors. Then he describes the experiments being carried out by the scientific fraternity, which invite comparison with the present-day craze for glue-sniffing, though it is claimed that Humphry Davy used these experiments to develop anaesthetics. As will be seen from the biographical note on that lady, Mrs Richard Lovell Edgeworth did not think much of these experiments about which Pictet allowed himself to become enthusiastic.

coachmen never using the whip, may be seen approaching from the distance. The horses, by their elegant shape, their shining hide, and their lively proud mane might take the eye of any judge of horseflesh. In your fancy you might see what you take to be standards of many colours floating on the imperial: what you really see are the ribbons and the petticoats of your English ladies who, so retiring otherwise, do not hesitate to mount on the top of a carriage there to expose their complexions to the rude winds, winds increased twofold in strength by the speed of the coach. But hardly has this leviathan drawn level with you than it is in the distance and out of your view no matter how keen-sighted you may be.

Last year we published in the *Bibliothèque britannique* an account of another discovery in relation to the nervous system, an account which found many people on the Continent incredulous. I refer to the effects of inhaling nitrous oxide gas into the lungs. An account of these effects has been published by Dr Beddoes in such an enthusiastic manner that his readers have received them with a mixture of doubt and wonder. The experiment which we made in Geneva fell short of our expectations. In the event we got no further than making ourselves dizzy. We did not experience any of those agreeable and unusual sensations of which both Dr Beddoes[2] and Mr Davy[3] have spoken, the latter being the first to inhale the gas.

---

[2]   Beddoes, Thomas (1760–1808). Physician and scientific writer. After graduating (MD, Oxon.) he visited Paris and met Lavoisier. Returned to England and set up, at Clifton, his Pneumatic Institution for the treatment of disease. Humphry Davy worked there under him.
     Married (1794) a daughter of R.L. Edgeworth, Anna, full sister of Maria, so becoming more intimately part of the curious network of relationships and connections between so many of the people Professor Pictet met.
[3]   Davy, Humphry, later Sir Humphry (1778–1829). Discoverer of the electric arc; inventor of safety lamps for coal miners; pioneer in electrolysis; with Beddoes he may be said to have laid the basis of anaesthetics. The poet Coleridge used to attend his lectures for the beauty of his speech and imagery, saying that if Davy had chosen poetry instead of science he could have been a major poet. Richard Chenevix, who

I was very much hoping that in the course of my travels I should have the opportunity to witness the effects, if not indeed to experience them on my own person. As it turned out my hopes were fulfilled in both regards. The subject came up in the first instance in a lecture on respiration given by Mr Davy at the Royal Institution and which I attended. The lecture over, Mr Davy observed that the meeting was too large to perform the experiment, besides, depending on the temperament of the subject, a degree of excitation could be produced which might well be frightening for some of the ladies present. However if there were those present who were willing to conduct the experiment after the lecture then the necessary facilities would be provided. In the event quite a number of enthusiasts, including ladies, waited behind for the experiment and two or three persons volunteered to undergo it. I shall now describe it. To begin with the gas is fed by the established method into a medium-sized bladder until it is about three-quarters full – regarded as the appropriate dose. The bladder is furnished with a tin-plate tube bent at the extremity. The subject sits. He voids his lungs of air by a strong exhalation. He holds his nose with one hand putting the tube from the bladder into his mouth with his free hand. He then breathes the gas into and out of his lungs.[4] Already very familiar with it Mr Davy was the first to undertake the experiment. Observing him with close attention I noticed that at the third or fourth breath he grew pale and that his lips went a violet colour. The movements of his chest became more and

more frequent, indeed violent and as he reached the final stages he was inhaling and exhaling all the

---

travelled with Professor Pictet to Scotland and Ireland, will have reason to be both thankful to and hurt by Davy.

Incidentally, is Pictet correct in saying that Davy was the first to inhale this gas? It was discovered by Joseph Priestley (1733–1804), chemist and theologian, born at Fieldhead near Leeds.

[4] One of Gillray's most mischievous cartoons depicts Davy, Rumford and other notables engaged in a gas-inhaling session.

contents of the bladder with each breath. Judged by the way the muscles of his face flexed he would have appeared to be in pain, but as we were to see he was far from being in any pain. At length he let go of the bladder and in an ecstasy he jumped up from his chair and began running about the floor laughing so heartily that all present began to laugh with him. He stamped with his foot, he swung his arms and appeared to be in need of muscular activity. The reactions did not endure more than a few minutes: by imperceptible degrees he returned to his normal state and then with his usual clarity he described the entire order of the sensations he had experienced.

One of the company anxious to try it out on himself came forward. Again I noticed the same external manifestations as with Mr Davy but when this person had exhausted the bladder he displayed a heightened state of agitation which rapidly became so extreme that an effort was made to have the bladder from him but he doggedly gripped it with one hand still keeping his nostrils closed with the other. Finally the bladder was taken from him. With his eyes raised to heaven he sat on his chair in a state of ecstasy still holding his nose in the most grotesque fashion. The entire company roared with laughter but this did not put him out in the least. At length still in uncontrollable laughter he rose from his chair entirely pleased with what he had experienced and still continued to experience.

Arrangements were made for a further session for the following day, a Sunday. Before that session Pictet attended divine service.

The following Sunday I eagerly made sure to attend divine service in the chapel of the Foundling's Hospital,[5] the institution which I had admired so much

---

[5] The Foundling Hospital was set up by the ex-sailor and colonialist, Thomas Coram (1668-1751) who was appalled at the sight of children literally being thrown on the scrap heap by besotted parents, themselves the victims of the cheap drink policy adopted to take grain off the market for distilling – 'drunk for a penny, dead drunk for

and which it gave me so much happiness to describe three years ago. I know of no religious edifice whose interior is laid out with such taste and so appropriate for its purpose as is this one. The organist rendered a very acceptable piece of music, a kind of lovely cantabile and by his light and shade, his very skilled variation of the stops, he created a truly moving effect, an effect which was complemented when the choir of children disposed amphitheatre-wise round the organ began to sing. I was simultaneously gripped in all my senses, it was a performance touching, more, overpowering – those heavenly voices, the devotion of all present, the sublime purpose; all these impressions combined begot in me an indefinable emotion accompanied by the tears I could not hold back. Though the Anglican service is very long it is varied and two hours went by without feelings of weariness, much less boredom, nor in any way dimming the sense of sustained elevation experienced all the while.

Later in the day Professor Pictet went to the premises of the Royal Institution in the company of Davy, Von Rumford, Chenevix, Wollaston and two Irish MPs, John Blachford and Henry Tighe for a further experiment with nitrous oxide laughing gas, which is described in much detail, especially the observations on the operation of temperament on the effects on the subject. Pictet arranged for Von Rumford to check his pulse. This behaved very irregularly. During the rest of his stay in London Pictet busied himself about meteor rock and with a visit to Sir Joseph Banks (1743–1820), President of the Royal

---

twopennies, clean straw for nothing' – children who, Coram thought, should have been peopling the colonies.

Handel's name is for ever associated with the Foundling's Hospital. In 1750 he gave a performance at which the anthem, since known as the *Foundling Anthem*, 'Blessed are they that consider the poor' was sung. His performance raised £728. He contributed an organ to the chapel. On his death he bequeathed 'a fair copy of the score and all the parts of the oratorio called *The Messiah*' to the hospital.

Pictet's delight at the service was well motivated. On the day he attended the reader was Rev. James Moore, the Preacher Rev. John Hewitt, the organist Wm. Russell. Only the best readers, preachers and organists were employed. The singers were under the wonderfully voiced, blind Blanche Thetford, a foundling. A naturally skilled musician, Blanche could deputise at the organ.

Society, scientist and the friend of scientists in distress (e.g. the imprisoned Dolomieu) and explorer with Cook on his famous voyage. The story is here resumed with Pictet describing how he and Richard Chenevix made the arrangement to travel via Scotland to Ireland.

As you are aware I left Geneva with the confirmed intention of travelling as far as Scotland and that I nursed a desire to get to Ireland also, though I was not optimistic about having that desire fulfilled. Fortune, which so far has treated me like a favourite child, has further pampered me with the means of getting to Ireland and I shall now be able to make the entire tour in the most pleasing manner. Von Rumford and myself have profited from the kindness of Mr Chenevix[6] who very obligingly performed some experiments for us in the Count's laboratory on the inflammability of the gas released by phosphorus of chalk in different circumstances and in contact with other gases. Mr Chenevix, the experiment completed, informed us that he was departing forthwith for Ireland where he was born.

"And I go to Scotland," I remarked, "though I wanted very much to go to Ireland also."

"Good then, if you come afterwards with me to Ireland I shall go with you to Scotland."

"I would not need much persuasion."

"When do you propose to set out?"

"Monday."

"That will suit me."

"For my part I would like to halt a day or two in York to visit an old friend."

"I shall have no objections to stopping whenever and wherever you have a mind to."

"Admirable. I shall go now to book our seats on the mail coach. We shall set out at eight o'clock on Monday evening and by Tuesday midnight we shall have covered the two hundred miles to York where we

---

[6] See the biographical note on Chenevix.

shall spend the next twenty-four hours. Catching the mail coach the following day we shall cover the next two hundred miles to Edinburgh in thirty hours. Are you completely decided?"

"Completely decided and at your service."

The mail coach is, to my way of thinking, one of those inventions which mark a civilisation at its highest achievement. Every evening at post-time, four-seater Berlins drawn by four horses set out for all the main ports from the Post Office by the main roads radiating from the capital. The rear of the Berlin projects to form a letter bin. To the lid of the bin is affixed a very comfortable seat for the guard. The entire body of the vehicle is suspended on a well-sprung carriage. The coachman and guard, befitting their service under the King, are dressed in red livery trimmed with lace. The guard armed with a blunderbuss carries a horn to announce the approach of the coach at every stage and to each town.

Four travellers can travel on the Berlin, but once on it the traveller is obliged to surrender completely to the timetable of the journey. An hour in twenty-four is allowed for a meal and in addition there are two more halts of twenty minutes each. If the passenger has not acquired the ability of sleeping in a carriage then there is no option but to stay awake though the roads are so well-kept and the carriages so good that it is not difficult to sleep in them. For the invention of the mail coach the country is indebted to Mr Palmer.[7] The Government, in recognition of the advantage it procures by having a substantial part of the cost of transporting the mail borne by the passengers who use the coaches, granted Mr Palmer a pension of £1,000 per annum fifteen years ago. Recently, I am informed, Mr Palmer, finding, as a consequence of the

---

[7]　Palmer, John (1742–1818). The owner of two theatres, one in Bristol, one in Bath. He was so weary of the delays and inconveniences in getting from one to the other that he proposed to the government the establishment of a mail-carrying service subsidised by passengers. This became the revolutionary postal system.

continuous departure of the real worth of money from its face value, that his pension was worth much less to him than when it was granted, petitioned Parliament to have it doubled in money terms. Parliament voted the increase.

You can imagine us then on the mail coach at eight o'clock on an evening of superb weather; there is little or no night in England at this time of the year.

The relays are for fifteen or sixteen miles, and the change is so quickly made that there is scarce time to notice it. The traveller rides on air, remote even from the ordinary remarks of his fellow travellers with no immediate regard for crops, buildings, or local customs. Hedges, houses, carriages go past and always in the twinkling of an eye.

Time itself flies. By eleven o'clock of the following day we are in York where I greet my old friend, Dr Belcombe,[8] there at the Inn to meet us and to bring us to his house.

Those who have had the experience of a reunion following a separation of ten years as was the case with us have no need for me to describe that experience: others would not understand it. I shall say no more on the subject. We had supper with the family.

Dr Belcombe had spent two years in Geneva and two of his six children were born there. It would be the next day before we should have the pleasing sight of all the family gathered together at one board. Mrs Belcombe appeared, as well she might, delighting in her family. Her three eldest daughters, already young ladies of consequence, combine in their persons all those sound qualities the better English education bestows and all the pleasing graces in which the French excel. In the privacy of the family we were to enjoy

---

[8] Belcombe, Dr William (1757–1818). In 1801 was visiting physician to the Retreat, an enlightened hospital for the treatment of mental illness. His son, who succeeded him at the Retreat, presumably one of the company who entertained Pictet and Chevenix, was, according to Hunt, the historian of the Retreat, a friend of Dickens. Perusal of the letters of the writer, on which this claim is founded, does not bear it out.

the display of their accomplishments – drawings, music, dancing, duos, ballets, even trios.

One by one all their friends of the Geneva days were recalled in conversation, for memory is most faithful in its recollection of friendship and for long we had to reply to the questions about those friends.

Next day they brought us on a sightseeing of York. In a very pleasant walk we made the tour of the walls to a vantage point where stands an old castle in ruins. Here there were several fully-grown cherry trees. The owner of the castle and cherry trees very kindly and hospitably did us the honours. I found the cherries of York just as good as our own though they are grown at the fifty-fourth degree of latitude. The view from this summit is superb, but the thing which most attracted my eye was a very large building of really fine architecture very close to us. Before the building there was an extensive plot of grass and there were two pavilions with colonnades on both sides. Expecting the answer to be an archbishop, at least, I asked who it was who resided in this palace, to be told that the place was the prison and that the persons to be seen walking about with the mere appearance of sightseers were in fact prisoners, some there as debtors, others were there for crimes, of varying degrees of seriousness. Those incarcerated for more serious crimes were in a second enclosure closed by an iron gate. A family of tame deer of the lovely spotted variety moved across the grass: if ever I am to be imprisoned and I am to have any choice in the matter then with my hands joined in supplication I shall beseech that I be sent to the prison in York.

The cathedral there is regarded, and rightly so, as one of the outstanding examples of the Gothic.

But the good Calvinist Pictet had really not much time for cathedrals.

We saw there what is normally to be seen in cathedral windows and memorials... Pressed to stay till the morrow we resisted the invitation. Tied as I was to rendezvous fixed for a definite date in Edinburgh I was very mindful of how short a time I had before me in which to make the journey there: I wanted to board the very next mail coach from London. It arrived – full to capacity, not a seat to be had for love or money. Robbed of the choice whether to go or stay, it was at once clear that to stay was what we most wished for.

Pictet, as ever, in a hurry was thus given the opportunity to engage in further experimentation with the 'laughing' gas. He gives an account, not recorded here, of these experiments which were interrupted by the arrival of the mail coach.

We were still engaged with the experiments when someone came to inform us that the mail coach had arrived and that there were places for us on it.

Farewells were exchanged just as if we were to meet again the following day. At midnight we were on our way to Edinburgh, a journey which was to take thirty hours. Here am I four hundred miles from London and six degrees of latitude further north from my friends in Geneva. I arrived in Edinburgh on Saturday; I leave today, Friday, for Glasgow where we shall stop for no more than one day whence we go straight via Portpatrick to Ireland with the Giant's Causeway, Edgeworthstown and Dublin my chief places of interest.

Letter III

Glasgow, 10 July, 1801

It is in Glasgow that I again take up my pen to tell you about Edinburgh. We left that city yesterday afternoon at four o'clock and we were drinking tea here in Glasgow at ten having covered in six hours, forty-three miles by the *Telegraph*, one of those flying coaches I have already mentioned to you.

Since people generally rise very late[1] in England my day is divided very distinctly into two parts. The first being entirely my own to do with as I please, I give a good portion of it over to my correspondence with you. The second, which does not commence before nine or even ten o'clock, belongs to everybody else. Once launched into the current of things to see and people to hear I live exteriorly, so to speak: I have no longer anything but eyes and ears so that it is goodbye to reflection, goodbye to the pen – at most a furtive pencil to label some observation for the memory, because you must not rely upon it on a journey: no matter how clear is a particular impression it is soon buried under what comes after and there is left for you a tangle of impressions which, without notes, you can only unravel with great difficulty. You get back late in the evening; you are weary in body and in mind; you think of your friends – but you do not write to them.

Before we arrived in Edinburgh we discovered that too much foresight can lead at times to

---

[1] Late, that is, by the standards of a man from Geneva where people rose at 4 a.m. in summer and 6 a.m. in winter.

disappointments. Among the people we wished to meet by coming to Scotland was Sir James Hall,[2] the author of some unusual experiments in the basalts and upon which we have reported.[3]

We understood him to be at his estate at Dunglass some thirty-three miles from Edinburgh and quite close to our way. To gain time we, in our wisdom, decided to leave the mail coach at the stage before Dunglass. We arrived at his home to discover that Sir James was in Edinburgh where he had been awaiting our arrival for several days. Sadly we took to the road again: a further misfortune befell us: a mile from Haddington, the next stage, we lost a tyre from one of our wheels. Perforce we shank it to Haddington. At Haddington there is not a horse to be had for there is a review of yeomanry [cavalry militia] which attracts the countryside as sightseers and with them – the horses. If this is not enough, the servant-man of my travelling companion,[4] subject, ever since he was poisoned by mushrooms, to violent spasms of the intestines, has one of his attacks. We bring him to the apothecary on the corner who administers to him a mixture of laudanum, ether, yellow amber, and such like which gives him considerable relief. We go as in the order of such things to pay for the medicine expecting that it will cost at least as much as in England, and that is saying plenty. "Gentlemen," comes the reply, "it has been a great pleasure to have been of service to you; I shall not accept a fee." This incident creates a favourable first impression of Scotland we are never to have belied.

Another favourable impression which endures with us is the superiority of Scottish agriculture. Nowhere are there better farms than those we have seen right

[2] Sir James Hall (1761–1832) of the Scottish School of Naturalists. See biographical note.

[3] *Bibliothèque britannique, Science et Arts* vol. X p.62.

[4] This is the only mention of Chenevix's servant man yet presumably he accompanied his master all the way.

and left on the recent part of our journey, and especially on the five miles it takes to pass through the Dunglass estate.

We have it from the landlord himself that there are among his tenants some large enough to be paying a rent of 2,000 pounds sterling. The question as to whether large farms should be encouraged would on the evidence of this countryside be answered in the affirmative – at least in the case of a resident landlord.

*

The entry into Edinburgh is by the dirtiest, the narrowest and the meanest street it is possible to imagine; but where this street ends at the top of a steep hill there comes instantaneously into view a city with an incomparable situation: its buildings of cut stone, a marvel of regularity, a city, indeed, the like of which there are few in Europe. It stands on a hill separated from a second hill by a deep ravine across which a very elegant bridge has been constructed to connect the two hills. Here, just as in London, the erection of new buildings is everywhere in evidence and if building work is a sign of prosperity, then Edinburgh abounds in prosperity; but the appearance of the middle and lower classes also suggest that the prosperity is not unmixed, for they are in general more poorly dressed people than the people of these classes we saw in England and much less clean. The common women go bareheaded and barefooted: I have often met them thus in the principal streets, clothed in silken mantle, becoming in all other respects – but barefooted. Going barefooted would appear to be a common custom here though it is a custom it would be difficult to explain by the weather which is neither dry nor hot.

The one thing wanting in this lovely city is a river; but then it is situated but a short distance from an inlet of the sea, the Firth of Forth, which resembles a lake – I had almost said the Lake of Geneva – and which gives much grandeur and life to the scene. In turn the tide converts this lake into a great sea on the edge of which, about one mile from Edinburgh, stands the highly commercial port Leith, from where boats sail for all parts of the globe.

Sir James, realising that we were hard pressed for time, made the very agreeable proposal that we make a lithological excursion into the surrounding countryside. Off we set hammer in hand, or, more correctly, hammer carefully concealed beneath our cloaks, for it was Sunday and we wished to avoid giving scandal. There are three hills overlooking Edinburgh and two of these could pass for mountains. We climbed all three one after the other for these areas contain geological features which have relevance to the controversy between the Neptunists and the Vulcanists[5] of which I have often spoken and which is again on the boil. Sir James, who has entered the fray, was anxious that we

---

[5]   The Neptunist-Vulcanist controversy centred on the origin of rocks and in particular on the origin of basalts and granites – what today are called igneous rocks.

The Neptunists were followers of the German naturalist Abraham Gottlob Werner (1750–1817), who felt that all rocks were by first origin the result of chemical precipitation which had taken place in a universal ocean. Werner gave a threefold classification of rocks: i) primitives; ii) transition; iii) floetz. Primitives were formed by chemical precipitation, pure and simple in the undiminished universal ocean. Transitions were formed in the ocean as it subsided when chemical production or action took place on the primitives in the course of formation. Floetz rocks owed their existence to combined mechanical and chemical action brought about by a still further lowering of the waters. The primitives contained granites, gneiss and some basalts. The transitions contained limestones. The floetz contained sandstones, rock salt and some basalts. The significance of the term Neptunist is thus evident.

The Vulcanists postulated, after a great deal of observation in the volcanic regions of the world, that basalts and granites were igneous in origin.

Briefly, Sir James was convinced of the igneous origin of basaltic rocks. His experiments with these rocks left him in no doubt of the matter. Much pioneering work on the origins of rocks had been done by James Hutton (1726–1797), who was in no doubt as to the igneous nature of basalts. His opinions, published in his *A Theory of the Earth*, were at the time revolutionary. Sir James was a follower of Hutton but with reservations which in one respect left him with if not a foot, at least a toe in the other camp. He believed that floodwaters, by which presumably he meant the flood of the Old Testament, had been a factor in the physical shape of things around him, as Professor Pictet is to say, quoting his old teacher De Saussure, who seems to have confused glacial activity, evidence of which abounds in Switzerland, with marine activity.

should know his thinking on the matter and he set to with animation but with ability to develop the theories to which he adheres.

Sir James, who prides himself in being one of Hutton's disciples, disagrees with his master on one point nevertheless: to explain the actual state of the surface of the earth he looks to a sudden and very violent activity of mighty flood waters descending from the mountains to the plains, an important event the evidence for which my illustrious colleague, De Saussure, has found to be established at every step in the vicinage of Geneva.

In referring to those who advanced the igneous explanation as Vulcanists – as opposed to the Neptunists who advance the agency of water – it would be unfair to represent them as advocating in their theory a motivating force analogous to that which produces the volcanoes we know. Their motivating force is an entirely different thing. It is a very high temperature affecting the entire crust of the earth at unknown depths coupled with an enormous pressure acting on the liquefied masses and resisting the release of the elastic fluids. Then finally there is a very slow cooling. Such are the characteristic parts of their hypothesis. Kirwan,[6] to avoid equivocation, has proposed what appears to me a very happy term. In his *Elements of Mineralogy* he designates those who are of his mind as Plutonists... Here it is no longer the forges of Vulcan; the explanation is sought much deeper; in the sombre plutonic kingdom which is, according to him, the furnace of that universal conflagration.

First of all we climbed Calton Hill which rises from the edge of the city and from the summit of which is to be had one of the loveliest views it is possible to imagine. On it are the Observatory and the post of the Corps of Signals. The rock of which the hill is composed looks much like lava; it is pitted with

[6] Kirwan, Richard (1733-1812). Irish scientist and mineralogist, met by Pictet when he reaches Dublin.

holes, some empty, some filled with calcareous spar. But nevertheless there is no sign of a volcano anywhere in the neighbourhood.

On our way from there to visit the two other hills. Salisbury Crag and Arthur's Seat, we passed the great block of basalt, or whin, on which Edinburgh Castle is built; its escarped promontory, rising above the hill on which the old city stands, constitutes a veritable fortress. Prehnites and zeolites are to be found here and in the massive rock Dr Kennedy,[7] the Vauqueline[8] of Edinburgh, has discovered, *inter alia* zeolite so phosphorescent that even the touch of a finger in the dark causes it to give off a train of light. He has very kindly given me a sample which you shall see on my return.

I have used for the first time in my letters the word whin. It has sounded so often in my ears in conversation with Scottish lithologists, and I shall, moreover, use it so often myself that I must, according to my ability, attempt to give it a precise meaning.[9]

Whin or whinstone is a generic term. It designates a type of rock, of which the basalt is, strictly speaking a specimen. In general it is a hard rock but varies in its hardness. In colour it is more or less dark, shading by time to greenish. It breaks under the hammer in no regular manner. Its grain, at times dull, at others brilliant and even, distinctly manifesting crystallisation, displays every degree of fineness. If the perfectly easily recognisable whin be taken as the centre, so to speak, of this type of rock, departures from the centre will embrace the traps at one end and the serpentine, the hornblendes, the porphyry and even the granites or the grits at the other. We have found all these varieties of the rock on our Scottish tour and we also found them in all the northern parts of Ireland. Mr Chenevix,

---

[7] Kennedy, Dr Robert. Scottish physician and geologist.
[8] Vauquelin, Louis Nicolas (1763–1829). French chemist.
[9] So called, though Professor Pictet does not say so, because whin or gorse grows very frequently above it. It is an igneous sill or dyke.

skilled in the principle of French chemical nomenclature has very felicitously suggested that that principle be applied to the varieties of this rock and that I designate them accordingly as they diverge from the indisputable and perfect whin by the epithets, whinney, whinnish and whinlike.[10] From that point onward classification became more easy for us and we readily agreed with each other in the application of these gradational adjectives to this or that sample it was our concern to identify and name. I conclude that this principle of nomenclature has a function to perform in lithology...

On our return from this first excursion Sir James had us to dinner with a few of the scientists from Edinburgh. This manner of getting to know people combines several advantages: the conversation is more varied and animated, the intellect is nourished simultaneously with the body. It would be difficult to put a given number of hours to better employment, and during our stay in Edinburgh Sir James never failed to favour us in this way with his hospitality.

He was particularly anxious that we should have the opportunity of examining certain geological features at a place on the east coast of Scotland near to his Dunglass estate about forty miles from Edinburgh. I demurred for a reason which has never ceased to constrain me on my entire journey, namely the shortage of time at my disposal. But Sir James would hear of no refusal and arranged it so that we should be back in Edinburgh in thirty-two hours, having, in the meantime, seen all he wished us to see. There was nothing for it but to give in to go with him. Setting out at 6 a.m. we covered the greater part of our journey by carriage following the London Road as far as Press

---

[10] In the original French, *whinique, whinneaux, whinatre*. Professor Pictet's enthusiasm for whinstone, as the *Edinburgh Review* wryly remarks, seems to have run away with his common sense. One might have expected differently from Geneva. Are we to assume that the canny Scotsmen in the company joined in this game of whins or only the Irish-Frenchman and the scientist from Geneva?

Inn, at which point we found saddled horses waiting us as arranged by Sir James. Mounted we made our way to the coast.

To observe this coast to the best advantage it is necessary to take a boat but in the event we were to be prevented from doing so for the wind was too strong and the sea too rough.[11] As we rode to the coast we suffered a regular downpour but I was well fortified against it by a type of cloak peculiar to Scotland, the plaid which an innkeeper, and not the one we stopped with, had, without my knowledge of it, provided for me.[12] I mention such small details in passing as they help to give an understanding of the national character of the Scots.

The rain was followed by a fog so dense that we nearly lost our way on more than one occasion. Finally we reached the coast close to the promontory known as St Abb's Head between 150 and 200 feet high whose face, though eroded almost to the perpendicular, still gives slope enough to permit a descent to the beach. The vertical section, constantly battered by a sea often furious in its force, would be picturesque for the landscape painter: for the naturalist it has especial attraction.

On the right of the first cove into which we descended we had St Abb's Head composed of a large whinnish, reddish mass of very irregular structure and texture even including in places pudding stone and in others breccia. On the left and without any clearly defined transition from the whin and other rocks were layers or strata of blackish schist which whilst the strata remain perfectly parallel with each other plunge down into the sea in a vertiginous sweep. Nothing, whether in composition or in arrangement could be

---

[11] Later when he and Chenevix visited the Giant's Causeway in the company of Dr Richardson the weather was equally unkind and prevented their seeing the Causeway complex from the sea.

[12] At the Causeway he will be protected from the weather, as bad as the Scottish, by the tattered coat of the guide.

more dissimilar than these neighbouring and adjoining masses.

The beach could be reached in only a few places, each in its own isolation. As we climbed the high cliff out of the cove to walk above the beach we returned into the clouds. Covered with grass and slightly undulating, the ground over which we walked reminded me of certain summits in the Jura; the resemblance was very much added to by the scattered flocks of sheep, an occasional cottage, the little lake of North-Field which came to view as we tramped along. Thoroughly soaked we reached Dowlaw, one of Sir James's farms where we made a welcome stop. From there we descended again to the sea close to some ruins known as Faste Castle. Here, the strata of schist which had originally been deposited in even beds were bent and curved in a manner consistent only with their upheaval whilst in a state of flexibility by some subterranean force and afterwards, when they had regained their solid form, retaining the curved form given them during the upheaval. Not far from Faste Castle at the base of a fairly high cliff at a spot known as Lumesden Burn this feature is even more striking. Here it was possible to observe over a fairly expansive area a vertical section of the beds of schist doubly bent in the shape of the letter N. A horizontal line, which we observed lower down on the cliff, breaking the continuity of the beds, indicates that above and below that line the mass, whilst without doubt in the solid state, had all at the same time been pushed laterally by some force without disturbance either to the inherent parallelism or to the regularity of the beds composing the mass; but that the force had so to speak chased them all together and broken them all at the same level. A sketch done by Sir James for the author depicting these features is to be found in the *Theory of the Earth* by Dr Hutton.

Sir James next brought us to another promontory known as Siccar where an otherwise inaccessible cove can only be reached by a track he has had etched on the steep slope leading down to it and which provides a descent right to the water's edge. I was astonished to learn from Sir James's wife, Lady Helen, that she had, despite the danger involved, made the climb down and up on several occasions. A very interesting sight awaited us here – the meeting of the schist with the gritstone. Here the schist is of a very fine slate nature, its colour that of the dregs of wine. Running parallel with the coast the strata are vertical, their edges where not overlain by the gritstone are exposed and form part of the shore, being visible when the tide is low, as it was at the time of our visit so that we were enabled to walk along the exposed edges. But, very close by, these edges are indeed covered by a mass of gritstone in the horizontal beds in which they are from that point found all along the coast. In the proximity of the schist which it overlies, the gritstone is in the nature of puddingstone or schistous breccia. By degrees away from the schist it assumes its more common form.

Not, in my opinion, to be seen anywhere else in so exemplary a manner, this relationship between the schist and the gritstone presenting a very real problem of interpretation. On the one hand you have immense beds of schist, not in high mountains but below sea level which have passed by some mysterious force from the horizontal state in which certainly they were formed to the vertical in which they are now found. Since their stratification is rigorously in plane and parallel they must have been in a compact state at the time of their upheaval. On the other hand, formed on the edges of the schists and covering them to a great height, you have these gritstones which required a very long detritus to be followed by consolidation. There is evidence here of alternating secular forces, at times of unequalled violence, at others slow and persistent. Fire and water can produce these forces and it seems natural to explain these great effects by the twin agencies of fire and water. Why rely on one to the exclusion of the other? In the controversy between the Neptunists and the Vulcanists I find it easy to persuade myself that both parties are wrong simply because each wishes to exclude the other; if they were to join forces they would put each other in the right.[13]

It was growing late. I was anxious to reach, before darkness took over, the residence of Sir James, Dunglass Castle, where we were to spend the night, so as to have light to see in his garden the model of a Gothic cathedral he has fashioned from trees by bending and curving the branches into the various shapes characteristic of that type of architecture. When we arrived at that beautiful home the day was too far spent to visit the model so that we had to postpone seeing it until the next day. In the meantime we were received with true Scottish hospitality, and that leaves nothing further to say, and despite our fatigue from the long day of travelling and excursion, the hours flew past in engaging conversation with not a thought of retiring on the part of any one.

We visited the model of the cathedral next morning before setting off. Having viewed it it is impossible not to be convinced of the force of Sir James's thinking on the origin of Gothic architecture and he has collected models from everywhere, not hesitating at the most complicated so as to reproduce them using the shapes supplied in the vegetable kingdom. The curving arches of his vaults are nothing more than tree branches bent naturally, so representing Gothic arches in nature's book. In this little church fifteen windows displaying variously carved traceries, and all of them copies of those to be found in some one of the English cathedrals are all executed from branches bent in all the forms

---

[13] Professor Pictet may appear to be more wise here than he was. He would have been wise if he were saying that some rocks may have been formed by the agency of fire i.e. igneous rocks and some by deposition in water i.e. sedimentary rocks, but that is hardly the case: his detritus is more likely to be the chemical deposition of the Neptunists than sedimentation.

which art would in turn have appeared to have borrowed from the branch forms in earlier times.

Though he was now returned home for the summer, Sir James was so kind as to accompany us as far as Dunbar, a small port eight miles from Dunglass, as there was something he wished to show us at Dunbar: a perfectly formed and beautiful group of prismatic basalts which form a small headland, the site as it happens of a redoubt containing a few cannons.[14] The basalt columns plunge in an almost vertical drop into the sea. The colour, not to speak of the composition of the basalt forming them, give these columns the appearance of brick; they are for the most part five-sided of very distinct form. The spaces between the columns are filled with coarse jasper which in this way forms veins enveloping the columns, the veins being determined in shape and thickness by the columns they envelop. Despite its toughness the jasper would appear to be more readily eroded by sea action than the material of the columns themselves for the interstices are sunken so that the prisms protrude slightly. Elsewhere the basaltic columns are criss-crossed with veins of calcareous spar at various angles. The ensemble of this site is strikingly beautiful and those who have never had the opportunity of seeing basaltic groups may, without going further than Dunbar, get a very clear and exact picture of this type of grand structures.

It is at this point that we took leave of our excellent friend. Everything in life has its counterbalance: the better is the company the harder it is to part. We parted just as if we were to meet the next day, always the best way. A long farewell, perhaps for ever, brings a variety of painful feelings which lying too deep for words are kept in the heart. No more can the joy of meeting again after a long parting be expressed: it is

---

[14] Reads rather strangely in the second half of the twentieth century. The scientists may not have been at war but England and France were and Pictet's account of the site of the cannons was read all over France a few months later.

then for the eye to speak what is in the heart; in those moments of intensity of spirit the best turned phrase can never convey as much as a single grasp of the hand.

The University was on vacation, all the main lectures, to my regret, over, and I was able to hear only one particular talk given by a Dr Allen,[15] on the same subject as that of the lecture I had attended at the Royal Institution in London, namely respiration. He treated his subject with understanding and order, but his mode of presentation, that generally followed in this country, of reading from notes and in a decidedly hurried manner, is to my mind, far from ideal. When a lecturer is master of his subject, and also has some facility of expression he teaches much better if he speaks extemporily to his notes than he can possibly do by reading them. Where he speaks to his notes he can observe his audience and can readily see if he is being understood; if he sees he is going too fast he can dwell on detail, expand when he sees this to be appropriate, he can give play to some topical reference, to some felicitous digression led on by his free-ranging talk. If in the exposition of some exciting discovery he has a real sense of involvement he will communicate it to his audience and they will likewise become involved. Nothing whatever of this nature can accompany lifeless detached reading from which the listeners cannot, except with difficulty, take notes, because the periods, the pause and the relative importance of the various details are but rarely indicated.[16]

It is not the practice here to question the students at the commencement of a lecture on the subject matter of the previous lecture. I am convinced that the practice of questioning the students in this way, introduced as it was at Geneva when the College and the academy were

---

[15]   Allen, John (1771–1843). Scottish physician, political and historical writer.
[16]   Professor Pictet angered the writer in the *Edinburgh Review* who reviewed his book on publication, but the professor should have been listened to with respect, coming as he did from Geneva Academy where the art of exposition was highly cultivated.

founded, has contributed, in our case, more than anything else to the good discipline and the success which have characterised our education. The practice is good for both professor and student. The latter listen much more attentively and take their notes with much more care and concentration when they expect to be questioned on them, and in replying to questions directed to them they acquire by degrees the ability to express themselves in exact and precise terms. As for the lecturer, he sees whether he is being properly understood and he can add the explanations which the experience gained from practice indicates to him as necessary and he masters an art necessary to his calling, that of matching and adapting his subject to the acquirements of his listeners.

From what I have been in a position to observe of English education and from what I have heard several English people say of it, I have reason to believe that it is rather poor. Young boys are sent boarding in public schools or colleges such as Harrow, Westminster, Eton, etc. There in great numbers, with little or no supervision, they are kept in subjection only by the fear of the rod, a pretty unenlightened type of discipline which indeed, if it is ever to be used, should be reserved for the gravest faults. The instruction is entirely classical; healthy rivalry is encouraged among the pupils to a minor degree only, and the example set is often more pernicious than useful in its effects. Some of these objectionable characteristics of the schools are also to be found in the universities and the distinction of person introduced among the students by the sons of the nobility and made apparent by a particular style of dress is, I believe, a baneful evil. The limited nature of the instruction is a further evil. Oxford is devoted almost exclusively to turning out men of letters and Cambridge mathematicians. It is only at Edinburgh that there is to be found a variety of the practical sciences aimed at turning out a man who will be useful to society and anxious to become so. It is to this latter circumstance and to the simple habits of the people of this city, resulting in a better employment of time, that the clearly marked superiority of the Scots over the English in the arts and in public affairs can, I believe, be attributed.

A Chair of Agriculture has been established in the University of Edinburgh a short while ago, a further illustration of the practical bent of the studies here. Dr Coventry,[17] the Professor who holds the chair has very kindly, in the course of a lengthy interview on the subject, gone into some details of the course and its development; it covers a very wide field. Dr Coventry interprets agriculture in the widest sense of the word: he regards it as the art of increasing and improving the produce of the soil but at the same time as being one branch of a more embracing science which he would designate as Husbandry but which we should most likely call Rural Science. His agriculture is the science of the farmer in the most generally accepted sense.

For completeness he would make it embrace: (1) the art of planting and maintaining forests; (2) the art of gardening, including the culture of fruit trees; (3) the art of landscape gardening, which he says is still in its infancy, notwithstanding the reputation earned by English gardens; (4) general estate management and agricultural economy by which we would imply the harmony between the type of farming conducted in a country, the state of population and the promotion of wealth through the various industries of the country.[18]

There was one place of exceptional interest in Edinburgh for both Mr Chenevix and myself and here I refer to the economical and up-to-date kitchen which Count Von Rumford had installed in the college known

---

[17] Coventry, Andrew (1764–1832). Scottish physician and agricultural scientist.

[18] Compare with what Pictet reports later of the work in the Dublin Society as the RDS was called at the time of the Professor's visit. (In Edinburgh as later in Dublin Pictet finds the hand of his friend Von Rumford at work.)

as Heriot's Hospital.[19] This is a very large building in which certain children are educated at the expense of a trust. It would be difficult to get oneself to accept, on going into that kitchen, no larger than that in a private dwelling, that it could have the capacity for the preparation of the meals for the very numerous community housed in this building. There was only one cook there and she appeared to be neither tired nor overworked. Neither smoke nor odour greeted our nostrils. I could not possibly give all the details of the layout and the purpose of the different stoves; to do so would require a volume complete with diagrams to match and were I to produce such a volume I should only anticipate the account which the Count himself intends publishing. It will have to suffice for me to tell you that, when the subject was broached with her, the cook was more than ready to talk and to do so non-stop on the advantages: in the economy of fuel and time, of the convenience which the entire installation provided. Even the porter, unsolicited, informed us that his lodge hitherto well-nigh uninhabitable by reason of the damp which attacked the place on all sides was now as dry as any other apartment in the building ever since he had had a Rumford stove installed.

I shall finish off this letter by remarking on what I find remarkable in Scottish agriculture.[20]

The plough here is an instrument so light and so cheap to buy that no great effort seems to be taken to care for it. It is simply left in the field after use; and we noticed so many of them left in this way without a care that we found it tempting to think that each field on the farm had a plough to itself.

In all areas near the sea, algae, wrack, everything which can be gathered on the shore at low tide, is used

---

[19] Founded by George Heriot (1563–1623) for the education of impecunious middle-class people 'for the honour and due regard which I [Heriot] bear to Edinburgh and in imitation of the public, pious and religious work found within the city of London, called Christ's Hospital'.

[20] To be contrasted with what he finds in Ireland.

with great success as manure. The carts laden with it leave a peculiar but not disagreeable odour in the roads where they pass. The effects of this manure are soon in evidence. In sown-out meadows which have had it spread on them recently, I have seen the grass very markedly verdant and consequently contrasting with the fields not so treated.

The corn crop has a very rich appearance. Though it has recently undergone a drought, the rain came in very good time to restore it all. I saw enormous fields of turnips planted in rows which allow the cultivator to pass between them and I learned that the cultivation of this crop is greatly advanced in Scotland, where it is claimed to be better understood than in England. It is confined to light soils, the heavy soils being reserved for beans, which are also sown and cultivated in rows from 20 to 27 inches wide; the rows being put at this width for the convenience of the cultivator the use of which for this purpose is almost universal in this country.

The potato has had an honoured place in Scotland for some fifty years and is mostly cultivated in the proximity of towns. It is not regarded as profitable as turnips or beans by the farmer. He plants what he needs for stock and for his family but the crop does not form part of his usual rotation.

Threshing and winnowing of corn are both done by machines, the machine for threshing being driven by two horses. The threshing machine is regarded as a wonderful invention for two reasons: the saving in labour and the more effective release of the grain. As the harvest was not ripe I did not see any threshing being done but I was promised a drawing of the machine and its action. It would seem to be too costly to be within the means of the smallholder. The winnowing machine is the very same fan used in German Switzerland, known to us all at home.

The flourishing state of agriculture in Scotland is generally attributed to the liberal system which has for

62

62

so long established a close relationship between the
vast majority of the landlords and the tenant farmers.
The leases are long and they have no arbitrary clauses.
The interest of the landlord is completely identified
with that of the tenant who has the legal certitude of
enjoying all the fruits of his industry for the duration of
his long lease; of seeing himself reimbursed for all his
improvements; and when his lease is beginning to run
out he does not have any reason to flag in the zeal and
the effort which up until then he has put into his work,
for he has the moral certainty that his lease will be
renewed on terms that he will not find
disadvantageous, These relations of patronage which
over several generations have obtained between the
land-owning families and their tenants, are the source
of an infinity of reciprocal advantages: they render
rural life most tranquil and happy. There is a highly
civilising force inherent in the goodwill generated by
people who co-operate in reciprocity of interest.[21]

But I forget. I have not come to Glasgow merely to
write. I am off to do the rounds, and I shall write again
when I can.

---

[21] Adam Smith's influence seems to have jumped over the University walls.

Letter IV

Port Patrick, 14 July, 1801

Yes Port Patrick and yet not in Ireland, we are still in Scotland though on board boat and separated from the land of Patrick by a 'step' not much wider than that from Calais to Dover. The legend has it that St Patrick made the step on leaving Ireland, and the small port in which we now find ourselves is the imprint of his footstep. Be that as it may, we have been condemned to spend twenty-four hours here, and that, truth to tell, for having risen too late yesterday morning back in the little inn at Girvan. To our chagrin we arrive, only to see the packet boat under full sail and to bemoan the fact that had we arrived a little earlier we should have been aboard and making our passage to the other shore. The boat sails from here every day but at times which vary with the tide. So it is in a way the luck of the draw to arrive at the time of sailing: in our case we drew a losing number. But we know how to take such disappointments in good part so that when fortune is minded to play us a trick we act so as to catch her in her own trap, and when she thinks she is arranging things as contrary to our wishes they are in reality what we really want. So you see, despite appearances, our real wish must have been to visit this coast, explore it, write up our notes, write to our friends, etc. All we needed for these things were lovely weather and twenty-four hours at our disposal. Fortune grants the weather and the twenty-four hours and we are much indebted to her. Nothing remains but to profit by the unexpected gift and here I am getting on with my writing.

I have mentioned Glasgow to you and it is indeed a pleasure for me to go back in thought to that interesting city. Nature has been bounteous to her and industry has been developed in her to a remarkable degree. Situated as she is almost at the centre of a neck separating the two seas, Glasgow has communication with the one sea by a navigable river and with the other by a very good canal. The area rests on seams of excellent coal extending twenty-four miles NE to SW and at a width of from four to six miles. Over all this area the seams of this fuel, to which England owes her riches and practically her existence, are found in varying thicknesses and down to a depth of sixty fathoms. With these natural advantages Glasgow has become at once the Birmingham, the Manchester, the Sheffield, indeed I may say, the Oxford of Scotland, for in spite of the great industrial and commercial progress of the city, the sciences are cultivated there with success, even among those classes of the inhabitants who in other places do not bother with such things. For example my travelling companion, Mr Chenevix, who spent two years at the University of Glasgow, was some years later, not a little surprised to discover one of his former fellow undergraduates in the person of his shoemaker. Nor was he less surprised on another occasion to recognise another fellow student of the earlier years in a countryman guide to sightseers at the waterfalls of the Clyde. This love of solid education is also to be found among the ladies who in appreciable numbers attend courses in physics and chemistry.

We were introduced by Mr Watt,[1] son of the celebrated engine-builder of that name, to Dr Cleghorn[2] one of the Professors of the University. Travellers pressed for time are indeed fortunate to find in a person to whom they are introduced as we were, to Dr Cleghorn, one who appreciates how they are fixed and who knows how, using understanding and

---

[1] Watt, James (1769–1848).
[2] Cleghorn, Dr Robert (1755–1821). Scottish physician and lecturer.

suiting himself to his guests' needs, to put every spare moment to its most profitable use. In Dr Cleghorn we met exactly this type of person and he joined with this precious gift of consideration for all our wants a richness of conversation and most agreeable company. We found ourselves in rapport with him right from the moment we met him, thanks to that indefinable affinity of the spirit which operates on the mind as does the force of gravity on matter, and we formed with him in one day a bond which will, I believe, endure as long as we do.

We had noticed in our first sightseeing outing of the morning a very large building of imposing architecture built close to a cathedral and on a height overlooking the city. This institution, the Royal Infirmary of Glasgow, was the first place we went to visit. As we walked there Dr Cleghorn let us know that the building had been completed only a few years before, that the money was provided by the voluntary contributions of the inhabitants of Glasgow and the surrounding areas,[3] and that it was to the plans of a commission made up of men chosen as the best architects and the most competent medical doctors and surgeons of France.

"Of France?" we interjected.

"Yes of France," he confirmed. "About fifteen years ago the French Government sent members of the Academy of Sciences to England to obtain all the information they could garner on the construction and administration of hospitals, to use this information in establishing the hospitals it was proposed to erect in France. The report of that commission and the plans it produced were a genuine masterpiece. Just at the time the question of building our own hospital was under consideration chance procured for us a copy of the report and plans of the commission from France and

---

[3] There is a great contrast between the hospital facilities as described here and what Pictet will later describe as obtaining in Dublin. In Glasgow a thriving industrial population finances what is provided: in what Swift described as 'miserable Dublin' the poor are degraded by charity – something Pictet will not understand.

we believed that we could do no better than to follow them in every detail. *Sic vos non vobis.*"

Certainly when we got inside that handsome building it was at once apparent to us that everything in it was perfectly designed to meet its function. Large lobby at the entrance for simple consultations; free movement of air in the wards; segregated wards for the contagious diseases; water on tap everywhere; well-lighted operating theatre; a garden for the convalescent to walk in; order, in fact everywhere complete cleanliness and a wholesome atmosphere prevailed. There is accommodation for 144 patients at any one time but at most times the hospital does not have to house more than a fraction of that number. Mortality here is low, not exceeding one in eighteen or twenty whereas in the Hotel-Dieu it is known to be one in four and a half. Precautions against contagious fever are so strict that as many as forty fever cases have been admitted to the hospital without in any way infecting the other patients.

The administration of the establishment is entrusted to twenty-five directors nominated on a yearly basis by different Glasgow bodies. Supervision is carried out by twenty-four visitors who have the right to enter the building at any hour of the day or night to satisfy themselves as to the conditions. The visitors write their remarks in a book which is always available in the assembly hall and which is read at every meeting of the directors. This, to judge by results, is an excellent system. As to the patients, they are admitted on the recommendation of subscribers to the hospital. A yearly subscription of one guinea gives a right on a yearly basis: an outright subscription of ten guineas grants a perpetual right to have one patient per year admitted. Five guineas per year gives the right to recommend four patients in the year, two of whom will be accepted at the same time.

Each year the directors publish accounts of receipts and payments as well as details of the number of patients treated, even giving the types of their diseases. Through the kindness of Dr Cleghorn I have details for the years 1795 to 1800, that is for six years, and I am arranging them here to show the most interesting details in tabular form:

Year	Patients M	W	Total	Cured	Relieved	Discharged	Detained	Dead
1795	186	90	276	142	28	38	50	18
1796	253	149	402	213	59	46	64	20
1797	387	218	605	337	79	90	60	39
1798	368	286	654	328	89	125	85	27
1799	459	262	721	420	59	120	90	32
1800	520	283	803	503	63	129	70	38

As can be seen from this table the number of patients treated annually has grown in the six years from 276 to 803. The yearly expenses are between 1700 and 1800 pounds sterling, a sum which is derived from private subscriptions and also from the income arising from foundation capital.

We went round the exterior of the various colleges which among them make up the university. Everyone was on holiday and nothing can be more melancholy than a seat of learning at that time of the year. We caught sight of some professors proceeding two by two with great gravity and in full academic dress but I have no idea of the purpose of that ceremony of which we were the only spectators.[4]

It was at this point that Dr Cleghorn took his leave of us to return to the country but before doing so he

---

[4]   The records supplied by Mrs Elspeth Simpson, archivist at the university, show that the procession was concerned with the conferring of a degree on a Bernard Calabris who on that day (10th July, 1801) was 'examined by the Senate, after which he explained the Aphorism and solved the Case prescribed to him; and, he having withdrawn, the Senate considered his several performances declared their satisfaction, and agreed that the said Candidate was worthy of having the Degree of Doctor of Medicine conferred on him... "*MDCCCI, Apud Collegium Glasguensem die decimo mensis Julii - Commitiis Universitatis legitime citatis programmate Vice Rectoris et in Aula publica legitime habitis... Vice Cancellarius eum Medicinae Doctorum more solito et solenni creavit.*"'

had introduced us to Mr Crichton,[5] a friend of his and a most competent craftsman, requesting him to go with us to the Clyde Foundries, situated a few miles from Glasgow, for me of particularly lively interest.

At four o'clock in the afternoon we climbed into a carriage for this excursion and we found, as we journeyed, that our guide, Mr Crichton, was a very well informed man and most interesting in his conversation so that in the very short time we were together in the carriage we learned many revealing facts about the country and its industries. Soon the sulphurous smell, the curling clouds of black smoke laced with a jet of flame, the dull measured sound of steam engines, the joyless and desolate looking soil, prepared us by degrees for the sights we were to see.

Mr Edington,[6] the principal partner of the works was absent but his junior partner Mr Bigley,[7] received us with every possible attention. He took us everywhere, went into every detail on which we desired information replying readily to our questions, some of them indiscreet possibly, with clarity and openness. He seemed even to take a pleasure in being unrestrained in his communication to us in contrast with the jealous reserve of his competitors in the same branch of industry.

With kettles, pots and home utensils of every kind, and those frightful agents of death, cannons and carronades ranged everywhere as we moved we came to the machine for boring and turning the artillery pieces which was in full operation. A steam engine of the old type, that is one powered by the alternate action of the pressure of air and steam was the driving force.

On the one hand a device connected to it rotates the piece of artillery, whilst a workman shaves off the metal in small flat ribbons from the outside by pressing a strong tool against the piece. This action produces

---

5   Crichton, James (1749–1830). Scottish instrument maker.
6   Eddington, Thomas (dates uncertain). Scottish industrialist.
7   Mr Bigley – nothing known.

very loud sonorous and musically varied vibrations. It is astonishing that cast metal, which is by nature very brittle, will still give off ribbons in almost the same way as a malleable metal just by being worked upon as it revolves in this way. So much for the action on the outside. The same steam engine drives the boring bit and it does so in a two fold manner, firstly, turning the drilling bit on its shaft, and secondly, simultaneously holding the bit firmly at its work on the interior of the artillery piece. This latter function is contrived by means of a weighted lever mounted on a trolley. As the boring progresses the trolley is drawn by a rake so that the bit works into the solid metal until the barrel is finally bored out. It takes about twenty-four hours to bore out a carronade. Boring, by reason of the fine finish, is much superior to hollow casting which always gives a honeycombed, less compact metal surface. In casting, a lump of metal of considerable weight is always left at the front of the piece where the mouth will open. This lump of metal compresses all the rest of the piece during cooling, helping to make it compact and homogeneous. It is removed before the boring commences.

These carronades are not generally known: they were invented at the Carron Foundries in Scotland and are at present very much used in the English Navy. They are artillery pieces, something between the cannon and the mortar. Not very elegant in form, they are without mouldings or ornaments, they do not even have a flange at the mouth. The absence of these features doubtlessly has the effect of making them less vulnerable to enemy shot at the portholes. Though it is very light the carronade fires a ball of very large calibre – usually about 48lbs. This ball, set in motion by a small quantity of powder so as to move at low velocity, has time to spend its momentum on any obstacle it encounters. Instead then of cutting clean through the timbers of the ship's side, as would a ball of high speed, it smashes and tears them along their length causing damage difficult to repair. Whilst the lack of weight in the carronade makes its recoil very trying to the gunners, it is nevertheless a simple and economical means of destruction, a very valuable implement of war. The Turkish government, not knowing, it would seem, the advantages of the carronade ordered a large casting of cannon of other calibre from the Carron Company.

The proprietors of the foundry very honestly informed the Turkish government that it could have a greater number of firing pieces of larger calibre using the same quantity of metal by accepting the artillery cast in the new process. That government in its reply insisted on the execution of the order as originally given saying it would place the order elsewhere if this were not done. The customer is always right! The Turks got what they asked for.

We went from shop to shop as we came to them without following the actual order of operations. In this way we came to an esplanade where the roasting of the iron-ore and the conversion of coal into coke (i.e. carbon of coal) were both being performed at the same time. The two minerals are tossed pell-mell, donkey-back fashion into long piles and the fire applied to them. Later the fire is extinguished by covering the piles with earth and dust. The sulphur and bituminous elements of the coal are driven off by this combustion and it is very important that this preliminary operation be well done, because it requires only a very small amount of non-roasted mineral finding its way into the furnace to spoil the quality of an entire cast. Though we were given this comment as a fact I cannot very well see the force of the theory behind it.

We ascended an incline to the mouth of a furnace some thirty feet in height. The ore and coke were all the time being fed into this furnace keeping it always topped up. The red, fiercely waving flame emerging from the mouth of the furnace gave the appearance of a volcano and this impression was heightened by the confusing noise coming from below. Natural curiosity draws your attention to the place from which this noise emanates. Here the ore, having descended bit by bit with its mixture of coke and the calcareous material which assists its liquidifying, runs as molten metal into a basin forming the bottom of the furnace and there it remains until it is drawn off in fiery streams to fill the moulds set for the purpose. Two such operations are performed in the twenty-four hours.

You continue on your way and eventually on the completion of a lengthy circuit you come, at the bottom of a kind of cavern, to the blast pipe by which the air is directed on the bottom of the incandescent pile. Here two of the senses are confused into one: all the power of hearing is absorbed in that frightening indescribable noise made by the current of air as it is blasted into the furnace by a force of which I shall soon speak; and the eye might as well look on the midday sun as on that spot towards which the terrible current of oxygen is directed, a spot of heat so intense that the metal as it falls into the path of the mad rushing stream and hurled into it is liquefied at once.

Interposed between the pipe leading the air to it and the blast pipe itself, which are both made of the same metal, is a hosepipe made of cowhide designed evidently to give the actual blastpipe what play it needs. The tension of the hide, which yields as little to the pressure of the hand as would a piece of timber, indicates the extreme force with which the encased air is blasted. You may wish to ask your guide questions, show your surprise, your admiration, but the noise is so powerful that all you can do is to make gestures and shape words with your lips. Anyway, you find it necessary to leave this place for fear of suffering lasting damage to the functions of eye and ear which endure so much.

We hastened to discover the driving force behind these effects. What else could it be but another steam engine? This one is constructed on the latest principle

of Boulton and Watt, and atmospheric pressure plays
no part in its action; the steam alone raises and lowers
the piston accordingly as it is alternately admitted and
condensed on one of the two faces.

It is said that Robert Burns went once to visit the Carron works but
was turned away. He retired to the quieter atmosphere of an inn and
wrote:

We cam na here to view your warks
In hopes to be mair wise,
But only lest we gang to Hell
It may be nae surprise.

Sour grapes or no his reflection is in delightful contrast with Pictet's
philosophising on the same subject.

I can never regard the steam engine without the same
feeling of fascination with which I was seized when I
first saw one in operation. The deft and regularly timed
action of the enormous beam which the steam causes to
rise and fall gives the notion of a sort of irresistible,
supernatural force applied to it which surmounts with
complete ease all the obstacles that could possibly be
set in its way. And that so mighty force is as obedient
as it is powerful. The degree of force employed,
though coming from a single piece of apparatus, can be
graduated to the need. The engines are constructed in
all sizes, whether to perform the work of one man or
one horse; for turning the millstone of a confectioner,
agitating the sieve of a mustard maker or doing the
work of 150 or 200 horses in lifting water in torrents
from the deepest mines. Nor is there any human
activity in their operation to help form a conception of
their movement. An old man from time to time putting
coal under a boiler is all that can be seen near them,
and the effect, out of all proportion to the apparent
cause, could drive one to believe in a god, a will,
animating these assemblages of metal, water and fire.

But it is man who, by directing his native intelligence to the better employment of those forces which Nature presents to him, has learned how to turn their action to his greatest advantage, and by imitating the supreme intelligence to make much of little.

We returned to our lodging with that feeling of fulfilment which a day well spent brings. We had the previous day reserved our places on the public coach which was to depart on the morrow for Ayr whence we bargained on getting to Portpatrick by post-chaise, but just as we were about to climb into the coach we were told that we were booked for the following day. This we disputed but we accepted a compromise. I remained in the vehicle where I had taken provisional possession of a place, and my companion followed post.[8] We arrived together at Ayr in a downpour of rain; the town, by no means beautiful, looked wretched in this inclemency. The rain eased a bit while we were dining, and the rest of the evening was tolerable. We arrived at Girvan at nightfall.

Girvan is a fishing village at the end of a little cove. I recalled with apprehension a village similarly situated on the Mediterranean coast by the River Genes – a village called Spiotorno ('*Non mai si ritorno,*' says the Italian proverb) apprehension was completely belied – a good inn, pleasant company and – no bugs! In fact, everything was too good; and of that I have told you the sequel.

From Girvan to Portpatrick where we now are, the road skirts the sea nearly all the way, in places reasonably above sea level. Offshore is seen the Isle or rather the rock of Ailsa, in shape rather like a sugar loaf. It is uninhabited save for the sea birds and the chance fowlers who have a mind to pursue them in that apparently inaccessible retreat. In the fifteen mile stage between Girvan and Ballintree I observed, both in the mass and as loose stones, the greatest variety of rocks I

---

[8]   Why did not both go by post? Possibly it was cheaper for Pictet to travel by public coach but then Chenevix must have had to foot the entire bill for the post-chaise.

have ever seen in a similar distance. Detached granites, whins of all shades, serpentines of very varied sizes, from the potstones to the jade jaspers, large porphyries of green, schists and finally gritstones; it would have been easy to collect in that piece of ground samples enough to fill several drawers of a cabinet.[9] From Ballintree to Stranraer where we dined the road borders a bay, and the sea becomes a loch, at the top of which stands the town of Stranraer; from there you cross a somewhat elevated peninsula to come to Portpatrick.

Yesterday evening was superb, and we took advantage of it to walk over the hills which border the sea, and for their greater length rise out of it. The sections here reveal whinstone approximating to the real basalt, although we nowhere saw any prismatic condition in all the mass. We visited an old castle situated on one of them; there were some tunnels to be seen and old towers with staircase railings falling into decay – everything suggestive of the *Mysteries of Udolpho*[10] and the sea lowing beneath the rocks made the spot even more romantic. In the distance, below the rays of the setting sun, we caught a glimpse of that semi-wild country, that Ireland whither our tracks were leading us. Flocks of unshepherded sheep moved around us, and their nervous wonder at sight of us showed that very rarely were they visited by travellers. A lovely summer evening has ever for me something

---

[9] Strange that it does not appear to Professor Pictet, so concerned as he was with the origin of rocks, to ask how this great variety of rocks materials was found together. The geological theory of the day could not have answered the question if he had asked it; but his not asking it indicates a lack of originality. His friend and mentor, De Saussure, had failed to respond to the same phenomenon in Switzerland. The great variety of rock material to be found on the Scottish and Irish shores results from the movements of former ice sheets.

[10] The *Mysteries of Udolpho*, by Mrs Ann Radcliffe (1764–1823). Published in 1794, it remained for fifty years required reading for anyone with a pretence to culture. Following on Horace Walpole, Mrs Radcliffe set her mysteries in the ruins of Gothic castles and monasteries but gave a natural explanation in the unravelling of the mystery – all of which is parodied by Jane Austen in *Northanger Abbey*.

of sadness in it; the circumstances in which I found myself that evening were conducive to melancholy.

'Why', I asked myself, 'am I going to run twice again the risk of the treacherous seas? Am I taking that risk for a bauble? And this search for knowledge which carries me to those shores – will it pay me for the risks I shall encounter?' I chased the thought. 'Away with this cold calculation! Where would science be if risks were never taken on her behalf? And what risk was I taking compared with those taken by the Cooks, and Banks and that fearless group of navigators who have illumined our times and made large the treasury of our knowledge. Here I am in their trail, though let the truth be said, very far behind them; here, nevertheless, and I feel within me a spark of that bright flame which fired then on. Onward!'[11]

The tide was low, no sign of a packet-boat, near as I was to the sea. But she will arrive later in the evening.

As I wrote to you, someone came to ask me to go to see an enormous crab which a fisherman had just caught. A crab resembles a spider as seen under the microscope, but with the legs of a lobster. We were driven by curiosity to weigh him; he weighed 5½ pounds, and had an overall length of eighteen inches from the extremity of one leg to the other. I bought it for a shilling and am bringing it with me cooked. It will give us a meal, and its shell, which I shall keep, will adorn my study.

I have seen here for the first time one of those *pounds* in which, according to the English custom, animals which cause damage in the country are locked up for punishment. The animals are starved here until their owner releases them by paying for the damage they have caused. If the beast could understand that it

---

[11] The inclination to laugh at Pictet's 'onward scientific soldier' here might well be tempered by the reflection that some hundred and fifty-one years later a modern ferryboat, *The Princess Victoria*, foundered with great loss of life in the same channel Pictet was about to cross.

had done wrong there would be some sense in treating it like this, but, as it is, it is starved to punish it for being badly fed. This kind of law could hardly be called humane. It contrasts with that other English law which authorises a man who sees another, even the owner, abuse an animal to take the part of the beast and bring the offender before the justice where he is made to make amends – explain if you can these inconsistencies.

I do not know from where or when I shall write to you next. For the present, farewell.

Letter V

Sonna[1] near Edgeworthstown, 23rd July, 1801

I take up my pen again in a lovely mansion right in the centre of Ireland. It is the home of my travelling companion's sister which circumstance, coupled with the so affecting Irish hospitality I have come to know, has assured us of a wonderful welcome. Here we find something of that rest of which we begin to feel the need; as well it provides the opportunity to continue my account.

We embarked at Portpatrick at six o'clock in the evening. The weather was delightful, little or no wind, and we had time before the night fell to survey in detail the vessel in which we were to make our passage. Distressingly it had the appearance of Noah's Ark by reason of the groups of unclean animals, which occupied all the quarter before the bridge, men, women, children clothed in the rags of misery and hoping doubtlessly somehow to better their lot on the other shore. I doubt very much from what I have seen to date if they can have gained anything by the change. That grievous sight was the cause of our going below to our cabin to settle in for the night earlier than we would otherwise have done. At half past five in the morning we found ourselves in Donaghadee without you may say our being aware of the crossing

I have never ceased to be astonished since my arrival here in Ireland at the differences I have observed between this country and the other parts of

---

[1] Sonna House, the seat of the Tuite family seven miles west of Mullingar.

78

the United Kingdom. I believe I cannot better convey these difference than to transcribe from my diary impressions of events and objects just as they presented themselves to me.

Here is the copy.

Tuesday morning 16th July.[2] The tide is out. From my inn I can see little carts coming and going to the beach. These carts are so small in the wheel that the shaft goes up by the side of the horse at an angle of 35 or 40 degrees.[3] As I watch them being loaded with algae and wrack left behind by the tide I imagine them to have been designed solely for that particular type of work, but in this Mr Chenevix my travelling companion corrects me, informing me that with the exception of the post-chaises I shall not see any other type of vehicle in Ireland used as it is for shifting the harvest, merchandise – everything in need of being moved. I take a closer look and make a detailed note of what I see – it is craft in its infancy. Two wheels 26 inches in diameter fashioned from a thick plank sawn in the round, are attached spitwise to an axle which turns with them and which is held in place in a notch made in the lower surface of each of the shafts by means of a large nail.

Here Pictet gives the following footnote:

From experiments carried out in France on the order of the Minister to compare wheels turning with the axles with those which turn on the axle, on average the conclusions were:

A wagon on fixed axles made of wood and drawn on the highway requires to put it in motion a force of... 14 myriagrammes. An ordinary wagon fitted with rollers in the nave of the wheels... 20 myriagrammes. A wagon with turning axle in rollers to reduce

2 Converting from the republican calendar to the Julian while crossing the Irish Sea must have confused Pictet. The date was 14th July 1801.
3 The famous 'low-backed' cart, now virtually extinct.

friction... 24 myriagrammes 5. From which it follows that the wagon with a turning axle even when that axle is furnished with rollers is more difficult to haul than the ordinary wagon with wooden axles and much more so than the vehicle whose nave is fitted with rollers in a box.

Fixed on the shafts is a horizontal almost square frame which, depending on what is being carried, has at times a box, at times a pannier, affixed as container whilst the harness is like the cart in its simplicity and the lot costs no more than a guinea. There is a world of difference between this simplicity and the wheelwright's art of the neighbouring country.

At eight o'clock in the morning we set out in a dirty tattered post-chaise drawn by two sorry nags and driven by a postillion more tattered than his post-chaise; the sleeves of the jacket in which he is rigged out threatens at each crack of the whip to say farewell to the rest of the garment and they are just about held there by the projection of the elbows which show through large holes. His figure is in keeping with the rest of the equipage, and in vain do I look for some traits of that so much vaunted Irish physique. The road is superb but on each side are unfenced trenches so wide and so deep that a start of the horse precipitating us into one of them would leave us there for eternity. Doubtlessly it is to the generally boggy nature of the soil that this method of road building owes itself.

The same reason, it seems to me, underlines a singular method of planting potatoes: they are set in flat beds of four or five feet wide and separated again by trenches.[4] Few or no trees, no hedges, the marches of the farms are banks or walls of earth and the appearance of the countryside gains nothing from these. Here and there houses – better still, huts – are to be seen, mostly thatched. They are built of mud mixed with straw, roofed with thatch on sods. For the most

---

[4]   The so-called 'lazy-beds' or rigs.

part without a chimney, the smoke issues through the door. The chimney when by chance it exists is an old barrel without a bottom, which brings the smoke through the roof; and when the roof is of straw it is so light that it is necessary to tie it in place by ropes of the same material attached to pegs driven into the mud wall. We went into one of these houses, there we saw a woman and six children; she was preparing the meagre dinner for her family on a small turf fire. The woman had handsome features but her face had the worn appearance of habitual misery. Our presence seemed to cause her uneasiness. She replied only in monosyllables to our conversation; we concluded that the class to which we were regarded as belonging did not give us a title to a warm reception in her cabin. It would have required more time than we had at our disposal to overcome her reserve to which we bowed and cut short our visit.[5]

At ten past eleven we arrived in Belfast – a pleasant town. It is situated at the head of a gulf which resembles a great lough and boasts of some fairly considerable buildings. It appeared to be well populated, but then, it was market day. I am given to understand that it is a very considerable commercial centre exporting linens, importing wines.[6] The surrounding countryside is covered with these linens spread out for bleaching. The country all about is well cultivated and here for the first time in Ireland we saw trees. Whilst our horses were being changed we went

to make a call on a merchant whose address we were given. He made us very welcome and gave us in writing, details of the way we should take to reach the Giant's Causeway by the shortest route. He

---

[5] It is also possible, since this intrusion must have been made somewhere about Ballygrainey Six Road Ends, that there were suspicions entertained towards well-dressed strangers. This was Betsy Grey Country: 1798 was only three years past. In the 1798 rebellion Presbyterians in the County Down were involved; one of these, Betsy Grey, is something of a legend.

[6] The father of Joseph Black the scientist was a Belfast wine merchant operating in Bordeaux.

recommended to us several castles as worth visiting, among others the celebrated residence of the Bishop of Derry.[7] Our coolness on the subject of castles and the eagerness we manifested to go to see stones built by nature created a contrast which astounded him and we felt that we read in his eyes a feeling of pity for our madness; we forgave him. At one o'clock we looked down on one of the largest lakes in Ireland, by name Lough Neagh near which is the town of Antrim, capital of the county of that name. We arrived there at three o'clock.

Between Belfast and Antrim the land is well cultivated and the soil appears to be good with the exception of the high ground which separates the two towns. The women go barefoot as in Scotland but their dress bespeaks much more poverty. We learned as we dined in Antrim that that county was one of the most troubled during the recent insurrection. We were shown the spot in the street where at the end of a battle of which the town was the main site, Lord O'Neale,[8] one of the chief peers of the neighbourhood, a man held in high esteem and who sought by words of peace to calm the tense feeling, was shamefully assassinated by a thrust of a pike aimed from behind. We do not know how far the fires of that rebellion have been extinguished; but we perceived no visible signs of them. Most likely a corps of red-coats stationed in each of the towns we go through and composed of English militia contributes essentially to the tranquillity.

We left Antrim at four o'clock and we arrived at seven o'clock at Ahoghill, a wretched village. It was raining cats and dogs; night was falling; the horses which should have brought us on our way had been out on the grass for most of the month, and nobody knew exactly where. There was nothing for it but to put up for the night in the most miserable of inns.

---

[7]   Harvey, Frederick Augustus, Earl of Bristol and Bishop of Derry (1730-1803).
[8]   O'Neale, John, first Viscount (1761-1798). Reportedly piked by his own parkkeeper.

We left the following morning at daybreak. It had settled in to a steady downpour. Our horses, it was obvious, had their education to begin all over again. The terrain became more and more undulating and we did practically nothing but climb up and get down. Everywhere bogs, cabins, and an appearance of poverty in the population which strongly contrasted with the rich quality of the soil, with the abundance of fuel for fires, for the turf there is excellent; and finally with the beauty of the well-made, well-kept roads. It is a paradox which he who would uphold must seek to resolve.

At nine o'clock we arrived in the well-situated town of Ballymoney, a much more lively place than Antrim. From here to Coleraine, which we reached at midday, our way frequently ran beside a river called the Bann, the Lignon[9] of the Irish poets. But on a wet day it resembles more the Styx than any other river for its waters which have washed the bogs have a blackish tint, something like coffee without milk.

My travelling companion entertained himself by getting the drivers to talk and I noticed in their replies an originality blended with naiveté and roguishness which is, he tells me, one of the distinguishing traits of the Irish. We had here for the first time a big well-made young fellow for driver.

"Why are you not in the army, a tall stout man like you?"

"Because they wouldn't have me."

"And why not?"

"Because I'm a lazy dog."

"Oh, that's it, you would have been made to do a bit of real work for a change."

"Aye, indeed; and that is the very last thing I want to do."

---

[9] Lignon, a small stream in the Massif Central of France, setting for a novel, *L'Astrée*, by Honoré d'Urfé. It is difficult to see the connection. The lower Bann is not a stream and the only romantic setting it offered was for the humorous ditty *Kitty of Coleraine*. The legendary origin, the uncovered well of Lough Neagh, might fit.

Mr Chenevix related to me on this occasion a reply once made by a driver which illustrates very neatly another trait of the Irish character. A traveller who had just suffered a spill in a ditch complained bitterly to the driver.

"Sure I spilled you," replied the driver. "Hadn't I the right to?"

"What do you mean, you rascal, hadn't you the right to?"

"Sure I had," came the reply. "Who but me yoked the young colts, so who but me had the right to drive them any way I liked?"

Coleraine is a rather handsome little town, a centre of a fairly extensive linen weaving area, linen being the principal manufacture of Ireland. People wishing to go to see the Giant's Causeway make their way direct from here in the ordinary course of events; but we had a call to make a little out of the way.

We had been given an introductory letter to Dr Richardson,[10] a cleric established for more than thirty years in the small parish of Portrush situated at the seaside a short distance from the area in which our interest lay and who has studied it with particularly close attention. The presence of a guide who was also most likely well instructed and who, we had reason to believe, was a hospitable man induced us to make light of the detour involved in going to the Giant's Causeway by way of Portrush.

As we headed for Portrush it was evident that we had long since left behind us the calcareous soil; now the rock, wherever it showed, in the loose or in the mass, was of basaltic origin. Near Portrush the road runs close to the bottom of a perpendicular rock in which I saw for the first time in this country clearly defined prisms or columns of basalt. We arrived at the Rectory[11] at one o'clock. Appraised of our coming by

---

[10] Richardson, Dr William (1740–1820). See biographical note.

[11] Not the rectory but the summer residence of Dr Richardson (information from Mr H.A. Boyd, MA, MLitt, Ballycastle, Co. Antrim).

some friends, I do not know who, Dr Richardson had been expecting us for several days. The most pressing and friendly of welcomes could not conceal the reality however, that we should have been better to arrive somewhat earlier or somewhat later for his house was already full of friends for a small party which was to be given that evening by the family; but this notwithstanding he was firmly resolved to put us up also. In this he succeeded: we had a bed and we were never to know whom it was we disturbed.

The day was too far advanced and the weather was too poor to permit of a visit straight away to the Causeway which was more than six miles off. Besides the worthy Doctor planned to bring us to the Causeway by boat and to give us the opportunity to obtain a magnificent and extended view of that singular coast, the object of our visit. We put off then the expedition until the next day but the Doctor, taking advantage of the first clearing in the weather, led us, hammer in hand around the area in the proximity of his house where he had geological features to show us as remarkable as those which the gigantic phenomena we were to examine on the morrow could offer us.

We spent two good hours on this outing, one of the most interesting I have made in my life from which I have carried back several unusual specimens. This is not the occasion to give an account of that visit, and I shall not depend on myself for that.

Dr Richardson had surveyed, it was evident, the neighbourhood systematically and in much detail; his conversation on these matters was so revealing and so rich that I have asked him very earnestly to be so very kind as to describe them himself. He has had the kindness to do so and the letter which I have received and which I shall translate will show you how right have been to insist.

As stated in the '*Avant propos*', the letter is not given.

When we got back to the house he showed us a small collection he had made from the most characteristic specimens of the district. An assembly of another kind awaited us in the drawing room. Shining youth of both sexes were there and music playing as we waited for dinner. The guests were received by Mrs Richardson, both she and her husband showing busy concern and all the social graces towards their guests. These were so numerous that it was necessary to have us seated at two tables in adjoining rooms. The dinner was merry without being noisy. The Member of Parliament for the County[12] was one of the guests so that politics became as much a topic of conversation as natural history.

I took the opportunity of satisfying my curiosity on the phenomenon of the excellence of the roads, even the minor roads which in that island are in as good condition as the main roads – and all without statutory labour and without cost to trade or the traveller since we had not encountered a single toll-house in our journey. Here, as I was informed, is the secret. Twice in the year the landlords of each district meet and form what is called a grand jury of gentlemen. At the meeting a report is compiled on the state of the roads of the district, of those to be begun, to be repaired, and so on. The report is accompanied by an estimate of the cost. If the majority of the jury approve it, an assessment of the cost is made on the landlords in proportion to their property; and forthwith the work is put in hand. If anyone feels himself over assessed he appeals to a smaller council known as a petty jury which examines his complaint with fairness. In this way, without any action by the Government or by the legislature, this very important problem of political economy is resolved to the great advantage of all concerned. The system is such however, (and my

---

[12] There were two members for County Antrim in the first Union Parliament – John Staples and Edmund Alexander McNaughton. Since McNaughton came from Bushmills it is the more likely that he was Dr Richardson's guest on this occasion.

observations on my journey confirm what I am saying) that work for which no provision has been made can be initiated inside the six-monthly interval between meetings of the grand jury so that if for example a bridge should collapse nothing can be done to restore it until after the next meeting.[13]

But such accidents are rare; the roads in general are extremely well made, they are no larger than is necessary, and the lightness of the cart in universal use, which I have described, and which never requires more than one horse to draw means that the roads suffer little wear by the transport of merchandise.

The dinner was followed by a very charming ball which lasted late into the night. For me it was as if I had found myself transported fairywise into the scene of an enchanted fête on the most northerly part of Ireland, the small peninsula of Portrush, beaten by the ocean waves whose roar, and the whistling of the wind, could be heard in the intervals between the dances. My head was full of what I had seen in that day so rich in experience, and the exciting display

---

[13] The traveller, especially if he is in a hurry, seldom hears anything beyond what his hosts want him to hear. Professor Pictet is unstinting in his praise of the Irish roads and what they owed to the grand juries. Roads were good but for additional reasons to those given by the MP for Antrim, who was most likely a member of the local grand jury.

'It is admitted that the state of Irish roads [in the eighteenth century] were exceedingly good; but many of the contracts for making them appear to have been grossly corrupt.

'Not infrequently', it is said, 'grand jurors got their own tenants contracts for making or repairing portions of roads at twice their proper price, and the tenants were thus enabled to pay out of public money arrears of rent.

'...enforced labour on the roads and the grand jury abuses were sources of continual complaint and were felt to be particularly burdensome.

'It is notorious', Captain Erskine reported to Viceroy Townsend in 1772, after his visit to the north, 'what use is made by grand juries of the power given them to lay cess for roads and bridges. Jobs upon jobs, one more infamous than another, serve to support the interests of some leading men in the country.' (Biggar)

The money from the roads as for the canals came from grants made by the pre-Union Irish Parliament and whose members, under a sense of grievance at having to make certain payments to the Monarch voted with liberality. It would be wrong to think that all Irish roads were good – 'Several roads in this country [Armagh] are in good condition: but the greater number are bad, many of them in the extremist degree.' (Coote)

which was bringing it to a close induced in me a
haziness, a kind of inebriation, making me fear at
times it might be nothing more than a dream.

Letter VI

Dublin, 28th July, 1801

Our movements are so rapid and my notes so tossed off that, far from being able to keep abreast of my correspondence with you as I had wished, my friends, I find myself more in arrears than ever before. I must indeed grasp on the wing the opportunities for writing; they become more and more rare and I can foresee that it will not be until I am in London again that I shall be able to complete for you the account of my experiences in Ireland which I am to leave very soon. As it is I have not yet even attempted to describe the place which was one of the main objects of my visit to Ireland, but this I now go on to do. We left off at Portrush.

A very wet night was followed by a morning hardly less so. The wind blew a gale and the seas were so high that it was necessary to abandon (not without much regret) the project of going by boat to observe from the sea the coast we were about to visit so as to get a panoramic view of it before coming in close to note the detail.[1] But as it was we were not at all sure for part of the morning that it would be even possible for us to reach it by any means; and we were strongly advised to put off our trip until the next day. But the weather assumed a more favourable appearance as the day advanced; and at eleven o'clock, after one of those pleasant lunches with the family which are unknown

---

[1] Professor Pictet and Richard Chenevix were thus unlucky for a second time in this respect. The Scottish weather had also prevented them, as was seen from viewing St Abb's Head from the sea with Sir James Hall. It is possible that Professor Pictet with his formula for seeing blessings in disguise welcomed the change in plans: he does not appear to have been much of a sailor.

outside the British Isles, we climbed into a chaise. Our excellent host, Dr Richardson, accompanied us as he was very anxious to be there to point out to us (and this was something we especially valued), features which had particularly struck him on his many visits to that very remarkable coast. With the courage of a true naturalist he braved on horseback all the inclemencies of the weather, making us somewhat ashamed of our protection in the carriage. When we arrived at the splendid scene it was necessary to proceed on foot: our privilege came to an end and in the event we had no further reason for feeling pampered; we became wet as he was. But we would willingly have paid an even higher price if necessary to gather from the rich harvest of the geological phenomena which that exciting day offered us. I shall now attempt to give you an account of them.

To get from Portrush to the Giant's Causeway you travel in general parallel with the coast, that is to say from west to east. You are all the time on basaltic soil but even so this basaltic soil rests for part of the way on very white calcareous rocks, something you do not notice until you come to a spot where an abrupt section of the coast covers them.[2] These beds fall away

---

[2] The white chalk cliffs topped with black basalt are the great characteristic of the Antrim coast and the offshore island of Rathlin. The outcropping of the chalk from Portrush to Glenarm is very picturesque but forcefully described by Rev. Dr Wm. Hamilton.

'The chalky cliffs may be discovered a little eastward from Portrush; after a short course, they are suddenly depressed to the water's edge under Dunluce Castle, and soon after lost entirely, in passing near the basalt hill of Dunluce, whose craigs, at a little distance from the sea, are all columnar. At the River Bush the limestone recovers, and skims for a moment along the level of the sea, but immediately vanishes on approaching towards the great promontory of Bengore, which abounds in every part with pillars of basalts; under this it is completely lost for a space of more than three miles.

Eastwards from thence, beyond Dunnseverick Castle, it again emerges, and rising to a considerable height, forms a beautiful barrier to White Park Bay and the Ballintoy shore. After this it suffers a temporary desperation near the basalt hill of Knocksoghy, and then ranges along the coast as far as Ballycastle Bay.

Fairhead, towering magnificently with its massive columns of basalts, again exterminates it; and once more it rises to the eastward pursuing its devious course, and

towards the south and quickly disappear under a terrain
of a very different kind which covers them to a great
depth.

On our way we perceived over on the right at a
distance of two rifle shots a very pronounced basaltic
summit which is called Craigahuler. We went over to
examine it; it was revealed on closer view to be a
regular grouping of prismatic columns rising vertically
out of the ground; it prepared our eyes, as yet
unfamiliar with this phenomenon, for what they were
to see. Further on in the village called Bushmills we
crossed a stone bridge, one of the abutments of which
rests on a tier of basaltic prisms. The tier has the
appearance of being part of the architecture designed
for the purpose. These basalts are to be found on the
left bank of the river crossed by the bridge and a little
below it. Finally, a mile on the other side of Bushmills
– and an excellent road all the way – we arrived at a
hamlet where the equipages are usually left. A number
of guides approached us eagerly offering their services
and it was necessary to be appraised beforehand that
they were well-intentioned towards us not to believe by
their dress and appearance that they were a sinister
band. Four, one of whom had accompanied Dr
Richardson on many occasions, came with us and as
we went along we realised that they were attentive and
obliging. Moreover, they answered our questions with
intelligence; they were, indeed, everything which could
be desired in guides. I have, I believe maligned in my
last letter to you the coats worn by the Irish; here fate
humbles me and by way of reparation obliged me to
wear one of these same coats, that belonging to one of
our guides which he readily offered to me to protect
me from the wind and the rain which hardly ever let
up.

Walking for a few minutes we came to the edge of
a fairly high cliff down which we descended by a path

---

forming, on the Glenarm shores, a line the most fantastically beautiful that can be
imagined.'

cut into the escarpment on our right and which gave a gentle decline. This path led to the famous pavement or Giant's Causeway.

It is a kind of promontory, or more correctly, a jetty which goes down to the sea in a gentle slope ending in a point on which the waves dash violently in foam. This jetty forms the western horn of a bay, crescent-shaped and surrounded on the landward side by a high precipitous coast which presents the most beautiful basaltic phenomena. There is nothing to be seen on all sides but grouped columns which are all vertical, with one notable exception to which I shall presently return. The guides have given to the various groups descriptive names derived from known objects: for example the one near the end of the bay is called the Organ; another is called the Weaver's Frame – and so on.

The Giant's Causeway is itself the lowest of these groups sunk so low below the others that the upper ends of all the prisms of which it is composed are practically at sea level. By contrast one sees only the lateral faces of the other groups. In the mass the horizontal section of the thousands of prisms which go to make up the Causeway itself give it the appearance from a distance of a pavement made up of polygonal stones. On closer view these sections are not really at the same level and as you move over the Causeway you step up and down continuously as if on the steps of a stairway.

All the prisms of which this natural jetty is composed, are in almost complete contact with each other without any intervening material; in this particular differing from the basaltic stack at Dunbar where the interstices are filled with a sort of coarse jasper-like material. They differ little in size; their diameter being from twelve to fifteen inches. The number of sides is not uniform, I have seen them of four sides and of eight; but by far the greater number conform to the hexagonal. It is known that the basaltic prisms are ordinarily composed of very nearly uniform beds superimposed on one another with an intervening jointing by which the prismatic continuity is decidedly interrupted. When these beds are separated it is found that their articulation always presents one face convex and the other concave. It did not appear to me that the convexity was more frequently in the bottom than in the top.

The basalt of which all these prisms are composed is a rock hard enough to generate sparks (although imperfect) on the impact of steel. It is blackish in colour when broken, but greyish on the surface exposed to weathering. The grain is compact; it acts on a magnetic needle; its specific gravity is about 2.9 in those samples which have no cavities. These cavities, which are to be found more commonly in the upper parts of the beds than elsewhere, are sometimes empty, at other times they contain fresh water, I am informed by Dr Richardson. I have not seen any which displayed this phenomenon. And speaking of water, there is in the centre of the basalts a little spring of which a sort of hermit has appointed himself guardian and offers glasses of water to visitors for a small payment.

There are a few foreign bodies to be found in the basalt – to wit some zeolites, usually rounded on the outside and radiant when broken, but sometimes also formed in small geodes. These are of all sizes – from a scarcely perceptible grain up to, it is said, a pound in weight. I have not seen any as large as that nor nearly so. Prehnites are to be found and some small veins of chalcedony, some steatite and iron-ore. To judge by the vast beds of red ochre which at various heights separate the beds of basaltic columns[3] this metal in its oxidised state is abundant in the region. Already to be

---

[3] The Causeway was formed by successive outpourings of lava punctuated by long geological periods which in desert conditions gave time for the tops of each layer to weather to a depth of a foot or more. The succeeding outpouring thus had between it and the one below the interbasaltic red layer. These layers are very noticeable in the structure of the columns.

seen in the amphitheatre which surrounds the bay is a phenomenon which becomes more pronounced in other vertical sections of the coast further on to the east – beds of that ochre alternating right up the cliff wall with basalts, some in regular columns, some very confusedly agglomerated and mixed with earth. These alternations are repeated several times; but the beds of ochre in particular occupy the lower levels in this enormous pile, the height of which can be put at 350 feet.

Almost opposite, where the causeway itself begins, all the beds are shot with vertical veins of basaltic material different from the rest; and this is one of those gaws or dykes to which reference was made in my last letter. This basalt is of a finer grain and under the hammer it breaks into small prisms whose sizes and number of faces vary infinitely; but with this peculiarity – the faces exposed by the breaking as well as the prisms they produce are like coatings of slender wrappings of a half transparent greenish matter which I have not yet been able to examine. It would be possible to construct from these small prisms a model of the grand spectacle which we came so far to see.

Very close to this singular vein and near the western face Dr Richardson drew my attention to a considerable stack of prismatic columns leaning forward at a remarkable angle. This is the exception, of which I spoke a short time ago, to the general vertical disposition of all the prisms when they form groups.

Time was running out and our kind and energetic conductor had other features to show us more to the east; but since it is not possible to go there by the shore, especially when the seas are high, we climbed up by the same path by which we had gone down and set ourselves to follow for two miles all the indentations of that escarped coast, coming at times, but cautiously, to the very edge of the cliff so as to enjoy the spectacle which these inaccessible bays have to offer, bays at the bottom of which the sea rushes in its fury to engulf the black rocks in white foam where they lie heaped on the shore. Everywhere the basaltic columns were ranged stage upon stage presenting as it were, by their being piled one on another, a vast architectural array and reaching almost to our feet.

At the bottom of one of these bays I discovered one of the gaws or veins of which I have spoken and which actually runs under the sea. Probably it continues into the vertical face but directly above as we were it stretched out in a straight line from below the cliff on which we stood and unable as we were to see the face of the cliff we could not observe if this be so. The tireless Dr Richardson has since returned to the spot to examine it from below and he has verified our conjecture.

Still moving along this so very remarkable coast we came to the extremity of a promontory known as Pleskin which rises as it approaches the sea to form as it were the head of a gigantic bastion rising almost sheer above the shore to a height of 322 feet.

Here language fails me to capture for you this awesome, magnificent view, which we edged over to take in. The Giant's Causeway and its immediate surrounds which had but shortly before so much impressed us were now but a toy, a miniature beside this abyss beneath us which our eyes gazed on with a curiosity difficult to satisfy. This advanced post was a vantage point for us to take in at once what up until then we had only been able to get in 'partial peeps'.[4] It was possible to study at leisure the magic super-imposition of those immense colonnades; to wonder at the regularity of the columns, thirty, forty feet in height, which go to make up some of them, and to attempt to reflect on the forces which at a period in the

---

[4]   The phrase 'partial peeps' to render Pictet's *'que des échappées'* is taken from a description by Dr Richardson of a panoramic view from a rowing boat off Ballintoy, in an article in the *Newry Magazine*, March–April 1817.

existence of the earth had the capacity of producing so remarkable effects.

Still further on at Port Moon we were told that there is a similar spectacle; but the day was growing late, the weather was atrocious and we should have been putting the kindness of Dr Richardson to too great a test to proceed further. We turned back therefore to the hamlet; and having decided that we should spend the night at Coleraine so as to make up for lost time, we had to tear ourselves away from this so very interesting man whom it had been so rewarding to meet. Again the sorrow of parting, the heaviness of heart. It is the price the traveller always pays for the happiness of making friends on his journey; and the greater the happiness the greater the price to be paid. But where in life are the unmixed blessings?

As to the origins of these basalts as we wait for the day when we shall know them we should rather move towards the truth by the process of elimination than to engage in *ad hominem* arguments as to what they are not. In the meantime you have had perhaps enough of these basalts and I shall not return to them again for some time. I shall have soon to talk at length with you of the interesting Edgworth [sic] family who have been constantly in my thoughts since I met them. Adieu. It is doubtful if I can write again before I get to London.

Letter VII

On board the packet-boat, 5th August, 1801

Lat. 53. 15' 30".
Long 5.30' W of Greenwich (Estimated).

Just in case you might think I am merely writing these numbers at random for a jest I must tell you that I am in fact giving you my latitude as obtained by observing the height of the sun at noon using one of those snuffbox sextants of which I once spoke in the *Bibliothèque britannique* and which whilst having only 18 radii still gives the minutes of degree. The Captain of our vessel when he saw me using it tried it out himself and when he had convinced himself that it was a real sextant, became spellbound before it: the sailors made a ring round me as I made my observations. They in turn displayed such an interest in it that I could not help being somewhat concerned about it especially as it is made entirely in gold. Besides it is not my own but belongs to the celebrated craftsman Troughton[1] who, because at the time of my departure from London had not yet completed the one I had on order from him and which he knew that I set great store to have with me, very kindly entrusted this one to me. I am very anxious to be in a position to return his own instrument to him when I get back to London.

We are having delightful weather and being only four passengers we have complete ease and space. One of our fellow passengers, a renowned comic actor from

---

[1]   Troughton, Edward (1753–1835). Mechanic and instrument-maker.

the London stage, appears so well pleased with his annual visit to Dublin on this occasion that he would succeed in making us glad even if we had, as I have, reason to be sad. I miss the good friend, the worthy companion of my travels to whom I said what may prove to be a long farewell on the Irish shore. I also regret having been constrained to give so little time[2] to the interesting country I am leaving, for a thousand memories of it haunt me. Whilst my fellow travellers besport themselves as they think fit on the bridge or cast a line for the excellent fish which abounds, I take the time to resume my correspondence with you. Let us take up then the account of my journey.

At the close of the tiring day at the Giant's Causeway we stopped at Coleraine. A good turf fire and a good supper re-established the balance on the physical side, and a discovery I made on a stocktaking of our belongings, contributed more than anything else to the charm of the evening. In this way chance placed in my hands a volume the appearance of which was not familiar to me. It contained dramatic verse by an unnamed author. "Ah," I said to Mr Chenevix, "chemistry and natural science are not enough for you; your needs must also have works of the imagination."

"Yes," he replied, "I do like poetry very much."

"And who is the author of these very beautifully printed tragedies?"

"That you will discover in a note at the end."

There I read that the 'second piece had been written in a prison in Paris where the author had spent fifteen months under the tyranny of Robespierre... etc.' (Mr Chenevix had previously told me of that sad episode in his life).

"What," I cried, "You are also a poet. Here we have been travelling together for a whole month and now only by a mere chance do I find this out."

---

[2] Pictet spent twenty days in Ireland, arriving Donaghadee 14th July, leaving Dublin 2nd August. He left Sonna on 22nd July, so he must have spent eleven days in Dublin.

"What would you have? I scarcely know myself as such. It was essential to keep myself occupied during the long captivity. As it is those pieces are not written for the theatre and the public will know nothing until the end of the year. Do, I beg you, say nothing of them on your return to London."

The next day, as you may guess, was spent in the post-chaise from early morning till late at night so that I had no time for geological observations. With nothing to report on that score I am entirely free now to give you an account of the volume I discovered. The two pieces it comprises are very different in content but each contain great beauty in detail. In the first piece, *Leonora*, the intrigues are perplexing and it is open to doubt whether the heroine can really have merited the terrors and punishment she undergoes but the interest is maintained throughout and there are some superb scenes. The second, *Etha and Aidallo*, is in a style practically new and as I read it I felt also impressions which were new to me. It is a high pastoral and the scene is set in those times which must have followed the first flowering of civilisation. The author has skilfully harmonised his material in keeping with that conception. The plot is simplicity itself centred on two women who are at once friends and rivals. Each of them engages in her turn our sympathy, and this sympathy is heightened in intensity and extends to both of them by the interplay of their characters and their situation. The language is what one would expect to have been spoken in that heroic age: all the time noble, sometimes sublime, it is inspired by an exquisite sensibility and generates in the soul of the reader a degree of exhalation which makes him forget the improbabilities. Those who have read the Sixth Book of the *Aeneid* will know the effect. Although I cannot, naturally, compare it for perfection with that great work I can still compare it with it in respect to the feeling engendered in me by reading it and I do not think that my friendship for the author falsifies my judgement here.

It was necessary to suspend reading, however, when we came near to having a spill through losing a bolt from one of the axles. A nail was substituted and this held good until the next relay. On the way I noticed an agricultural practice which appeared to me a good one, to wit the removing of weeds from the corn with a pair of pincers or tongs made of wood and having a long beak. The method seems to me to be less onerous than pulling the weeds by hand and also less disturbing to the corn in the proximity of the weed being removed. Also I witnessed a practice in domestic economy though at first I did not divine the purpose. Not far from the road as we were passing a woman with her skirts raised without undue concern for propriety was stamping with her feet in a bucket. On my enquiring I was told that it was the method used locally for clothes washing. Well, well: *honni soit qui mal y pense*; but the method would hardly recommend itself to our own lye washers.

We passed through Garvagh, Maghera and Stewartstown where we had dinner at six o'clock in the evening. Here the land becomes very fertile and the crops have a magnificent appearance, in singular contrast with the atmosphere of poverty of the inhabitants. Above all prodigious numbers of children are to be seen and all in rags. Frequently whole families are encountered on the move, apparently in the process of changing house which consists of going from one cabin to another a few leagues distant. The mother and the older children carry the belongings which amount to a crock for water and a pot to boil the potatoes. The rest of the children follow as best they can, but the head of the family rarely forms part of the procession – the only kind of movement we met on the roads. To my great surprise, none of these people ever asked for alms, even once.

Journeying through this country the traveller, though the hills are small, is for ever getting down from the chaise and climbing up again. Going downhill the postillions have a mania for never reining in their horses and since such local habits have always a reason behind them I have a strong suspicion that this one has its origin in the uncertainty of the drivers as to the ability of their very small horses – as poor in their harness as their drivers are in clothes – to hold back the vehicle were the attempt made to make them do so. In the circumstances there is nothing else for it but to abandon yourself to Galileo's law of acceleration and to recommend yourself to the mercy of Providence who certainly accords a special protection to the traveller.

As night descended we drove past Charlemont Fort[3] beautiful in its situation. It is a military post and I believe I dimly saw artillery pieces. It was eleven o'clock when we reached Armagh[4] – without once having to prime our pistols.

There is little less readiness in this country, it would appear from what I have learned, than there is elsewhere to resort to the service of the pistol. Mr Chenevix has given me an account of how one of his countrymen, whom he mentioned by name, was travelling recently with a friend in a post-chaise by night. They had fallen asleep. They woke with a start, the chaise being brought to a sudden stop. In the light of the moon they saw a man near the door of the carriage and one of them let fire with his pistol, stretching him dead on the spot. On questioning the postillion they were told that the dead man was a poor wretch of a soldier who had been making his way peacefully along the road and had come alongside the

---

[3]   Pictet uses the word château: what he must have seen was Charlemont Fort.
[4]   It thus took seventeen hours for the sixty miles journey from Coleraine to Armagh in stark contrast to the six hours for the fifty miles journey Edinburgh–Glasgow (LETTER III). Pictet would appear to be in error in giving the latter journey as forty-three miles.

carriage at the request of the driver to help him to disengage his whip which had become caught in the wheel. That ball should weigh forever on the heart of the man who fired it.

I had time to go sightseeing in the city next morning since we were not to set out before six o'clock.[5] Armagh occupies a lovely site on the slope of a richly cultivated hill. It has a college. It has good winter society, among others Dr Richardson, well known to you by now. The houses are built of a red calcareous stone from quarries in the vicinity. I have noticed that many of the loose stones in the district break under the hammer to reveal themselves as schist and all but basaltic.[6]

The time came to be off again and as we were getting into the chaise I was seized with the temptation to joke at the expense of the horses on which we were to rely for the first stage of our journey. They were so very small that I was preparing some witticism on the subject as telling as I could invent at the time when Mr Chenevix sensing my drift checked me.

"Take care", he warned, "not to speak ill of his horses, we shall be lost if you do. Praise them, put him on his mettle and everything will go well. It is another trait in the character of my fellow-countrymen."

As it turned out on that stage, the most arduous of our journey, we had plenty of occasion to admire the skill of our driver and the grit of those same little animals. We became so attached to them that any assistance we were called upon to give them on the steep hills was given with a ready heart. Ah how hard-hearted is the man who ill-treats a horse and how inconsiderate, each new act of ill-treatment adding as it

---

[5]   An instance of how early Pictet rose each day. He must on this occasion have been up shortly after 4 a.m. However, it is well to remember that 6 a.m. say, today, would have been approximately 4:30 a.m. then. Irish time was some twenty-five minutes later than Greenwich and in 1801 there was no advance of the clock to give Summer Time.

[6]   It is difficult to see how a stone could be 'all but basaltic': the observation reflects Pictet's uncertainty as to the origin of basalt.

does to accumulation of wrongs. If such a bully were
to change roles with the brute beast for a single hour
he would almost certainly be cured of his cruelty for
all time. The terrain we crossed is remarkable for its
undulations, generally uniform but very pronounced for
all that. It gave the impression of a remote sea where
enormous waves had been balanced and left fixed in an
imprint. It is one continuous succession of hills and
valleys, the valleys always floored with bogs which are
being exploited, the hills covered with well-farmed
land, except for the higher summits which unfarmed
and devoid of trees, very much resemble the hills of
the former Burgogne. The only sign of manufacture we
saw was that of printed linens.

And apropos of linens, especially those justly
famous Irish linens, I do not know where they are
made or the source of the material which goes into
them. I have seen little or no hemp or flax grown in
the countryside we passed through and the cabins we
saw here and there gave little impression[7] of housing
spinners or crafts: finally shirts are such a rarity
among these poor people that it is tempting, were it not
for the display of it in the famous Dublin Hall, to doubt
whether linen is known in the land at all. That display
in Dublin Hall where linen forms the chief item of
trade proves the contrary. I shall have more to say on
the Hall later.

We made a halt at Castleblayney where there is a
mansion built in the modern style occupying a
delightful position at the foot of a richly wooded hill,
by the edge of a small lake and overlooking an island
in the lake[8]. All the way from here to Carrickmacross

---

[7] Just as the Professor was wrong about the horses he was wrong about the lack of
industry in the cabins. He could have found looms at work in the cabins almost
anywhere between Coleraine and Castleblayney: anyway this statement seems to be at
variance with that made in the previous paragraph.

[8] From information now available it has been possible to identify the house described
here as that of the Whitsitts of Kilcoran, petty landlords and Quakers. Converting an
older house into the mansion which caught Pictet's eye so taxed the family resources
that they were obliged to sell off their property to meet the debts incurred.

are schists which break under the hammer to reveal themselves as prismatic and rhomboidal with basaltic grain and all the time excellent roads, small good-going horses, a very rich soil, a benign nature, but the wretched humanity forming with all these blessings a sad contrast. At seven o'clock in the evening we arrived at Kells where, as we found in any spot worthy of the name of town, there is a garrison. Kells is a lovely little town. The precaution of having a garrison in every town must have effectively curbed all signs of disaffection for certainly we saw none; yet there are many marks of the late rebellion by which this country has been so cruelly affected.

There are, I may say in this locality some very fine mansions belonging to titled families.

Another half day and we shall arrive – I can now say home – for I was received and treated as a brother. That thought gladdened us and we managed to make ourselves gay by drinking the healths of distant friends in negus, a kind of lemonade with wine, a drink too little known on the continent.

The morrow comes – a Sunday. We set out early in superb weather on a very lovely and varied route. Often we skirt parks and rich pastureland. We make a stop at Castledelvin; and it is not until Mullingar that we come at length on a main road, having traversed the greater length of the greater part of this country, until a year ago a kingdom,[9] by byroads, all of them good, and finding at every stage at least one four-wheeled carriage to carry us further on our way, sometimes very passable inns and never an accident. *Éire go bréagh.*

We arrive at two o'clock at Sonna House, hidden until you enter a park when it reveals itself in all its grace and beauty – lawn on one side of the avenue, a stretch of ornamental water on the other, here and there lovely trees, a very rare sight in this part of the

---

[9] The reference is to the absorption of Ireland into the Union by the Act of 1800.

country, clumps of flowering shrubbery, serpentine ways, sheep-grazing meadows, well-appointed outhouses – in a word everything which betokens a noble and lovely house is before my eyes. We are welcomed by friendly children who fling themselves on their uncle's neck. We learn that the rest of the family are at church a good half-league away and off we set in that direction. We meet on the way. There is no surprise for we have been expected and you can readily imagine the joy experienced by a much attached brother and sister[10] on their reunion after a long separation and the guest for whom time can be found to welcome in a first moment like this may feel that he can expect much from Irish hospitality but however favourable might be his expectations from this circumstance the reality will far exceed them.

As I am going to spend two or three days with the family of this house and as you as yet know no member of it except my travelling companion I now introduce you to the others. Sir Henry Tuite,[11] whose ancestors came to Ireland at the Conquest, is the titular owner of the estate but takes little to do with it, living by choice in a corner of the house by himself in a sort of voluntary seclusion though he has nevertheless been out in the world and has travelled. To meet him I should have never attributed to him his misanthropic tendency. Mr Tuite,[12] retired officer and one of those who endured the memorable siege of Gibraltar, is the husband of my friend's sister. They have three children and I have never seen a couple more suited to each other: they spread around them their inward happiness so clearly made manifest in their countenances. An émigré French priest,[13] talented and intelligent, performs the functions of tutor to the children. I can see at once that the abbé is far from displeased at the

---

[10] Mrs Sarah Elizabeth Tuite (1768–18?). See following footnotes.
[11] Sir Henry Tuite (1742–1805).
[12] Hugh Tuite (1747–1843).
[13] Abbé Nicolas Cabley.

opportunity for speaking his native tongue presented by our arrival, though not because he has not acquired English, for at least he has enough to prepare his sermons, duly corrected by the governess for grammar and meaning. These he delivers and, I am told, are wonderfully received, in a neighbouring Catholic chapel. The zeal of this good man is not merely tolerated but indeed encouraged by the family, good Protestants though they be, a circumstance which, it appears to me, is to the honour of all concerned.

During dinner I noticed that the windows of the dining room were partly built-up and that loopholes had been contrived in the walls. On my enquiring as to the cause of these precautions I was informed that the house was very seriously under siege during the late insurrection; indeed that one of the chief rebel camps covered a neighbouring hill and that a like situation, often very critical for them, ensued for all the big land-owners during those disastrous times now no more than two or three years in the past.

At this juncture it occurred to me that it was now seemly that people who had just been reunited after a long separation should be left alone to themselves so I betook myself quietly to my room to occupy myself by writing to you. My letter is now on its way to Geneva. Later we all reassembled to pass a charming evening with Mr Chenevix and his sister giving us a reading of *The Heir at Law*,[14] a comedy with some very engaging Irish characters, which has had a capital success in London.

The following day after one of those family lunches which have for me a charm for ever new, Mr Chenevix and I took a carriage for

---

[14] By George Coleman the younger (1762–1836). Dramatist with twenty-five plays to his credit of which *The Heir at Law* and *John Bull* were the most important. The author of some very coarse verse himself, he became censor in 1824 and was very strict as such. Sometimes he used the pseudonym Arthur Griffinhoofe. Published his autobiography in 1830 under the title *Random Records*. Managed the Haymarket 1789-1813.

Edgeworthstown for that visit I had long looked forward to and with ever increasing interest. It is a two hour drive and even when we are in sight of the lovely house we are further away than we realise because to reach the house itself it is necessary to go round part of the estate which is fairly extensive. But at length we arrive. Mr Chenevix is known to Mr Edgeworth as a neighbour and I beg of him not to introduce me by name but as a stranger who has come a long way to meet him. Mr Edgeworth is in the peristyle and receives us unbooted. He greets us both by name. Who has given me away? At any rate my little ruse has to be abandoned and at once Mr Edgeworth and I are on the footing of old friends. As we enter the doorway I notice that there is a large number of people at tea; but no one stands on ceremony and places are found for us at the table. I look around the faces trying to determine who in the company is the celebrated Maria. Mr Edgeworth reads my mind.

"I see", he says, "that it is not to see me alone that you are here; perhaps Maria has even precedence over her father and I am not going to dispute her right but just to punish you you are to know that she is thirty miles from here and you cannot see her before tomorrow. Stay the night with us; I shall have a messenger sent directly to her; she will travel post tonight and be here midday tomorrow."

"I regret, Sir, we cannot stay the night as we are already engaged to return to Sonna for a special dinner."

"Very well, but in that case, promise to come again tomorrow and I shall still keep my promise to you." We willingly accept the accommodating proposal, the messenger is sent off and three short hours begin their swift course for us with that interesting family.

Mr Edgeworth is, I should think nearly sixty years of age and has every appearance of being in the full vigour of life, extremely active in body and in mind. He has had seventeen children by four wives, the

present Mrs Edgeworth being several years younger
than his eldest daughter, Maria. He has ten children
alive and an eleventh is expected in a few months. The
portraits of his four wives are hung in the hall and
among their children there are evident manifestations
of harmony, friendliness and accommodation
prevailing, very pleasant to behold, and a testimony to
Mr Edgeworth's *Principles of Education* and his
capacity for running his house. Right from the first
moment spent in their company a characteristic trait
exerts itself and that is an intellectual curiosity which
ensures that anything which is likely to promote new
ideas is listened to and examined with serious attention.

I had with me to show to Mr Edgeworth that little
sextant I have mentioned to you. He had scarcely
examined it himself when he explained its purpose to
Mrs Edgeworth; she in turn passed it to the eldest of
the children, he to one of his sisters, she to a younger
brother, who is not the least intelligent of the family,
and so on. On seeing so delicate an instrument pass in
this manner from hand to hand I was not without
unease, but I need not have worried, it met with no
mishap.

The conversation turned to Maria who, it was
evident, is appreciated in her family. In the drawing
room stood the little table at which she writes her
appealing works amidst the talk and chatter of her
brothers and sisters. Before the lovely novel, *Belinda*
which is at present appearing, she published a small
volume entitled *Castle Rack Rent* in which her main
theme is the portrayal of the customs, habits and
indeed the idioms of the Irish through the medium of
the narrative of an old steward, of a certain mansion,
relating the histories of four families who one after the
other have occupied it. The piquant and inimitable
naïveté of the language she gives to the old man, the
oddities and absurdities he describes without ever
questioning them, his manner of jest – all together give

an effect which is full of salt and gaiety, though it would for the most part defy translation.

"Would you like to see the original of the worthy Thady who has made you laugh so much?" Mr Edgeworth asked us. "I shall introduce him to you." He called over to him an elderly male servant who was supervising some haymakers in the meadow and as we listened, put some questions to him on matters familiar to him so that we might have the pleasure of listening to him.

"Haven't we still about the house", he asked the servant at length, "the worker who some time ago saw the fairies dancing on the lawn?"

"Yes, your honour."

"Bring him here."

The workman came over.

"Tell us, John, what was it you saw the other day?"

"Your honour, with the respect I owe you, I was on the roof replacing some tiles when I saw them coming one after the other."

"What, the tiles?"

"No, your honour, the fairies and they set to dancing a reel on the lawn."

"But are you sure that you made no mistake?"

"Mistake is it? I saw them as much as I see you, your honour, and your honourable company."

"And what height were the fairies?"

"Nearly as tall as my leg, your honour."

"I see; and how were they dressed?"

"Faith, your honour, I didn't pay much attention to their clothes, but particularly noticed that they were in boots."

"In boots?"

"Yes, your honour, but in tiny boots; then I lost sight of them in a cloud of dust."

"You see, gentlemen," said Mr Edgeworth, "Maria has invented nothing in *Castle Rack Rent.*"[15]

One of his sons, a lad of seven or eight years, had impressed us by his reflective appearance. "I warrant you", said Mr Edgeworth, "that one has a good head and that he will be a mathematician, he is for ever making calculations." We came on our walk in the park to a seat missing as to one of its four legs.

"Come here, William," said he. "You see that seat which has only three legs: how would you draw a line on it so that if you sat on one side of the line you would be in no danger of falling but if you sat on the other side of it you would be sure to somersault?"

The tight little fellow stopped before the seat while we continued with our walk and, on our return, we found him still there but with his problem solved and he drew on the seat for us the diagonal line between two of the three legs as being the required line.

Two or three robins, instead of flying off on our approach fluttered after us from branch to branch as if they wished to follow us.

"You see those little birds," remarked Mr Edgeworth to us, "they let you know that our children do not torment them as do other children with a thoughtlessness which often amounts to cruelty."

We returned indoors and Mr Edgeworth who has a mechanical turn of mind and an inventive talent expressed a desire to show us some of the useful and interesting inventions in which the house abounds. He showed us to begin with, a clock with an escarpment of his own invention and which is wound up by being geared to a device attached to one of the doors most used in the house.

Next we saw pulleys of a simple yet ingenious construction for closing doors automatically. In another place is a passageway with two doors arranged to form a lobby; when one of the doors is open the other is

---

[15]   Perhaps: but the Irish countryman knew how to please 'his betters' and moreover it would not have been the first time one of them regaled the stranger with a tall story.

closed so that the passage itself is always closed. For
ease in dismantling, the bedposts have special screws.
As is known the drawers in a chest of drawers are
difficult to pull straight: those in the Edgeworth home
are made with a central groove along the bottom.
Although this necessitates some lifting of the drawer to
open yet the total movement of the drawer is smooth
and uniform.

Windows made in the English or contrepoidal
manner are difficult to open when they are a tight fit
and yet they are draughty if they are not so.
Mr Edgeworth has had his windows made slightly
wedge-shaped. The wedge-shaped edge of the sash
enters to a nicety when the window is closed and
makes a complete seal. It requires very little pressure
when opening the window to undo the seal for there is
no retaining friction. We saw a little private theatre
with very cleverly laid-out turning-wings. We saw a
small rolling mill to pattern lead for the glazing of
windows and in all the windows there is a very well
arranged military device for crossfire to forestall a
robber. However, if I were to attempt to give an
account of all the inventions I saw in Mr Edgeworth's
house I should never be finished.

Mrs Edgeworth has also her own share of talent.
She both draws and paints with plenty of taste and
ability whilst her father, Mr Beaufort[16] is a
distinguished man. An excellent map of Ireland owes
its existence to him and others, the most up to date, the
most correct map of Ireland yet made. Noticing that I
was examining a copy which was there with attention
and interest, Mr Edgeworth insisted that I accept it. As
this map is not to be purchased anywhere I prize the
present of it all the more.[17]

But still we had to leave and when it was time to do
so, as he was determined to have our company as long
as he could, he had the horses put in his own carriage

---

[16] Beaufort, Rev. Daniel (1739–1821).
[17] The map was issued to subscribers only.

and we joined him in setting out with our own carriage following. Eventually we parted until the morrow, he returning home, we to Sonna.

When we arrived there it was to a party of guests already assembled with others expected at any time. Present were an Irish peer,[18] a general,[19] officers from a detachment in the neighbouring town, the minister of the parish,[20] the Abbé, ladies in proportionate numbers, all forming what is called good society in any country. I was privileged to be at table with Mr Malone,[21] deservedly known in English literary circles for his *Commentary on Shakespeare*, and more recently for his astuteness in discovering the fraud of an impostor who claimed to have discovered some unedited manuscripts of that celebrated writer, including, among others, an entire tragedy entitled *Vortigern*. We gave an account at the time of this literary event,[22] and that circumstance provided a meeting-point of which I fully availed myself... I was lucky to be taken up with these interesting matters, because the meal had the usual, it could be said, the regulation, phrases of all gatherings of that type where the guests, knowing little of one another, behave in a manner dictated by duty established in custom rather than in one which their own choice or their genuine sociable inclinations would have them behave. The evening commences with the assembly of the large number of guests who invariably have to rely on the weather for conversation and when the weather is neither lovely nor unpleasant the conversation based on it becomes entirely meaningless. After the assembly comes the dinner, and when the appetite has given out (and it is generally recognised that that faculty has its limitations) resort is had to all

---

[18] Edmund Malone's brother, Baron Sunderlin (1738–1816). Distinguished Irish lawyer.
[19] Unidentifiable.
[20] Meares, Rev. Thomas, BA, (1759–?).
[21] Malone, Edmund (1741–1812). Distinguished scholar.
[22] *Bibliothèque britannique*, vol. II, p.269.

those dainties which extravagance piles up in complete irrelevance and the conversation, for which these laboriously thought-up dishes form the usual basis, is of a consequence robbed of all interest. The third stage comes with the ladies retiring to the drawing room and the men, the master of the house presiding, get round a well polished mahogany table on which there is a battery of glasses brimming with a variety of dessert wines which are set going from hand to hand among the guests, right and left, while time seems to have ceased to exist. I did not at all feel myself minded nor did I have the perseverance to hold out until this ritual would come to an end, and having drunk patiently for two hours without any desire to do so – a sort of rack which, if I mistake not, was administered in former times to those guilty of some heinous crime – I took advantage of my privilege as a foreigner who would be ignorant of the local social rules to slip into the coffee room. Alas I escaped from Charybdis only to be caught by Scylla: here the circle of ladies had just about reached the freezing point and had it not been for the genteel noise and the movement produced by the occasional cup of tea being passed I could have believed myself alone looking at the wax models I have seen on the boulevards of Paris.[23]

The mistress of the house made the most praiseworthy efforts to nourish some general conversation; but at length the men reappeared sometime around eleven o'clock. Some took coffee, others tea; the carriages arrived at the front and the guests made their departure – not without having first engaged to meet again within the octave at the house of another one of the set for an equally enjoyable evening.

---

[23] It is just possible that the ill-mannered gatecrashing of Professor Pictet froze the conversation. Whilst there was much merit in his criticism of the lifestyle of the Irish landlord class what irritates here is his holier-than-thou preaching to people who, on his own admission, had received him with the utmost hospitality. Besides, the Tuites seem to have been like the Edgeworths, caring landlords.

"And this is society life in the country," I said in despair to my excellent hosts, when the guests had departed; "This is how you employ your time, your fortune, your moral and physical faculties – to reciprocate boredom, to the profit only of your publicans and grocers."

"Unfortunately", was the reply, "that is how society is constituted here. We also have often the feelings about it that you seem to have; many reasonable people would wish to change this mode of life, but nobody is brave enough to make the first move because there is a fear of being accused of selfish motives by a certain class of upstarts who are feared: so like many others it is necessary to pay social impost and to regard ourselves as fortunate to get off, as today, with only five or six hours lost."

"It is well and good for you, my dear friends, who have more than enough time to spare; but as for me for whom hours have to serve as days, I would have found it so very charming to have spent these hours in your company alone so that I can scarce forgive you for having traded them away as you have done."

The following morning we sped to the rendezvous at Edgeworthstown and I have forgotten to tell you that the house is quite close to the little town of that name which nominates a member of parliament (need it be doubted that this is always an Edgeworth?). The family, as on the previous day, were at table, but today Maria and the eldest of the sons, Mr Lovell Edgeworth, were of the company as well. As I went in I had eyes only for her. I had persuaded myself that the author of the work on education and of so many other useful and readable books must be singled out by some very distinguished outward feature. I was wrong: of small build, with eyes nearly always downcast, of profoundly modest and reserved appearance, with little expression in the features when she is not speaking –

this was the sum of my first observation.[24] But when she spoke, something which for my liking happened too seldom, there was nothing more thoughtful and well said, though always timidly expressed, than that which fell from her lips.

What, might it be imagined, was the first subject of conversation launched by Mr Edgeworth?

"To what extent, do you think", he asked, "can a gasometer measure the pressure of an elastic fluid?"

I shall spare you the reply and the conversation on chemistry which that question set going. It ended with the announcement of dinner.

We moved into the drawing room, in the middle of which was a large table covered with drawings and charts and the opportunity was taken to show me an extremely ingenious but simple apparatus which was thought out and designed by the children for drawing perspective and which is described in *The Treatise on Practical Education*.[25] I admired it.

"It is yours," said Mr Edgeworth on the spot, "kindly accept it as a souvenir of a family which holds you in high regard."

I accepted with gratitude.

We referred briefly to his tiff with his brother who had reproached him with failure to mention religion in a work in which it would have appeared natural to have it introduced. He justified himself at once, giving the reason he had advanced to his brother in his reply to his criticism, namely that it is difficult to treat of this subject in a country where there are sharp differences in religious beliefs, and moreover he made me read a very clear exposition on the propriety of associating religious concepts with other educational ideas, which he had inserted on the second edition of this work.

---

[24] Professor Pictet seems to be too egotistical to realise that being dragged thirty miles from enjoyable company was enough to make any lady less than expansive with the cause of her transportation.

[25] By Richard L. and Maria Edgeworth.

We went on then to discuss various philosophical subjects and in doing so I experienced such a genuine pleasure in finding myself in perfect agreement with the thinking of Maria that often, as they listened to me, she and her father glanced to each other, surprised in the extreme to discover that a stranger coming from a distance of three hundred leagues should appear, in a manner of speaking, to have thought with them. We discussed at length the problem of happiness, especially the happiness of the middle classes in society. Maria informed me that she has written on this, perhaps the most interesting subject in philosophy that can be considered. I gave them those simple notions on happiness of which my friends have heard me speak and which my experience has convinced me are sound. I spoke with them also of that serpentine curve by which I am pleased to represent my life. Its axis is a horizontal line which represents sleep; above the line is the area of good fortune, below that of adversity. At the end of the day I ask myself whether I should have preferred to have slept all day rather than having been awake and on the reply which I give to that question will depend on which side of the curve will be traced the ordinal of the day; and that ordinal is distanced whether above or below the line corresponding with the average memory of pleasure or pain which remains with me, and how vivid is that memory. Whoever will amuse himself by plotting his life in this manner will see, when he makes a reasonably long time into appraisal, a year, say, that his happiness oscillates about the average line with striking regularity: the compensations of life make it so.

With the aid of a small apparatus I had with me on the journey we performed some experiments in chemistry while the ladies attended to their toilet. We took a turn in the park before sitting down to dine and what a contrast to the dinner of the previous evening. I strongly desired Maria to write on this subject with the weapon of ridicule she uses with so much talent, to destroy that so-called social institution; that absurd round of the upper classes which prevents them, as a body, from attempting to employ the talents each of them possesses for the advantage of the community. It bars the way to participation in the joys of the mind and acts like a snuffer on the noble candle flame of the spirit, the sole attribute which marks out the intelligent being from the brute, and, without which, man is reduced to the ignoble state of seeking his pleasure only in eating and drinking, in unworthy feelings of self-love, with a little gossiping thrown in for full measure, and in the event, nearly always counterbalanced by humiliations of equal weight. What a result! Let it be contrasted with what the total potential of human faculties could yield when everyone, reciprocating the efforts of others, directed that potential towards the procurement of the maximum of human happiness. But, as I see it, to obtain that maximum it would be necessary to reconstitute society on the base of education, to ask for a kind of revolution so as to change the heavy gothic structure which, as an excuse for civilisation, is in some countries their ornament. Perhaps some apt and courageous spirits will arise to work in common for a gradual reform; but it will not be the present generation which will gather in the harvest.[26]

There are many other things I could have noted to you about this family. For example, I have said nothing of Mr Edgeworth's eldest son, a very well informed young man just fresh from the mould of the University of Edinburgh, an institution where the dedicated will become indeed learned. Nor have I said anything of Miss Charlotte, his sister, a young lady of sixteen, lovely and fresh as a rose, whose eyes, beaming with intelligence, show that without daring to put in a word of her own in the conversation she does not lose any of those which circulate about her; she

---

[26] Professor Pictet might at least have acknowledged his inspiration, the Geneva-born Rousseau. The Edgeworths were much influenced by Rousseau.

knows how to listen, a quality rare enough in the young. But, then, in that house nothing is as it is elsewhere.

The moments were passing with the most desolating speed. The family had been counting on keeping us over until the morning but in this they had forgotten our duty to our hosts at Sonna House to whom we had only the remaining evening to give. I saw in Mr Edgeworth a sign of disappointment which was almost beyond his control. But at the same time he understood our reason and had the horses yoked in his carriage and, as on the previous day, accompanied us a part of the way. Again one of those farewells which are the inevitable portion of the traveller and whose bitterness is always in strict proportion to the pleasure obtained in the company left behind. I am not without hope of one day seeing at Geneva some member of that so very friendly and distinguished family.[27]

Night has stolen up on me, so that I can scarcely see in the cabin where I write. The English coast is within sight and we should in a few hours drop anchor if the wind should decide to freshen a little. Here I end my letter; it is long enough to convince you that I have some time left me to call my own and that I have not been bothered with seasickness. I shall post it when I get to Holyhead. I still have to tell you of my experiences in Dublin and when I write I shall add a few general observations on the country I am about to traverse. There you have the plan of my next letter. Adieu.

---

[27] The Edgeworths did go to the Continent in the autumn of 1802, returning to Ireland in 1803.

Letter VIII

Holyhead, 6th August, 1801

Although my friends, I sent you a long letter only hours ago here I am beginning another. By an incident you will soon learn about I saw myself condemned to spend more than twenty-four hours here despite the fact that the mail coach leaves every day. I fretted this morning at the disappointment but by evening I have seen nothing more interesting geologically than the marvels of this coast which I spent so much of the limited time at my disposal to visit. I do not even know whether the geological features I saw there have, or have not, a more basic quality from which to infer causes than that of any other basaltic phenomena no matter how striking. My head is so full of them, I am so impressed by them that I can barely resist the temptation to go on talking about them in this letter but all the same, I feel I should rather take up again my chronicle of events; and who knows I might even bring myself right up to date in this letter. I am going therefore to bring you back with me to my excellent friends at Sonna House where indeed my thoughts are, and where on our return from Edgeworthstown we spent an evening not indeed gay – with the parting of the morrow hanging over us – but all the same one which had its own sweetness. There is in the recesses of the heart a place for the feelings which such a situation produces; one experiences some pleasure in storing away those memories there where they will remain for what remains of life.

Mr Chenevix would have it that, to the many obligations I was already under to him, he would add the further sacrifice of parting from his family with whom he had just been reunited to go with me to Dublin and remain with me for as long as I should be there. We set out early without saying farewell; a single look as we broke up the evening before had said all we needed to say. We travelled post all day on a main road which, on the approach to Dublin, becomes pleasant, even picturesque in the varied views along the banks of the River Liffey. Not a single incident did we encounter except once that our horses were frightened at a sight to which they were as new, as was the sight of our post-chaise to the jades we met along the way in single harness in the small carts I have already described for you. What provoked the fright in our horses was the sight of a four-wheeled wagon, the only one I have seen in my entire Irish journey and which belonged to an iron foundry some Scots have established near Dublin.

But apropos of vehicles, just as I have spoken lightly of the small carts so I have admired one which is, I believe, peculiar to Dublin and which is called the jaunting-car. It is a runabout vehicle on two very small wheels on which is attached a horizontal rectangular body. There is room on each side for three persons; each seated so that his legs are out over the wheels from which they are protected by a footboard, well cased at the back and sides against splashes; the six passengers sit back to back so that the wits call this equipage an Irish vis-à-vis. There is room between the two groups sitting back to back to pack a small amount of baggage and to the front, room for the jarvey, as the driver is called. The lot is drawn by a single horse. No sight can be more pleasant than to see a father, mother and four sisters on one of these cars driven by a young brother at a good pace heading for run in the country. I believe that this vehicle solves the problem of how to obtain the maximum effect from a single horse. It must be acknowledged that when it rains there is no protection except that given by an umbrella – if there is one; but to make up for this, if there is the slightest fear of a spill it is as easy to climb down from the seat on to the road as it is to rise from a chair to move across a room – and as easy to climb back up again.

Some time before we arrived in Dublin we passed on our right an enormous building of fine appearance which I learn is the college or seminary of Maynooth where Catholics destined for the priesthood make their studies.[1] About five o'clock in the afternoon by a road which skirts a canal or river which the ebb and flow of the tide renders alternately lovely and unsightly, we reached the capital of Ireland.

The desire to meet again the celebrated Kirwan,[2] the Nestor of chemists in Great Britain was one of my

---

[1] Under the Penal Laws – largely in abeyance by the 1790s – students for the Catholic priesthood were educated on the Continent: at the time of the French Revolution out of a total of 478 of these students 348 were in France. As happens so often in public affairs religion became the football of politics so that it was argued that these students in France should be saved from the poison of the Revolution by having them educated in Ireland. At any rate, the old Irish Parliament contributed eight thousand pounds towards the establishment of the college Pictet mentions here – with generous subsequent grants. As can be seen from what Pictet says earlier, Penal Laws or no Penal Laws, the Catholic religion was being freely practised in the 'chapels' throughout the country by 1801.

[2] Kirwan, Richard (1733–1812). Scientist of great distinction, he was born at Cloughballymore, Co. Galway. He made important contributions to analytical chemistry by his experiments and he was a figure in the study of mineralogy; his *Elements of Mineralogy* mentioned by Pictet was for many years the standard work on the subject. An exceptional linguist, he maintained a communication with the scientists of Europe.

We learn from Pictet of Kirwan's plans to have a mining board for Ireland established. Charles Abbot (1757–1829), first Baron Colchester, during his short term as Chief Secretary, encouraged Kirwan to draw up the heads of a bill for the establishment of the board – Charles Francis Greville MP (already mentioned), according to Richard Griffith, the Inspector of the Royal Marines in Ireland, felt Kirwan's plan was worthwhile. Writing in 1814, Griffith says, 'the late Right Honourable Charles Greville, the enlightened patron of mineralogical science, was also very anxious on the subject [the board]: and a very short time before his lamented death, he addressed a letter to the Earl of Liverpool pointing out the benefit which Ireland would derive from a general examination of mines and minerals'. Later Griffith says, 'Our celebrated countryman, the late Mr Kirwan, laid a proposal before the Government for a Mining Board, similar to those under whose guidance the German mines are conducted; but it was imagined that the control, which this Board was

motives for coming to this country. On my arrival I wrote a few lines asking him to meet us as soon as we had dined; he gave us a pleasant surprise by coming to make his reply in person and he fetched us to his house where we spent a most interesting evening. I have never known a mind more richly furnished than his; his memory is completely reliable and embraces a unique variety of knowledge. At the moment he is concerned with the subject of meteors and he would appear to be convinced that there is now a sufficient fund of facts to establish a body of knowledge on the subject and to deduce from it principles and laws. There is no one more qualified than he for that type of work which demands a vast amount of correspondence. He corresponds over a wide area; he places much store in procuring for himself everything published in France, in Germany and in the northern countries, on all the branches of science he cultivates; and the orderly and scholarly life he leads gives him plenty of time which he knows how to use profitably. He has a considerable library in which I noticed a copy of our journal[3]. I was looking forward to seeing his laboratory, but he did not bring us there. Not infrequently the painter is reluctant to let his studio be seen.

When we returned from this first interview we put what we left of the day to good use by visiting some of the finest places in Dublin; and if I were an expert on architecture I could write to you of facades, colonnades and all the rest; if these are not as plentiful there as in Rome, they are at least more so than in London. The former Irish Parliament was much better housed than is the Imperial Parliament in the capital of the British

intended to possess over all the mines in the country, would interfere too much with the property of private individuals, and could not be carried into effect consistently with the freedom of the British Constitution'. (*Report on the Leinster Coal District – 1814*).

Kirwan was sixty-eight when Pictet met him in Dublin and by that time he had developed the oddities which marked his later years. (Pictet does not mention these.) Afraid of catching a cold, for example, he would sit before a blazing fire, even in summer, wearing a hat and coat. He received his visitors reclining on a couch.

[3]   *Bibliothèque britannique.*

Empire. The college, that is to say the University buildings present an equally noble appearance; and it is a pity that the area which these two lovely buildings front is little more than a large street. Further on we came to a place or a square which seemed to be as spacious as any in London but not so well kept.

I find in my notes three observations I made as we made the round of the streets: the contrast between the frightfully tattered dress of a great part of the population and the wealth so obvious in many buildings; the many gambling houses, well lighted and in good state where can be seen in hordes resembling in every aspect what would in France be called 'the riff-raff'; on display on the stall of a bookseller a work with the title *General Instructions for all Seconds in Duels* by a ci-devant Captain (leading me to the conviction that in the art of killing one's fellow man, en mass, war, or singly, duelling, the latter is the more in favour in this country, and moreover since seconds are involved in the diplomatic end of the business the principles thereof should, fittingly, be laid down in a body of Principals).[4]

The following day we had much to see. Mr Chenevix, who had been away from Dublin for several years, was afraid that he was out of touch and in the morning he found two of his friends to accompany us. They never left us during our stay. It would have been impossible for us to have had a better choice. One was Mr Weld,[5] the author of *A Canadian Journey*, a work from which we have given an extract

---

[4]   "Duelling in the eighteenth century was very frequent in England, but the fire-eater and the bravo never attained the position in English life which was conceded in Ireland. The most eminent statesmen, the most successful lawyers, even the fellows of the university, whose business was the training of the young, were sometimes experienced duellists. An insolent, reckless and unprincipled type of character was naturally formed." (Leckey)

[5]   Weld, Isaac (1774–1850). Traveller and writer. Weld gave the account of his North American travels, in which he met Washington, in his *Travels* (1799). Other publications were, *Scenery of Killarney* (1799), and *Survey of Roscommon* (1848). He was half-brother to Charles Weld (1813–1869) the historian of the Royal Society.

in translation in our journal, the other was
Mr Higgins,[6] Professor of Mineralogy and Chemistry
with the Dublin Society. Together we arranged our
affairs so as to put every available minute to the best
possible use over two days, and the plan was followed
to our complete satisfaction. There is no better, no
more friendly man than Mr Weld. I very much fear
that I began abusing his exceptional good nature in the
vain search I made for a sample of gold from a mine
recently discovered in County Wicklow: we had seen
some in the homes of several persons but no one
wanted to part with any. These pieces were irregular in
shape though rounded as if they had been rolled.
Nobody had any of the matrix and their weight could
have been anything from three to six pennyweights.
This mine is presently being exploited I was told, and
our two friends offered to go there with us if we
decided to make the trip: it would have involved only a
matter of three or four days but it was necessary to
resist the temptation – as so often.

Mr Kirwan had arranged to meet us in the
mineralogy theatre of the Dublin Society – an
institution of which I was anxious to get detailed
information. In the interval before going there we
visited the Custom House built on a much grander
scale than anything the trade of Dublin would seem to
demand; it would be on a par with the one in London I
believe. It is capped by a cupola which we climbed.
From the top we had a lofty view of the entire city
lying right beneath us. The principal tax offices are
magnificently lodged in the centre of the building
which is really enormous and the style of architecture
is in keeping with the function. The buildings of the

---

[6]   Higgins, William (?-1825). Born in Sligo, Higgins became a brilliant chemist but
was indolent. He gave the first account in English of Lavoisier's system of chemistry.
In his *Comparative View of the Phlogistic and Antiphlogistic Theories* (1799) he is said
to have been the first to enunciate the law of multiple proportions. For a time chemist to
the Apothecaries' Company of Ireland, he became librarian and chemist to the Dublin
Society and eventually professor of that body. Elected FRS in 1806, he proved too
indolent to present himself for final admission.

124

Dublin Society[7] whither we then betook ourselves, have little exterior appearance to recommend them but the interior bespeaks activity, grand design and great circumstances. The Society was founded in 1749 by Royal Charter with the title of *Society for Promoting Husbandry and Other Useful Arts*; it has a large membership.

It owes its existence mostly to Thomas Prior, and Samuel Madden, a very benevolent and very able clergyman of the Established Church, for the purpose of improving husbandry, manufactures, and other useful arts. The part which this society plays in the history of Irish industry during the eighteenth century is a very eminent one. It attracted to itself a considerable number of able and public-spirited members, and it was resolved that each member, on his admission, should select some particular branch, either of natural history, husbandry, agriculture, gardening, or manufacture, should endeavour as far as possible to make himself a complete master of all that was known concerning it, and should draw up a report on the subject. The chief object of the society was as far as possible to correct the extreme ignorance of what was going on in these departments in other countries which, owing to poverty, to want of education or enterprise, and to the isolated geographical position of the country, was very general. The society published a weekly account of its proceedings, collected statistics, popularised new inventions, encouraged by premiums agricultural improvement and different forms of Irish industry, brought over from England a skilful farmer to give lessons in his art, set up a model farm and even model manufactories, and endeavoured, as far as possible, to diffuse industrial knowledge through the kingdom. The press cordially assisted it, and for some years there was scarcely a number of a Dublin newspaper that did not contain addresses from the society with useful receipts and directions for farmers, or explanations of different branches of industry, whilst offering small prizes for successfully following the instructions given. Thus – to give but a few out of very many instances – we find prizes offered for the best imitation of several different kinds of foreign lace; for the best pieces of flowered silk, of damask, of tapestry, of

---

[7]   The Dublin Society. The most important of the signs of public spirit in Ireland was the Dublin Society, which was founded in 1731.

wrought velvet; for the farmers who could show the largest amount of land sown with several specified kinds of seed, or manured with particular kinds of manure; for draining, for reclaiming unprofitable bogs, for the manufacture of cider, of gooseberry wine, and of beer brewed from Irish hops; for the best beaver hats made in the country; for the baker who baked bread or the fisherman who cured fish according to receipts published by the society; for every crop crimped in the method that was in use in England and Holland and brought on a certain day to the market on Ormond Quay.

Such methods of encouragement would be little suited to a high stage of commercial or agricultural activity, but were eminently useful in a country where, owing to many depressing circumstances, industrial life was extremely low... In 1750[8] it received a Royal Charter..." (Leckey).

> At the entrance I observed – march of progress – all the models furnaces, stoves and fireplaces of my illustrious friend, Von Rumford.[9] They were all there on show, next door to the physics laboratory. Further on was a very long gallery – a place dedicated entirely to the fine arts – replete with drawings, paintings, sculptures, in my view, many very interesting showpieces. In still another hall were models of useful machines as well as of every variety and size of agricultural and farming implements. Another room housed the fine mineralogical collection which the society has acquired from a certain Mr Leske[10] and which Mr Higgins is at present classifying. It was at this point that Mr Kirwan joined us and meeting him thus made me determined to use his knowledge of this wonderful collection to the greatest possible advantage.

---

[8] Leckey is thus at variance with what Pictet says – 'founded in 1749 by Royal Charter'.

[9] In the spring of 1796 Von Rumford was in Dublin as the guest of the Chief Secretary, Lord Pelham. He left behind him a collection of his inventions and improvements.

[10] Leske, N.G. (1751–1786). German mineralogist.

We fixed a time to go together to the country to pay a visit to the second highest person in the land,[11] for my part, being anxious to renew a relationship begun some fifteen or twenty years before.

I have given you only a very cursory account of this society. It has a very ambitious programme mapped out for itself, a programme it cannot possibly fulfil without generous government assistance. Let me outline some of its commitments. There is the Botanical Garden, of which I shall soon speak, employing seven professors with salaries ranging between £100 and £300 sterling annually. These professorships are:

(1) Botany and Husbandry,
(2) Veterinary,
(3) Figure Drawing,
(4) Landscape and Ornament,
(5) Architecture,
(6) Natural Philosophy,
(7) Experimental Philosophy.

The Revenue of the Society is about £5,000 per year. In addition the former Irish Parliament did at times supply capital when the need for such was established. Its requirements have always been many: it does everything on a liberal scale. To encourage agriculture and the arts it gives many premiums.

You can share with me the pride I felt when I discovered that its Department of Fine Arts is to all intents and purposes modelled on our Society of the

---

[11] The second highest person in the land would almost certainly be the Chief Secretary, who in July 1801 was Charles Abbot, first Baron Colchester (1757-1829), barrister, a parliamentarian who did a very great amount of work in the legislature. Abbot introduced the first census of population in 1801. He became Chief Secretary of Ireland in February 1801 and resigned in January 1802. A friend of Sir Joseph Banks and Sir Charles Blagdon, (an associate of Von Rumford), it seems likely that it was through one of these that Pictet had met him earlier as indicated here. Abbot was interested in reclaiming bogs. He asked Sir Joseph for advice on the Irish bogs. Banks knew something about draining fenlands but nothing about peat bogs so he was not able to help. Abbot encouraged Kirwan in his proposal to have a board of mining established. On his relinquishing the Chief Secretaryship of Ireland he returned to England to become Speaker of the House of Commons.

A view at the head of the canal or basin at Paddington.
© *British Museum*

Scientific researches! New discoveries in pneumatics or an experimental lecture on the powers of air.
© *British Museum*

The famous 'low-backed' cart, now virtually extinct.
© *Ulster Museum*

Girls setting seed potatoes.
© *Ulster Museum*

Selling the water.
© *Mrs Marie Don*

Sonna House.
© *Irish Architectural Archive*

Edgeworthstown Manor House.
© *National Library, Dublin*

Customs House, Dublin.
© *National Gallery, Dublin*

Count Von Rumford by his 'ain fireside'.
© *British Museum*

The Canal Quays at Coalisland, Co. Tyrone

'The Ackiedock'.
© *Democrat Photograph*

Arts in Geneva. Listen whilst I translate from the 'Introduction' of the *Transactions of the Society*, the first volume of which has just appeared, and acknowledge that we can without vanity say with Correggio,[12] *Anche noi*; we too.

'The Society has established schools of architecture, ornament and figure drawing for boys whose parents are not in circumstances to afford this kind of education. The school of architecture is free to all journeymen, carpenters, masons, stonecutters, etc., so that they may learn the true proportions of cornices, basements, indeed of all features in a building, should they come to work for themselves. They have also opened an academy for live figures where regular artists are admitted free of expense. As they are sensible that it will be an advantage to the kingdom to cultivate the art of drawing, annual premiums are given to the pupils of their schools, and they propose to extend their premiums to established artists, being convinced that the art of drawing is no sooner become common than it keeps all artists and manufacturers, as it were, in awe. It obliges them to give plans and models to everything they promise to perform – it enables all eyes to judge of a work not yet executed – it conveys into whatever is done for us, a truth and symmetry, which ensures us the enjoyment of a thousand beauties, in things that seemed in no way relative to drawing.'

The authors of this same introduction state that it will be possible to procure separately each of the essays appearing in the *Transactions* so that any farmer or manufacturer to whom they may be of any interest may conveniently acquire them, and in keeping with

---

[12] Allegro, Antonio, called Correggio (1489–1534). One of the greatest Italian painters. In a blinding appreciation of the art of painting when he gazed on Raphael's St Cecilia he cried out *"Anch'io son' pittore"* ("I too am a painter"). It is to be hoped that Pictet is speaking here in jest. It would be a bit presumptuous of him to compare himself and his co-founders of the Society of the Arts in Geneva with Correggio before Raphael's masterpiece.

the humility and the public spirit which animates the members of this worthy society they end with these words:

'Were the members of this Society actuated by the mean ambition of commencing authors, then indeed their *Transactions* had probably appeared in another shape. But different motives required different conduct. Their intention is not to amuse the public with nice and laboured speculations, or to enrich the learned world with new and curious observations; but, in the plainest manner to direct the industry of farmers and common artists; and to bring practical and useful knowledge from the retirements of libraries and closets, and from foreign languages, into public view. In short, to be universally beneficial is their only end; and whether they attain it, by making new discoveries, or publishing those already made; by increasing the present fund of knowledge, or by conveying it into more hands, is to them perfectly indifferent.' – Ideals when they are expressed in this manner deserve to meet with success. I have before me these *Transactions* but so far have not been able to run through even the first volume. There are a number of essays which would appear to have an interest for me.

Our projected visit to the country[13] drew a blank, to my own great regret but by way of compensation allowed me to spend two hours in the coach with Kirwan. His horses were somewhat fresher than one would associate with a naturalist; but though they were too bothersome to allow uninterrupted conversation, I had still the opportunity to learn much and to admire what I saw in passing through the park known as The Phoenix, truly the phoenix of parks – in its entirety there is simply nothing in the neighbourhood of London to equal it.

---

[13] Presumably to visit the Chief Secretary or the Earl of Clare.

The conversation turned chiefly on a favourite project of Mr Kirwan, the setting up of a Board of Mines in his country; here are his main ideas.

This body would be composed of a dozen members who would have to be thoroughly expert in prospecting and exploiting the minerals of the country. There would be a laboratory for conducting tests. Four of the twelve members of the Board would receive an annual honorarium of £500 sterling; two of £400; and six of £300.

The candidates for these positions would be expected to know Latin and French in addition to being versed in all the knowledge and experience demanded of their profession. They would have to spend two years at Freyburg, travel for a year in the mining areas of Germany, and a further year in similar areas of England.

Their ability would be attested by rigorous examinations. Each summer at least two of the members would be sent on a mineralogical survey in the different counties of Ireland.

Once it was established, no owner of a mine could work it without the permission of the board.

Every owner of a mine would, on its discovery, send a sample of the gangue to the board which would, inside a month, depute one of its board members to make the survey with all necessary detail and report on the area in which the mine was situated. If this initial report were favourable one of the senior members of the body would subsequently be sent out to make a further survey; and if the findings from the second survey were encouraging the board would then freely give to the owner a certificate of approbation and with this he could go about forming a company to undertake the exploitation on his own. The board would ensure that the funds necessary to begin operations were deposited in the bank; and the operations would be supervised entirely by one of the members of the body

which would receive such aliquot of the profit as would
be expedient.

These ideas are in part suggested by what
Mr Kirwan tells me of the German system of
exploitation; in other words they are the product of
long and fruitful experience. I pass them on to you in
this report to publish in our journal.

On our return I took leave of Mr Kirwan, not
expecting to see him again: I was very sensible of his
obliging welcome. If the pursuit of science had no
other result than to establish such relations among its
practitioners as to put them on their first meeting on
the footing of old friends, this would already be a
wonderful blessing.

The following day was set aside almost entirely for
our visit to the Botanic Garden and to a few hours of
work at my lodgings to send you extracts from the two
Memorials which are to appear in the forthcoming
volume of the *Transactions of the Royal Irish Academy*
presently in the press and which will have in our own
journal the merit of novelty, at least. There is a work
by Mr Knox[14] on the Calp. There is also an article by
Mr Chenevix on sulphuric acid.

Accompanied by our two friends we set out
betimes. The Botanic Gardens are situated to the north

---

[14]   Knox, George, Rt Hon. (1765–1827). Politician and MP, Knox was the fifth son of
Thomas Knox, First Viscount Northland of Dungannon and of Anne, daughter of Lord
Knapton and sister of the Viscount de Vesci.

Knox was an enigmatic figure. He is represented by the historian Leckey as a
moderate, a liberal in favour of Catholic emancipation and all his speeches in the old
Irish Parliament support Leckey in this view. In his speeches he was also eloquently
and consistently against the Union (1801). He is later in correspondence with Viceroy
Hardwicke, advancing his claim to a pension on the grounds that he had at one stage so
managed things as to prevent the opposition from bringing in an anti-union motion at a
critical time.

He was appointed a lord of the Treasury, March 16th, 1805, an office he held only
till February 1806.

Dublin University conferred on him the degree LLD (*hon. causa*) in 1791. He was
an MRIA, and in February 1802 he became a fellow of the RS, London.

The paper to which Professor Pictet refers was published in the *Transactions of the
Royal Irish Academy*, Vol. VIII, p.207; read 9th March, 1801.

of the city in a district known as Glasnevin. On our
way there we skirted and then crossed a very fine
navigational canal brought down to sea level by a
system of locks but we saw for all that, little or no
navigation. I am led to believe by a certain amount of
evidence of this kind that the people of this country are
characterised by a lively spirit for promoting schemes,
but with little perseverance for seeing them through.[15]

The garden is a vast enclosure of twenty-seven
English acres bounded by a river, on the other side of
which is a wood of high, long-established trees as a
shield against the north winds. In it is every variety of
soil to suit all the wide variety of plants which are
grown within its borders. At the entrance there is a
very lovely house for the Professor of Botany. Here
the lessons are taken and here also we saw a choice
library for the use of the course. Near it are five large
hot houses all, including the roof, of glass; and you
will understand that nothing has been overlooked when
I tell you that to provide native conditions for the
saxatile plants in the garden, a special hillock, well
supplied with large blocks of quartz, has been built at a
cost of six hundred pounds sterling. Further on there is
an excellent spring enclosed in a grotto built of
artificial lavas supplied by a glass-making furnace.

---

[15] The correctness of Professor Pictet's remarks here can hardly be denied, at least in
relation to inland navigation. One might identify four reasons for the gross underuse of
the canals:
  1) the generally underdeveloped state of the country industrially: the merchandise
     was not there in the volume required for transportation;
  2) the abundance of peat for fuel: coal was always an important element in canal
     transport but here it has to be admitted that the canals could have been used to
     transport peat to the capital, as the railways were used in the Second World
     War;
  3) the difficulties of containing water in channels which ran through so much bog
     and limestone, coupled with a lack of expertise in the problems involved;
  4) the policy of the old Irish Parliament which, as a counter to paying certain royal
     revenues to which it objected, was all too ready to engage in speculative
     ventures just to give out grants; this has a bearing on what has been said on
     roads. This policy led to too many unfinished projects.
Irish canals will get a fuller treatment – or at least one will – when the relevant part of
Letter XI is given.

Some pieces resemble the tremolite of St Gothard – so much so that they could have been taken for the real thing.

But leaving aside all question of the exotic, the layout of the garden appeared to me to be as useful as it was ingenious. The shrubs are all arranged together, as are the fruit trees; then come the medicinal plants, elsewhere are the indigenous trees; then, in another area, are the culinary plants; in still another the plants used in dye-making. Then there are the creepers and the climbers, then the cryptogames, the herbaceous, the graminaceous plants. There are a number of species whose names I have forgotten; but I have made a note of two departments which merit our special attention. The first is that for cattle and farm animals according to five types on the basis of those kept in the country; namely sheep, goats, cows, horses and pigs. Each type of animal has four plots: in the first are the species of plants for which it has a preference; in the second those which suit it; in the third are those which it refuses and in the fourth those which are noxious to it. All the plants are clearly and legibly named instead of being numbered as is usual in the designation of the plants in collections such as this.

The other department worthy of imitation is the experimental garden. Here each plant has conveniently placed near to it a record of the experiment being conducted in relation to it: this is given in sufficient detail to attract the interest of the visiting observer. I would willingly have devoted several hours reading these informative labels. It seemed to me that potatoes figured particularly in these experimental researches; and indeed there are few plants which merit so much attention as that precious root, especially in Ireland, where it feeds, as is known, a very considerable proportion of the population.

You would agree that in such a setting so ideally suited to it a course in botany would be pursued with great interest. But the Dublin Society does not rely on chance enthusiasm alone in its effort to promote the scientific method which derives from attendance at the course; it is equally concerned with sustaining interest so that it employs a further incentive to combine emulation with a more reliable spur as it is generally called, or more simply, monetary rewards. I do not know of any other institution for instruction where this type of promotion is employed; and since the idea is novel, even in Dublin, I cannot prophesy the outcome. In the meantime here is the programme; it is by any standard remarkable enough.

'Being as it is that Dr Walter Wade[16] has begun his lesson in Botany the Society, desirous of encouraging them as well as the study of Botany to the advantage of agriculture is offering the following premiums.

'*1st* To the person who in a public examination to be held in the winter of 1801 or the spring of 1802 as shall be advertised, shall give the best answers in General Botany – fifty pounds sterling and a gold medal.

'To the first person with honourable mention in the same examination, thirty pounds sterling with a gold medal.

'To the second person with honourable mention, twenty pounds sterling.

---

[16] Wade, Dr Walter (?-1825). Physician and botanist. Wade became *accoucheur licentiate* in 1787. He practised in Dublin. In a Latin work he published on botany in 1794, *Catalogus Systematicus Plantarum in Comitatu Dublinensis*, he described himself as 'M.D. Licentiate of the King's and Queen's College of Physicians, the Lecturer in Botany'. It has been claimed that this Latin work was the first systematic work on botany produced in Ireland. In any event the author was the pioneer in diffusing a general taste for botany in Ireland. He himself went everywhere in the country in search of plants. He is credited with being the first person to find the pipewort in Ireland.

It was through his efforts that a grant of £3000 was obtained to establish the Botanic Gardens. Professor Pictet's account of Wade's methods of spreading an interest in botany in Ireland is a timely memorial to his practical vision.

In 1802, the year after Pictet's visit, Wade published a full syllabus of a course of lectures in botany. He described himself on the title page as 'Professor and Lecturer on Botany to the Right Honourable the Dublin Society'. He has several other works to his credit.

'*2nd* To the person who, in an examination of the same type, shall give the best answers on useful and noxious plants for each type of animal with respect to their quality, botanical description and the soils which suit them, fifty pounds sterling, and a gold medal.

'To the first person with honourable mention, thirty pounds sterling and a gold medal.

'To the second, twenty pounds sterling

'*3rd* To the person who shall give the best answers on the various type of fodders, their qualities, their botanical description and the soils which suit them etc., twenty pounds sterling

'To the person with honourable mention, ten pounds sterling

'*4th* To every person who in the years 1801 and 1802, shall produce to the Society a plant, tree or shrub native to Ireland and not described by Linnaeus or the most modern botanist, five guineas besides a premium of twenty guineas'.

'I transmit to you another idea which seems to me to be equally favourable for procuring for oneself and for the public choice seeds of the principal grasses to be found both in natural and artificial meadows; it is all part of the same plan.

'For each of the seeds named below, which shall be collected and sent to Dr Wade at the Botanic Garden before the 1st January, 1802, entirely pure and well cleaned namely:

Poa trivialis,
Poa pratensis,
Poa annua,   A premium of four shillings
Festuca ovina,   per pound weight
Dactylis glomerata,
Festuca pratensis,
Avena Flavescens,
Avena elatior.

'Should more than four hundred pounds of these reach the Society, no more than the first four hundred will be accepted.

'A premium of eight shillings the bushel will be given for the following seeds:
Alopecurus pratensis,
Antoxanthum odoratum.
'The first of these two is the earliest of the grasses and the one to give the most hay.
'The second gives the hay its pleasant odour, and should be increased in all meadowlands.'
'The Society proposes to distribute the seeds at cost price and it recommends that they be sown in ground that has been well prepared so as to make sure that they will be profitable and harvested in their purity.'
In the brochure on which I rely it is said that the Dublin Society is the only society serving the public in this country. Be that as it may there is not, I believe, a country in the world in which philanthropy shows itself as active in so many varied forms as in Ireland, a land, it maybe said, which in some other respects is but half civilised.[17] I have informed myself precisely on this question of philanthropy, and the manifestations thereof pass the bounds of credibility.
I have lost count of the societies involved but I have made an attempt to classify them.
First of all the Dublin Society has a little sister born in 1800 which is specially dedicated to the advancement of husbandry; it derives its title from its purpose.
Then there are the hospitals both public and private, fifteen in number. I single out the following:
The Foundlings: three thousand children are fed there.
That for Lying-In founded in 1745 by a private individual. Between the time of its establishment and 31st October, 1800, 44185 women were admitted to it;

---

[17] A man who was to have no objections to service under Napoleon, who judged progress in industrial and suchlike terms was hardly qualified to pronounce on civilisation. He seems quickly to have forgotten the kindness he received from the poorly dressed guide at the Causeway. But then he is most likely parroting the views of the class with which he is exclusively associated.

and 23510 male children and 21458 female were born there. 767 women gave birth to twins, 14 to triplets and 1 to quadruplets.

Next there is the Industrial School founded in 1773 where since that date 148000 inmates have sojourned for varying periods. The poor here are placed in classes according to their abilities; the children are clothed, fed, cared for and instructed separately from the adults; and the sick have a special infirmary for themselves. I regretted all the more that I had not time to visit the infirmary for as I should have found there additional proof of the philanthropic labours of my friend Von Rumford.

There is the Orphanage for Male Children.

A similar house for Young Girls.

A Society for the Education of Children. 1457 children are cared for, of whom 998 are boys.

A Society for the same purpose but intended exclusively for the children of soldiers.

A Society for Weekly Schools. Since its foundation in 1786 it has provided instruction for more than 10000 children irrespective of religion, the subjects taught being reading, writing and arithmetic. The children being instructed at present number 1415.

A Society for the Welfare of the Poor.

A Society for Charitable Loans. Anything from two to five guineas is lent to any individual borrower who must return 1/40th of the sum lent each week. Since the month of March, 1780, 14010 persons have taken advantage of this arrangement, and a sum of 11102 pounds sterling has been put in circulation. Loans are not made at the time of a lottery.

A Society to help people dedicated to Literature and Polite Learning who no longer have the abilities for earning their living from their work.

A Society to discourage vice and to promote the Knowledge and practice of the Christian Religion. It has been in existence for ten years.

A Society for the Encouragement of Domestic Servants. It gives pensions to recommended old servants and those who have become invalids.

An Asylum for Repentant Girls founded in 1766. It is directed by ladies of the highest rank.

A General Asylum for the same type of unfortunate girls founded in 1798.

An Industrial House, again for unfortunate girls, founded by a private individual in 1794. The net product of the work done in this institution raises 300 pounds sterling per year: and 220 women have regained their moral health and their welfare there.

Add to these three dispensaries to supply medical assistance free to the needy and medicaments at a reasonable price to others, and you will be as hard put to it as I have been to explain the contrast which exists between a policy of charity so clearly manifest and the ferocious character which the poorer classes evinced in the insurrection which has recently tormented this country.[18]

The spirit of the Dublin Society extends itself also to objects which are as a rule outside the scope of philanthropy. It has for example created several learned societies.

First there is the Royal Irish Academy whose institution dates from 1786 and of which Mr Kirwan is the President. It is organised under three committees; one for the sciences, one for *belles lettres* and one for antiquities. It has to date published seven volumes of *Memoirs* or *Transactions* which have often supplied interesting material for our journal.

The Dublin Society for Reading which possesses a fine library which is open for ten hours each day.

On our return from the Botanic Gardens we visited the Linen Hall. It is a vast building containing many courts surrounded by porticoes leading to a considerable number of shops which the merchants

---

[18]   Pictet was hardly told that many of these societies were proselytising in purpose.

occupy in the trading season. The bales were piled in such numbers in these porticoes that I was obliged to form a high opinion of this branch of Irish commerce.

Mr Weld had us engaged to dine with him for the last meal I should have in Ireland. But I was obliged to break the engagement owing to the preparations I had to make for my departure and the necessity I was under to put order in the chaotic state of my notes whilst the facts were still fresh in my memory. Mr Chenevix undertook to make my excuses. I then had in my humble lodgings an honour I did not expect. Mr Kirwan came to spend nearly two hours tête-à-tête with me before taking leave of me. May that famous and worthy philosopher enjoy for long the esteem he has earned in his own country and in all Europe.

At nine o'clock Mr Chenevix had the goodness to accompany me in the carriage to the usual place of embarkation. It is an immense jetty which I was able to see only by the light of the moon but I believe it is one of the wonders of the country. I would not have wished to see it by daylight; the realisation that the moment for the painful parting had at last arrived occupied me entirely. Let us not talk of it.

The simple ease of embarking here contrasts with the botherations and the complexities with which the unfortunate traveller is burdened at certain ports elsewhere. You board the ship from the jetty. Both are at the same level. No one says a word to you, you are not even asked your name, and it is not until the ship is well under sail that the captain draws up the list of his passengers. I had my passport all ready yet I embarked and disembarked here as at Portpatrick and Donaghadee without being asked for it at all. I can only suppose that I was always taken for an Englishman.

We were in sight of the English coast when I closed my letter; but a complete calm befell us and a very strong flow set up by the run of the tide carried us considerably off course. We passed close to the

Skerries, small islands, or more correctly, rocks, on one of which is a beacon tended by a family which live there in complete solitude. Occasionally the long-boat from a passing ship is sent there to purchase lobsters and crabs. Two of our passengers climbed down into the long-boat to purchase some and one of our sailors who on one occasion passed a whole night there informed us of a singular fact of natural history, to wit, that these rocks are infested with fleas which allow no one to sleep on them. Be that as it may, we had very good soup with the crabs brought back to us.

Finally, at two o'clock in the morning in superb moonlight we reached the beach and as it was low tide we were taken aboard the longboat. Those of my fellow travellers, who knew better than I did how to proceed, whispered to good effect in the ear of the inn-servant when we had all landed, so that when I went to book my place on the mail coach at the office it was only to be told that all the places were already taken and that I must resign myself to wait till the morrow to continue my journey. But as I have told you at the beginning, all is for the best in such circumstances, and my time has been spent in, what has been for me, a most interesting manner. I am now up to date with you and... for this once you have not got the advantage of me. Scheherazade[19] stopped when she saw it was day; I stop because my eyes close. Farewell until London.

---

[19] Scheherazade, the heroine of the Arabian Nights, who, by her all-night storytelling, won the trust of her sultan husband Chahriyar who, fearing to be made a cuckold, always had his bride of the previous day killed the morning after. Scheherazade, his latest bride, by her skill in storytelling, especially in leaving the sequel in suspense each morning, not only saved her own life but persuaded the sultan to abrogate the law requiring the death of his bride.

Letter IX

London, 15th August, 1801

I had thought, my colleagues, that I could take up my pen again directly I arrived in London so as to give you an account of the rest of my journey; but for eight days since I returned here to my hearthstone, and I am as it were at home with my illustrious friend, engagement after engagement has prevented me from doing so. Today, to my annoyance, I have learned that a complete embargo is being placed on all direct communication with France,[1] other than by letter. The

---

[1] The closed ports. This would appear to be a further instance of the special position which scientists in England and France maintained for themselves during the war: they were not at war.

Direct travel between England and France was banned for nine years during the Revolutionary Wars. The movements of Pictet and Von Rumford would suggest that the ban was not absolute, that ships were available for passenger transport when it came to the travel of selected people – in this case two scientists.

Following the Peace of Amiens in the spring of 1802 the ports were open again for a short period for all travellers. They were closed again in 1803. During the short period the ports were open again, the Edgeworth family went on Professor Pictet's invitation to France. With the closure again in 1803, one of the family, Lovell, the eldest, did not get out of France and was held in detention for eleven years. Richard Chenevix's cousin, the widow Mrs Melesina St George (*née* Chenevix), went to France in the spring of 1802 for a 'short vacation ramble in Paris'. She was, however, detained at first by indisposition, then by preparations for her second marriage and then by her second husband's captivity. The intended few weeks became in the event five years.

At this point Professor Pictet engages in a long dissertation on the geological phenomena suggested by the rock bedding uncovered by the ebb tide at Holyhead. His dissertation, in which he makes an imaginative attempt to formulate a theory of the metamorphosis of rocks and to force a shotgun marriage between the Vulcanists and the Neptunists, might be of interest, if at all, to the students of the development of geological theory. The translator proposes to leave the dissertation to the specialists, who may wish to read it, and go on to the account in the same letter of the Professor's comments on the Christian Sunday as practised in Wales and denied to the citizens of revolutionary France, comments actuated by the sight of church-goers in Holyhead. As

crossing by Dover is closed; if this measure is of long duration and I can hardly believe so, I shall be forced to return by Hamburg, something I dare not think of.

To distract myself and you I shall begin by transporting you in the space of a few moments so that you can traverse with me that very interesting coast of which I said not one word in my last letter.

When I had set out on my excursion everyone was at church as it was Sunday so that I met nobody in the street. The tide was low and all the boats on their sides on the beach might well have brought the remark that they also were obeying the Sabbath commandment. As I returned I found the entire place alive with strollers of all types and ages. It was a wonderful day and all were intent on getting the most out of it. I met every variety of group, entire families, children, husband and wife, everywhere were people of good appearance, well-dressed, faces alight with gaiety and with every show of happiness. Alas, I said to myself when will the Sabbath day, so well celebrated here in this country, return for the Christians of France? That day on which the people, drawn purposefully to thoughts of religion, inspired by the sublime and consoling ceremonies of public worship, find, in their spending of the rest of the day a relaxation and enjoyment (which the idle cannot experience and of which too many in our day do not know the need) the happy association of the duties of religion with the pleasures of a day of rest earned by honest toil.[2] In what new institution will this reward be

---

stated elsewhere in the biographical note on Pictet there is most likely more in these comments than appears on the surface.

The rest of LETTER IX deals with Pictet's return to London, a description of Von Rumford's house and begins the biography, to be completed in LETTER X, of Von Rumford. The Professor's description of the house will not be given but its present location will be. There will be comments made on the biography and some extracts given. A longish biographical note on Von Rumford is given in the appendix to this book. LETTER IX is written from London, 15th August, 1801.

[2] The Christian Sunday, gaiety and toil. It is appropriate to quote here the reflections of a traveller (Mrs Chenevix-Trench) in France in the summer of 1802:

142

found? I was saddened by the gaiety of these good
people, I was jealous of it for my fellow-countrymen.
[Original footnote. 'Our author could have hardly
surmised that the very time he was penning these
sentiments the negotiations which have led to the
historic law on the restoration of public worship were
in progress, that a peacemaking and conciliatory
government was in secret preparing the great charter
soon to be published which it would honour'].[3]

I have spent the rest of the day writing to you
whilst I have experienced a certain amount of regret at
finding myself only a few miles from the famous
copper mine of Anglesey yet not visiting it: and if I
could have had foreknowledge of that fatal embargo
not only would I have given myself the pleasure of
making that piece of sightseeing, but most assuredly I
would have prolonged my stay in Ireland.

But enough of regrets. On Monday morning in
lovely weather I boarded the express mail coach, and
on the next day but one I found myself in London
having covered the 272 miles in forty-seven hours, and
that is about all I can tell you of that part of my
travels. The Welsh country, through which I moved all
of the first day, is very picturesque and engaged my
eye by its variety. I often thought myself in

July 8, Breteuil

*Where is the gaiety we have heard of from our infancy as the
distinguishing characteristic of this nation? Where is the original of
Sterne's picture of a French Sunday? I have seen no dance. I have
heard no song. But I have seen the pale labourer bending over the
plentiful fields, of which he does not seem, if one may judge from his
looks, ever to have enjoyed the produce; I have seen... men, women
and children working under a burning sun... and others giving to toil
the hours destined to repose, even so late as ten o'clock at night...*

[3]   This footnote was the work of the editors in Geneva. One may be forgiven for
suspecting Professor Pictet of sycophancy here to Napoleon. He was always pleading
the cause of public worship; he had influence with Napoleon and it is possible that he
had been involved in the negotiations leading to the concordat. Anyway, judging by
what Mrs Trench was to see one year later, the concordat was not to make much
difference to the lives of the peasantry.

Switzerland when in Wales and on one occasion the scene could have been that of the cherished borderland of Leman.

Since it is at times necessary in the interest of justice to speak out, I warn the traveller against the inn at Chester where we supped; it is one of the worst in England where the meanest service is rendered for the highest payment.

There were places for only four people in the coach. The travellers I met were going only short distances: they were constantly changing and so kept presenting me with varied little episodic scenes. One of them was a good merchant of sixty who, every year at this time, so he told us, makes a tour for his pleasure and instruction, getting in this way to know England. But his manner of studying it is not very deep.

At dawn we were going through some town the name of which I have not recorded. We were going at a spanking pace. Our man glanced out through the carriage window and announced to myself and the other travellers with an air of complete satisfaction,

"I am delighted to have observed that town; I have never before called there though it has always been my desire to get to know it." We congratulated him on his achievement; but here am I jesting about the good man and he in his turn could have turned the laugh on me if I had told him that I was returning from a trip lasting only five weeks which had included England, Scotland and Ireland and yet I had the presumption to think I had seen something. So I refrained from comment.

For eight days now I have been living the Elysian existence which is the lot of Count Von Rumford leading the finest life it is possible to imagine.

Professor Pictet returned to London on 7th August, 1801 hoping to embark at once for Calais but found himself unable to do so owing to the embargo. He spent most of his time at the home of Count Von Rumford in expectation of receiving permission to travel from Dover to Calais, dreading the sea voyage to Hamburg. He finally got away on 20th September, 1801.

Von Rumford's house was at Brompton Row. Brompton Row was then outside London. It no longer exists as such. Since 1860 it has been absorbed into Brompton Road quite close to Brompton Oratory. A row of shops at numbers 130 to 170 Brompton Road represents the transmutation of the Row. These shops, which include a bank, sit back somewhat from the road. At the rear and parallel with the road is Cheval Terrace, dwelling houses most likely converted from the stables of Rumford and his neighbours.

Mr Melvin Barnes, Borough Librarian and Arts Officer, Central Library, the Royal Borough of Kensington and Chelsea, confirms that Von Rumford lived at 45 Brompton Row which is now 168 Brompton Road. It is occupied by a secretarial college. Pictet refers to the house as 'ingeniously planned'. This description can have little meaning with respect to the overall plan of the building, a large terrace house; it must have referred to the extras Von Rumford supplied such as a glass partition for double glazing effect, under-bed wardrobes and not forgetting what the cartoonist, Gillray, referred to as 'the comforts of a Rumford stove'.

That much said and Gillray notwithstanding, Rumford's forward-sloping heat-projecting grates were regarded as the last word in modernity at the beginning of the nineteenth century. Thus, Jane Austen in *Northanger Abbey*, to shatter Catherine Morland's expectation of the romantic in her arrival at the abbey, can do no better than equip the drawing room with an example of the Count's inventiveness: 'The furniture was in all profusion and elegance of modern taste. The fireplace, where she had expected the ample width and ponderous carving of former times, was contracted to a Rumford, with slabs of plain though handsome marble, and ornaments over it of the prettiest English china'.

On a map printed 28th January 1794, Brompton Row in the parish of Kensington is shown as two terraces in series, twenty-seven houses in the first and twenty-eight in the second. Von Rumford's house, number 45, would be number eighteen in the second terrace. Coming out of London one would not have got a straight frontal view but an oblique one so that it is difficult to see how number 18 in the second row could be seen to stand out from all the other fifty-four, as Pictet says in his LETTER I. It is hardly to be doubted that the Professor is flattering Von Rumford and indulging in a bit of self-commendation towards his readers by lauding the house in which he stayed.

As stated, the rest of LETTER IX and all of LETTER X is concerned with the biography of Von Rumford; here extracts only will be given from this biography.

The first of these shows Von Rumford confronted with the desertion, twenty-eight years earlier, of his wife and daughter, then an infant in arms, and Pictet putting a gloss on it, describing Von Rumford's recollection as one of sorrow for something which the Count had not willed, an explanation the reader would have difficulty in accepting – a guilty conscience being the very obvious cause of the discomfort occasioned by that recollection.

Extract I

"But", I asked him, "at the age you were then, is a young man the master of his own affairs? How were you able without obstacle to pursue the instinct, as I may call it, which led you on towards a career different from that laid out for you?"[4]

"Unfortunately", he replied, "shortly after my father's death my mother contracted a second marriage which turned out to be a misfortune for her. A tyrannical husband forbade me her company. I was yet a child. My grandfather, who survived my father by a few months only, left me hardly enough to subsist on, so that I was at a very early age pushed out into a world for which I was almost completely unprepared. I simply had to adopt the habit of thinking and acting on my own, and to live at my own expense. My ideas were not constant; one project followed another, and it is likely that I should have acquired the habit of indecision and vacillation, and perhaps I should have been poor all my life had it not been for a woman's love: a woman who gave me position, a home and independent means.

"I married or, more correctly, I was married at nineteen years of age. I espoused the widow of a

---

[4] i.e. that of scientific study and independent living.

Colonel Wolfe and daughter of the Revd. Mr Walker,[5] a highly respected ecclesiastic. One of the first inhabitants of Rumford, he was already connected with my family. On no less than three occasions he had made the voyage to England in the public interest. Very well informed he was a man of a very generous disposition. Wholeheartedly approving of the choice of his daughter, he himself united us in matrimony. That excellent man was sincerely attached to me; he directed my studies; he formed my tastes: my position was in every respect as happy as it is possible to imagine..."

His grief stopped him in his narration. I brought him back to it the next day. I rely on my notes for what follows.

Unexpected events drew Thompson from his peaceful seclusion and tore him from his favourite studies, which otherwise would probably have constituted the main occupation of his life, to send him on to the grand world scene to play a part for which he did not appear to be prepared.

On the outbreak of the troubles in America which led to the War of Independence, Thompson, at the ripe age of twenty-one, was bound by ties of friendship to the Governor[6] of the Province and attached to the Government. He was a compatriot of Thompson. These facts as well as the civil and military offices with which, young as he was, he was already invested, could only lead him by duty and conviction to the side of the Royalists.[7] When the opposing side was successful in his Province there was nothing for him but to leave home and seek refuge in Boston, which was still held by the English forces. It was about the end of November, 1773 that he secretly left his home,

---

[5]   Mrs Sarah Wolfe (*née* Walker), (1739–1792), was the widow of the local squire. She was thirty-three when Thompson, at nineteen, married her. She had a son by her first marriage and a daughter by her second.

[6]   Wentworth, Sir John (1737–1820).

[7]   Shortly after his marriage his wife introduced Thompson to the Governor of New Hampshire, Wentworth, who liked him so well that he at once made him a major in the Second Provincial Regiment of New Hampshire.

his wife and the daughter to whom she had given birth. He was fated never again to see his wife and it would be twenty years before he would meet the cherished child she had given him. Twenty years later when the daughter had lost her mother she came to Europe where she joined her father. But the contrast between the peace and the ease of life in her native place and the court of Bavaria where her father then resided was too much for her. Her health suffered. She sighed for America and returned there. She has since kept up a most consistent and interesting correspondence with her father as I judge by the portions of it he has allowed me to read.

Letter X

Extract II

The second extract concerns Thompson, the self-centred poseur, doing his act to attract the attention of Prince Maximilian; it is taken from LETTER X in which Pictet continues the biography of Von Rumford. The American war is over and Thompson, the fever of the soldier in his veins, decides to test the glories of the battlefields of Europe prepared to offer himself to whomever is willing to engage him.

By now the American war was over and Thompson asked to be employed with his regiment in the East Indies. However the peace brought with it a reform of many brigades, his included, and he was freed from the obligation of service. Accordingly he obtained leave from the King to travel on the Continent. Apparently his motive for so doing was simple curiosity coupled with a search for opportunities for extending his knowledge, though he was by now being devoured by a passion for things military, and he nursed the hope of serving in the Austrian army against the Turks.

"I owe it to Divine mercy", he told me one day, "that I was cured in time of that martial madness. At the house of the Prince of Kaunitz[1] I met a lady of seventy years old of lofty soul and exceptional accomplishments, the wife of General Bourghaussen.[2] The Emperor, Joseph II, often spent an evening at her home. That excellent lady took a liking to me. Her

---

[1] Kaunitz, Rietberg Wenceslas, Prince of, (1710–1792), Austrian Ambassador to France and minister of Emperor Joseph II.
[2] Bourghaussen and his wife – nothing known.

advice was wisdom itself and her counsel gave a new bent to my thoughts, opening up to me a perspective of glory above and beyond that of victory on the battlefield."

He returned to England but leaving again in September, 1783, he disembarked at Boulogne-sur-mer. Chance had given him as a travelling companion the celebrated Gibbon[3] but Thompson's manner of driving his horses caused Gibbon to be terror-stricken as he confessed in his published correspondence with Lord Sheffield[4] describing the driving of the horses by three epithets which show how well he knew the driver whom he described as the 'Soldier–Philosopher–Statesman Thompson.'[5]

Travelling on the same boat was a wartime enemy, the famous Laurens, President of the American Congress.[6] He had been made prisoner whilst coming to Europe and brought to England, where he was imprisoned in the Tower of London until the ending of hostilities.

Now there commenced a new era in the life of my illustrious friend though it would appear that a purely chance circumstance was the deciding influence on his destiny. He made his way to Strasbourg where Prince Maximilian of *Deux Ponts*,[7] the present Elector of Bavaria, at that time *marechal-de-camp* in the French service was garrisoned. Taking the salute, the Prince noticed an officer in foreign uniform mounted on a fine English horse. It was Thompson observing the review. The Prince addressed him and Thompson let it be known that he had just returned from service in

---

[3] Gibbon, Edward (1737-1794), English historian.
[4] Holroyd, John Baker, first Earl of Sheffield (1735-1821). English statesman.
[5] The phrase Gibbon actually used was 'Mr Secretary Colonel Admiral Philosopher Thompson' which would indicate that he regarded the cavalier driver as something of an upstart.
[6] Laurens, Henry (1724-1792). American revolutionary statesman of Huguenot origin; President of Congress (1777-1778); prisoner in the Tower (1780-1781).
[7] The Electors Charles Theodore (1724-1799), Maximilian Joseph (1765-1825).

America. The Prince waving his hand in the direction of several officers in his company remarked:

"These gentlemen have fought in the same war as you, but on the opposing side."

The officers in question were attached to the Royal *Deux Ponts* Regiment which had engaged in the American war under the command of the Comte de Rochambeau.[8]

The conversation, begun casually in this manner, became very animated. Colonel Thompson was forthwith invited by the Prince to dine with him at his quarters and there he met a number of French officers against whom he had fought in America. There was much talk of the incidents of the war and the Colonel sent for his portfolio which contained precise plans of all the principal battles, the fortifications, the sieges and above all, a collection of excellent maps. Each person present recognised on these maps some place or places which had for him something personal in his service. The conversation was long drawn-out and the party broke up under promise to meet again, the Prince himself being passionately devoted to his career and most keen to expand his knowledge. He invited the Colonel to meet him next day.

When the party reassembled the conversation was renewed with the same gusto as on the previous day and when the traveller took his leave of him, the Prince prevailed upon him to include Munich in his itinerary, giving him a letter of recommendation to his uncle, the Elector of Bavaria.

At this point, my friends, notice the chain of circumstances, all apparently without connection – a meeting of some military enthusiasts, a conversation on military events – which open up for Count Von Rumford that noble, beneficial and beneficent career which today is his chief claim to fame and which is the joy of his life.

---

[8]   Rochambeau, Jean-Baptiste, Comte de (1725–1807). Commander of the French troops who aided the Americans in the victory at Yorktown, 1781.

He returned to England in September, 1795 having
been out of that country for eleven years. The main
purpose of his visit to England was to publish his
essays and to draw to the attention of the English
nation the ideas on public and domestic economy he
had conceived and executed in Germany. Lord Pelham,
one of the most respected men in England and today a
Minister, was at that time Secretary of State in Ireland.
In the spring of 1796 the Count accepted an invitation
from him, giving the opportunity to visit that
interesting country of which I have spoken at length
elsewhere. During his visit there he was responsible
for many important improvements in the hospitals and
workhouses of Dublin and he left behind designs for
several useful mechanical appliances. These, you will
recall, were among the first things to catch my eye on
that visit to the Dublin Society of which I have already
given you some details.

Appreciation and honours expressed in the most
exalted terms were accorded him. The Royal Irish
Academy, the Society for the Encouragement of the
Arts and Manufactures, each elected him an Honorary
Member, whilst on his departure from the country he
received an address of thanks from the Grand Jury of
County Dublin, an official letter from the Lord Mayor[9]
of the city, and one from the Viceroy[10] of Ireland. I
have seen all these memorials: they are replete with the
most flattering expressions of recognition and
gratitude.

[9] In 1795–1796 the Lord Mayor of Dublin was Sir W. Worthington and in 1796–
1797, S. Reid.
[10] Pratt, John Jeffries, 2nd Earl of Camden (1759–1840).

Letter XI

The hold-up in London waiting for permission to sail via Dover–
Calais enabled Pictet to make visits he might not have otherwise
made. One of these was to the 3rd Earl of Stanhope (1736–1803) at
Chevening. The Professor had come to know Stanhope during the
years the latter had lived in Switzerland for his health. Three things
distinguished the 3rd earl: his love of experimentation, his love of the
principles of the French revolution, his inability to manage his
domestic affairs. The first of these had caused him to turn one of the
best rooms in Chevening into a laboratory, the second had earned him
the nickname of Citizen Stanhope, the attentions of the cartoonish
Gillray and the mob to his door in an attempt to burn him out. As to
the third, after the death of his first wife, Lady Hester, a sister of Pitt
by whom he had three daughters, he married an heiress, Louisa
Greville, by whom he had three sons. By the time Professor Pictet
visited him in September 1801, his three daughters had left him, the
first at the age of sixteen to marry the family doctor, a man many
years her senior. The boys, aided by their half-sisters, had either
quitted the house or were about to do so.

One of the girls, Lady Hester, extremely intelligent and forceful,
was the right hand of her prime minister uncle, Pitt, living with him at
Downing Street where her high-handedness made her many enemies.
On Pitt's death she quitted England for good, and roamed over Egypt
and the Middle East before going to Palmyra where, in the Valley of
the Tombs, she had herself crowned 'Queen of Palmyra'. Six feet tall,
good-looking and fearless, she did not hesitate to settle with a remote
tribe in the mountains of Syria, putting herself at the mercy of the
tribesmen from whom she might have expected revenge for the
murderous incursion of savage punition she had had inflicted upon
them. She spent the last twenty-five years of her extravagant, bizarre
life in a bastion of her own design and construction where, in oriental

dress, none too clean, the narghile seldom out her mouth, she ruled a household of virtual slaves; she died in utter solitude.

As 'Queen of Palmyra' she once addressed Queen Victoria in a letter as an equal – 'Madam'.

Professor Pictet saw several inventions to interest him and to record as he said in LETTER XI,

> My head is so completely filled with what I have seen and learned in the two days I have spent with Lord Stanhope at his beautiful estate at Chevening that I shall lose myself in all the detail if I do not get my notes sorted at once.

Concern here will be with only one of the inventions the Professor saw, that of an inclined plane for canal navigation because of what he had to say of the canal he saw in Ireland and also because an inclined plane was used in an Irish canal in the 1770s, the first ever used in the United Kingdom. In the light of Stanhope's inclined plane, an account will be given of the Irish canal which opened in 1777. Pictet's account of Stanhope's plane follows.

Brompton Row, 1st September, 1801

> Engineers have for a long time been searching for a method of bypassing canal dams so that boats may go from one level to the next. It is said that the Chinese have found a method in the inclined plane. The Duke of Bridgewater[1] has successfully employed this method also. Lord Stanhope, concerned as he is with transport to his estate in the south of England, has directed his inventive mind to the use of the inclined plane for this purpose. He has devised a method whereby empty boats and the weight of water in them will counterbalance that of boats full of merchandise, which it is desired to raise to the higher level so that all that is required for raising these full boats is the force required to overcome friction. Since I have seen the model designed to this end, very ingenious as it is,

---

[1] Egerton, Francis, third and last Duke of Bridgewater (1736–1803). Canal builder.

built on a sufficiently large scale to prevent any detail from being overlooked, I shall attempt to explain the paradox.

Imagine then, an inclined plane going from the lower to the higher level of a canal.

The inclined plane is made of two parallel sets of wooden planks covered with iron, one set of planks intended for the ascent, the other for descent. We shall call them ascending and descending slipways.

The boats using the slipways are rectangular chest-shaped hulls rather longer than broad and they can be attached one to another in any number. When they come to a pound dam and it is necessary to go, say, from the lower to the higher level, there are waiting for them a number of hulls of the same type but somewhat larger, designed to carry them from the bottom end of the slipway to the top. These carrier hulls or wherries are equipped with four rollers, friction-reduced made as they are as large cast-iron tyres, the exterior surface of which rolls on the plane of the slipway and the interior surface on a system of rollers centred on the axle on which the hull is mounted. This arrangement reduces friction so much that a weight of forty pounds puts one of these hulls weighing 2000 lbs in motion on a horizontal plane. I have seen the experiment performed.

When the boat or barge to be transported is placed inside the larger barge or wherry there is still room around and beneath it for water so that it floats in the carrier. The boat and carrier are well caulked so they are watertight, special care been given to the joints.

A strong, endless chain carries the laden carrier up and down. Here is how the chain operates:

Let us begin with it in the lower level of the canal whither we shall trace it back again. It rises out of this lower level and goes up the length of the ascending slipway. When it reaches the brink of the higher level it crosses a pulley to go straight down into the water along a ramp sinking to a depth slightly lower than that of the barge and its container together. There the chain enters the groove of a great semicircular pulley, the diameter of which is equal to the combined widths of the two slipways and the plane of which is bedded in the water in such a way that when the chain has passed through the grove in the semicircular pulley it comes up out of the water again along the ramp (still on the same plane by which it descended into this water); at the top it crosses another pulley to go down along the descending slipway. That slipway goes right down into the water of the lower level of the canal as far as the arc of a second pulley, of the same diameter as that bedded in the higher level. The chain, when it has passed through the groove of this pulley, comes up to the ascending slipway that is to say with the circuit complete for it was here we began to follow its course.

Now let us imagine two vessels attached to that chain, the one at the bottom of the ascending slipway is the wherry containing the floating barge laden with merchandise; the other, at the top of the descending slipway, is a wherry carrying no boat but filled with water, yet equal in weight to the boat-carrying wherry at the bottom because, the boat with its merchandise floating in that wherry represent the weight of the volume of the water they have displaced. This being so, it takes very little force added to the descending wherry filled with water to upset the equilibrium and start the ascent of the other. Arrived at the higher level of the canal, the boat-carrying wherry comes to the ramp which descends under the water. Down this ramp it goes under its own weight and the force of the chain still being pulled by the descending water-laden wherry, which in turn goes under the water in the lower level and as it does so the pulling power of the chain lessens.

But the wherry at the higher level does not bring down the boat and the cargo which it carries with it; the wherry alone sinks from under the laden boat which is now left free to float off in the water of the

higher level. The wherry, itself by its immersion fills
with water so that when it goes across the canal under
the water and rises up the ramp at the other side it is
ready to perform the function of hauling another boat-
laden wherry up the other side of the inclined plane
pulling the chain as it descends.

I have mentioned two wherries but it will be easily
understood that as many pairs of wherries may be
attached to the chain as there is room for pairing them;
thus equilibrium will be maintained.

Nor have I said anything of a number of ingenious
refinements in the execution of the system, as for
instance a certain curvature given to the ramp at the
higher level by which the wherry enters the water, a
curvature calculated to make uniform the reciprocal
action of the two wherries: one at the top of the
inclined plane, the other at the bottom, which are
immersed at the same time.

In all this can be discerned the genius of the man
who anticipated all the obstacles and acts to overcome
them.

The Inclined Plane: Stanhope; Ireland

The farmers of Devon had long been in the habit of fertilising their
upland fields with sea-sand containing shells. Stanhope had an estate in
Devon and it was of his tenants that he was thinking when he planned
his canal to transport sand from Bude into the hills. Ingenious as was
the system he proposed for raising the boats containing the sand, or
for that matter, other merchandise, it was never used on the canal as
he planned but was left to his son to complete. The inclined plane was
used on it but not the water–and–boat–carrying wherries. Other
methods of supplying the power to raise the boats (and lower them)
from one level to another were adopted.

For those not versed in canal navigation it might be thought from
Professor Pictet's description that the inclined plane was an attempt to
solve an as yet unsolved problem, namely to lower or raise a boat
from one level of a canal to another but in fact that problem had been
solved more than three and a half centuries before Lord Stanhope

showed Professor Pictet his model. It had been solved by the invention in 1440 of the pound-lock by Philippe Marie (1392–1443), a member of the ruling Milanese family of Visconti.

As to the inclined plane itself, it had a special function, that of carrying materials or merchandise through hilly country not generally suited to the construction of a pound-lock canal and of utilising much smaller craft than those normally using the pound-lock canal i.e. boats of 60–80 feet in length and capable of carrying, 60, 70 even 80 tons. The boat associated with the inclined plane was called the tub-boat owing to its small size; a flat bottomed craft six to ten feet long with capacity of something like a horse wagon. It was a device to avail of the navigational potential of winding upland steams or rivers. Here it might help to think of the 'lavets' as a mountain road with the difference that for navigational purposes the bends have been eliminated so that a series of channels at progressively higher levels are connected by means of inclined planes. A plane could be as long as 800 or 900 feet with rises of anything from 120 to 150 feet. The plane could be and was used in the case of fairly straight-flowing streams or rivers made navigable by weirs but requiring a connection of passageways at the weirs. It was also used for a canal whose waters were fed from a neighbouring stream. But the concept of the 'lavets' with the analogy of the climbing road does give a good picture of what is involved.

The plane itself was a kind of carriageway on which cradles or buggies carried the small boats piggie-back up or down to the next level. Its surface could have been made of any material which allowed for the expeditious movement of the small craft-carrying buggies or wherries on wheels but wooden planks were usually employed or indeed wooden rollers. In their passage up or down the plane boat and wherry were entirely independent of the water. Stanhope's boat of course was afloat in its wherry.

STANHOPE'S INCLINED PLANE:

PLAN

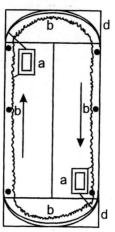

ELEVATION

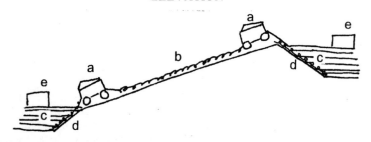

(a) Wherry carrying tub-boat (tub-boat shown also afloat as (e))
(b) Endless Chain
(c) Upper and Lower Pounds
(d) Ramps
(e) Tub-boat

Forms Of Traction On The Plane

To begin with, the plane was usually as described by Professor Pictet, double so that the movement of a wherry (and boat) down it could assist in the hauling of another wherry and boat upwards. But counterpoise whilst of help could not of itself effect the raising of wherry and boat up the plane. Three forms of motive power were employed: (i) the tub–in–the–well, (ii) the water wheel and later (iii) the steam engine. Apparently none of these would have been necessary with Stanhope's system in which a weight of 40 lbs was sufficient to overcome friction with a load of 2000 lbs. No doubt the horse, which was the usual means of hauling on the level sections of the canal, would have been more than sufficient to execute the raising of the boat-laden wherry up the plane aided, as the horse would have been by the counterpoise of the water-filled wherry.

(i)   The tub–in–the–well. This method was the brainchild of the Pennsylvanian-born inventor and mechanic Robert Fulton (1765–1815) who in the early days of his sojourn in London earned his living as a miniature portrait painter. Fulton also developed a submarine and he was the first person to apply steam propulsion to navigation.

Two shafts were sunk side by side conveniently close to the canal and from the level of the higher pound, both shafts being provided with outlets to the lower pound. At the bottom of each was a trip device. Out over the plane was a windlass round which a rope coiled, the two ends of which were separately attached to separate wherries. The rope's effective length was something longer than the length of the plane. When the rope was extended the length of the plane one wherry was at the bottom of it, the other at the top: when the rope was half extended the two wherries were level at the centre of the plane, each on its own side thereof.

Over the windlass was another rope which when extended reached to the bottom of either shaft. On each end of this rope was suspended a large container with a capacity of fifteen tons of water. In the nature of things it will be understood that when one container was aloft the other was at the bottom of its shaft. That at the bottom was either empty or in process of being emptied by the trip, that at the top was either full or in the process of being filled from the upper pound. A wherry was at the bottom of the plane waiting to be raised; one was at the top waiting to be lowered. So when the tub at the top was full and the restraining device released it sank into its shaft and, as it did so, operated the windlass to a) raise one wherry and lower the other and b) raise the other (empty) tub.

(ii)   In the case of the waterwheel the windlass for raising and lowering the wherries operated in the same way as for the tub–in–the–well but the power was supplied by the waterwheel coming from the upper pound or from a race.

(iii)   The steam-engine needs no explanation.

It is of interest to compare the practical approach of the mechanic Fulton to a problem, with that of the scientist Stanhope applying a principle (in this case that of Archimedes) to gain the solution to the same problem.

The Attempt to Use the Inclined Plane on an Irish Canal

Since this account of Professor Pictet's tour in 1801 emphasises its Irish part and since the Professor comments on the non-use of the fine canal he saw beside the Phoenix Park in Dublin, it is appropriate to give some account of canal building in Ireland in the eighteenth century with reference to an attempt made to employ the inclined plane in the construction of a particular canal. This can be done with reference to the Tyrone or Coalisland canals: (a) the pound-lock canal between the Blackwater river and Coalisland, (b) the tub-boat canal between Coalisland and coal-mines some four and a half miles above the basin of the pound-lock canal, the first in the British Isles to employ the inclined plane.

The latter canal had been mooted and talked about since the beginning of the eighteenth century but it was left to one Daviso D'Arcort, whose name has passed into history as Ducart, to complete the venture. The canal never proved a success[1] and indeed by draining funds from the former, prevented necessary improvements to that

---

[1]   It is fair to state that the ultimate success would have depended on the coal–mining venture – which was a failure.

canal, leaving it open to people like Professor Pictet to comment on the poor development of yet another Irish canal.

Both the Coalisland–Blackwater canal and Ducart's canal were developed with a view to bringing coal via Lough Neagh and inland canals to Newry; thence by sea to Dublin. All of this under the old Irish Parliament when Ireland had also a separate economy.

In the digging of the Coalisland canal the first step was the excavation of a channel at Derrywurragh, Maghery over against the mouth of the Upper Bann, a river which had been partly used in the making of the Newry inland canal. This channel opened into the Blackwater which was made navigable to Annaghbeg where the Coalisland canal began.

It was at this point also that the Tarn river, the main feeder – and, at times of flood a nuisance feeder, of the canal also entered the Blackwater. Canal and river ran beside each other for some two and a half miles whilst the basin or harbour of the canal in Coalisland was fed partly from a diversionary race from the higher reaches of the Tarn. There were seven locks including a double lock at a place called *Macs* at which point one of the three roads to do so crossed the canal by a high humpback bridge.

The canal was some four miles in length from the Blackwater to the basin in Coalisland. The digging and maintenance of this section proved difficult for the comparatively inexperienced engineers employed. Briefly these difficulties arose from:

(1) the boggy nature of the terrain;
(2) the nicety required in placing the seven locks;
(3) the Tarn river for:
   (a) bringing down vast amounts of silt;
   (b) its proclivity to share the bed of the canal;
(4) running sand which at the first two locks at and near Coalisland made lock building very difficult;
(5) starvation of funds and especially by the attempt to extend the tub-boat canal to the collieries which were above Coalisland.

Completed about the middle of the eighteenth century, by 1800 it might well have merited Professor Pictet's strictures: it was unusable. But a determined salvage operation at the beginning of the nineteenth century made it very usable and for more than a century it was a valuable economic factor in the industrial compound which was

Coalisland, transporting coal[2] to Coalisland as well as maize[3] and other agricultural requirements – the last named for the most part in pre-railway days, and of building-sand and fireclay products used in the rapidly expanding Belfast.

It ceased for all practical purposes to be used in 1939, as it was taken over by the Ministry of Defence. It was finally closed in 1954 having given some hopeful signs of coming to life again immediately after the War.

But in the context of Stanhope's inclined plane it is the tub-boat canal above Coalisland that merits special attention, always remembering that the canal from Lough Neagh to Coalisland had to exist before a tub-boat canal above it could have been thought of. Constant agitation for the development of both canals had been made in the Dublin Parliament from the beginning of the eighteenth century by the owners of coalmines – the Knoxes of Dungannon who had strong influence in that Parliament. The Coalisland–Blackwater canal, had, as stated, been somehow completed in the middle of the century and various proposals had been made as to how the coal could be transported from the mines to it, for example using the bed of the Tarn river; building a horse railway; building a good carriageway; even, at one stage, digging a 45 foot wide canal to go all the way from Newry and through Lough Neagh right up to the mines themselves. Finally the scheme proposed by Ducart was accepted even though Ducart himself was not completely settled in his own mind as to the shape his canal would take: he at one stage, in imitation of Bridgewater, thought of digging a tunnel into one of the pits and combining this with a huge shaft by which coal from other pits would be lowered into the barges; for the coal was being mined in several townlands – Derry, Brackaville, Congo, Drumglass. He finally settled on a tub-boat canal employing three inclined planes to meet the 200 feet rise involved in the four and a half mile scheme. The project was somehow finished in 1777 with the distinction, as stated, of being the first canal in the British Isles to employ inclined planes.

His canal predated Fulton's tub-in-the-well or Stanhope's boat-floating wherries. Though a large water-wheel which might have

---

[2] For domestic use over a wide area, for the kilns and power of the fireclay works and potteries, for the forge of the spade–making works and for powering the linen mills and factory.

[3] For grinding in two mills for agriculture over East Tyrone.

helped him was subsequently installed to drive the mighty hammer in a spade-making works near his canal – now to be seen at the museum at Cultra. His planes employed rollers on wooden ramps. These did not work very effectively. He had difficulty in getting his boats over the sills in the upper pounds. His plane was too steep. His boats sat uneasily on their buggies. Eventually, by accepting the advice of a visiting engineer, he made his plane double and using a pulley at the top introduced counterpoise to enable the descending buggy to aid the ascent of the other. He installed a winch to help the boat clear the sill, and he replaced the rollers with railway rails.

The canal had to cross the Tarn river and in the solution of the problem involved, the Italian blood in Ducart's vein manifested itself leaving to posterity a thing of delicate though robust beauty, a cutstone three-arched aqueduct. He also left to posterity two new words. His inclined planes though much altered by age are still to be seen under the name of 'dry hurries', his lovely aqueduct under the name of 'ackiedock'. By 1777 Ducart would appear to have been only interested in avoiding legal action for failure to complete the work: he possibly realised that his canal had no real future in its imperfections. He 'proved' himself by transporting coal from the mines to the Coalisland basin. Some boats (as local tradition would have it, one boat) made the journey. The coal they contained was uploaded in Coalisland into waiting barges and presumably the boats had to be carried on buggies to the quayside as Ducart's canal finished fifteen feet above the Coalisland basin.

On their way from Stewartstown to Armagh on the Friday evening of 17th July, 1801 Professor Pictet and Richard Chenevix, had they known about it, (and if Professor Pictet could have spared the time) could have, by descending from their post-chaise and walking a field length at Drumreagh,[4] examined one of Ducart's inclined planes which had not been used since the day in 1777 when 'one' or 'some' boat(s) on their buggy had rolled down it. The plane would hardly have changed as much between 1777 and 1801 as it has since then, though

---

[4] In the early nineteenth century the main road from Stewartstown to Armagh passed through Brackaville, Derryvale, Laghey, Moy and Charlemont. It thus passed over Ducart's canal, though the track thereof, at least where the road was concerned, had disappeared most likely by then. The former channel of the canal can be traced even today from the ruins of Drumreagh House to the Newmills aqueduct. It is interesting to note that the full name of the townland which gave the house its name is 'Drumreagh Etra'. 'Etra' is likely the Gaelic word *eitre* meaning a channel.

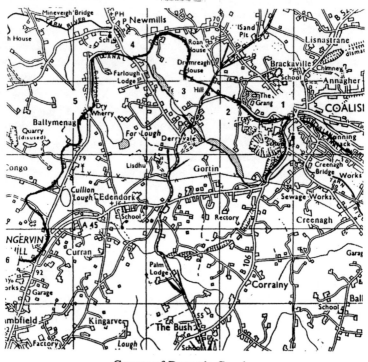

Course of Ducart's Canal
(Superimposed on 1:2500 Ordinance Survey Map)

Canals ━━━━━━━━━━━

Pictet's Route; Stewartstown–Armagh - - - - - ➤ - - - - - -

1. Foot of Ducart's Canal – some 50 yards above Coalisland Basin.
2. First Dry Hurry (Wherry).
3. Second Dry Hurry (Wherry).
4. The Ackiedock (Aqueduct).
5. Third Dry Hurry.
6. Head of Canal – Former Drumglass Pit.

Also shown – Myer's experimental Canal: Coalisland Tarn, dug mid 1760s: not mentioned in text.

almost certainly the wooden timbers would have gone. Pilfering was always a plague on the Coalisland canals.

Sequel to Ducart – the Proposal of Robert Owen

This account of Ducart's canal would be incomplete without mention of a subsequent proposal to reactivate it, a proposal made by Richard Owen (the engineer who was responsible for bringing the Lagan canal to Lough Neagh) when in 1787, that is ten years subsequent to the pretence of completion, he was asked for his opinion on possible rehabilitation – if that is the correct word.

Owen identified two main defects in Ducart's canal: i) the porous nature of the limestone rock through which it ran above the aqueduct, making it impossible to retain water; and ii) the impracticability of the original 'hurries'.

Presumably he felt that the first defect could be remedied by puddling,[1] a method subsequently successfully used on the channel of the Coalisland–Blackwater canal. As to the second, he had a plan which can be described as revolutionary, anticipating, as it would have done by something like a century and a half, the technology of roll-on roll-off so important in present-day transport especially ferries. Owen[2] would have reversed the roles of Ducart's buggy and boat whilst making Stanhope's water-filled wherries look like extravagant playthings. He would have had four pounds rising by 27 feet, 50 feet, 50 feet and 62 feet for the 189 feet needed to attain the higher ground of the Drumglass colliery. The legend of Owen's illustration states his detailed plan:

A, A Float of flat bottomed Vessel 40 Feet in Length, 13 Feet in breadth, and 2½ Feet in depth, may answer the purpose, with a broad Bow and Stern. B, Box Wagons 4 Feet 6 Inches long, the same in breadth, and depth 2 Feet 6 Inches, each of which will hold one Ton of Coals, made with common Wheels, and may answer from 2 Feet to 2 Feet 6 Inches in height. The Float will hold two rows with ease; that is 14 in number and of

---

[1] 'Puddling' – mixing clay and water to give a water–tight bottom.

[2] It has to be observed that Owen was concerned only with transporting coal from a higher to a lower level: Stanhope was moving merchandise both ways.

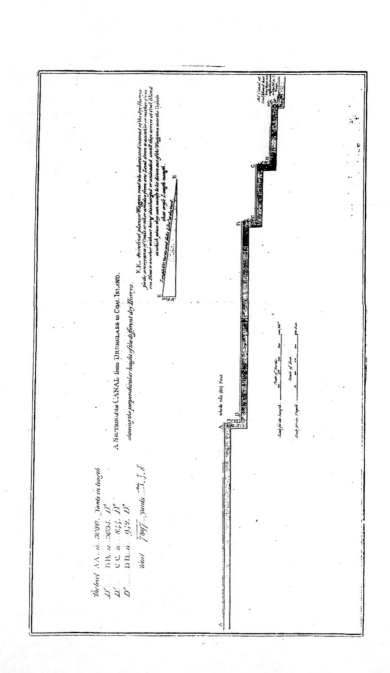

A SECTION of the CANAL from DRUMGLASS to COAL ISLAND.

shewing the perpendicular height of the different dry Harras.

consequence must be 14 Tons. Two of these Vessels may be fastened together one before the other and drawn by one Horse, that would make 28 Tons, or they may be made 60 Feet long with the same breadth and depth, such would carry 26 Tons each. C, An Inclined Road that falls 4 Inches at every running yard and may be either paved or gravelled as convenience suits, all or part of the Wagons may be taken down together at pleasure by locking some of the wheels. I am fully persuaded that more business may be done by this mode of conveyance where all the Articles may be carried down the Hill which is the case with the Coals from Drumglass to Coal Island, than by the use of Locks, especially as there is such a considerable rise between these two places, the advantage of this new Scheme must be amazing and of infinite importance to the Country when it is considered that one Twentyth part of the expence of making Locks will answer the purpose and be practicable where Locks Cannot be made for want of sufficient supply of Water. I do not in the least doubt but two Men and two Horses will be able to take 28 Tons of Coals from Drumglass to Coalisland and bring back the empty Wagons in one day. Please to observe the distance between Coalisland and Drumglass colliery is about 3½ Miles, and three different Levels of Water, also three sundry Inclined planes or paved Roads, the fall of which when taken together is 189 Feet [i.e. Irish miles].

Thus with Owen's scheme the wagons would have been filled with coal at Drumglass, they would have been floated on the flat-bottomed boat in the first pound, rolled off the boats at the inclined plane, down which they would have rolled to be rolled on to the boat waiting in the next pound and so on down to the waiting lighter in the Coalisland basin.

In 1787 the channel of Ducart's canal would have been substantially in existence. It had been dug 24 feet wide and 4 feet deep. It was 21½ feet at the aqueduct. His planes could have easily

A SCHEME *for the conveyance of goods upon a Canal without the use of Locks by Richard Owen.*

A. *A Float, or flat bottomed Vessel 40 Feet in length, 13 Feet in breadth, and 2½ Feet in depth, may answer the purpose, with a broad Bow and Stern.* BB. *Box Waggons 3 Feet 6 Inches long; the same in breadth, and depth 2 Feet 6 Inches, each of which will hold one Ton of Coals, made with common Wheels, and may answer from 2 Feet to 2 Feet 6 Inches in height. The Float will hold two rows with ease, that is 14 in number and of consequence must be 14 Tons; two of these Vessels may be fastened together one before the other and drawn by one Horse, that Would make 28 Tons. Or they may be made 60 Feet long with the same breadth and depth, such would carry 26 Tons each.* C. *An Inclined Road that falls 4 Inches at every running yard, and may be either paved or gravelled as convenience suits; all or part of the Waggons may be taken down together at pleasure by locking some of the Wheels. I am fully persuaded that more business may be done by this mode of conveyance where all the Articles are to be carried down the Hill, which is the case with the Coals from Drumglass to Coal Island, than by the use of Locks, especially as there is such a considerable rise between those two places; the advantage of this new Scheme must be amazing and of infinite importance to the Country when it is considered that one Twentieth part of the expence of making Locks will answer the purpose, and be practicable where Locks can not be made for want of a sufficient supply of Water. I do not in the least doubt but two Men and two Horses will be able to take down 28 Tons of Coals from Drumglass to Coal Island and bring back the empty Waggons in one day. Please to observe that between Coal Island and Drumglass Colliery is about 3½ Miles, and three different Levels of Water, also three sundry Inclined planes or paved Roads, the fall of which taken together is 189 Feet.*

10 Feet.

been adapted to Owen's scheme so that in all that the scheme was entirely feasible.

Owen envisaged four planes: his reference to three planes is to the existing three Ducart planes – or their remains – and it is as well to remember that Ducart's canal ended a short distance from the basin and 15 feet above it. But Owen's scheme was not adopted and today hardly a vestige of the canal beyond the remains of the arches used in the construction of the planes and the aqueduct remain. Its most likely course is given as superimposed on a present-day OS map in the accompanying illustration.

Letter XII

Before his departure for France on 20th September, 1801 in the company of Von Rumford, Professor Pictet made an excursion, accompanied by Von Rumford to Woburn Abbey, the seat of the Russell family, to attend one of the agricultural seminars – as they might be called today – given frequently by the 5th Duke of Bedford. With many others in attendance they were shown the model farm, the various breeds of cattle including the fantastically heavy bullocks which were prepared each year for the Christmas market at Smithfield. The numerous group of visitors were the Duke's guests for the night and they had a long and animated discussion on agricultural matters, including such Epicurean mysteries as the differing tastes of a cut of meat whether taken from the animal on the side on which it fell when slaughtered or the other side, and the taste of the flesh of different breeds of sheep; the talk went on well into the small hours.

There Professor Pictet and Von Rumford met Sir John Saunders Sebright, an eccentric ever anxious to waylay people, no doubt of distinction, to bring home with him to show them his dovecote and his library, to participate in the art of falconry with him and most importantly to listen to him. But apart from his being a member of the squirearchy of olde England, Sir John was a member of the scientific and literary club, confraternity or set to which reference has already been made – Sir Joseph Banks, Dr Beddoes, William Wollaston, Richard Chenevix, Maria Edgeworth, Sydney Smith, members of which the reader of Pictet's book are for ever meeting.

Interesting in itself, Pictet's account of the visit shows him at his anglophile best, a statement which will, it is hoped become clearer when the biographical note on Sir John Sebright is read. For all his visits, with the exception of that to Mrs Tuite where he was downright rude, our journalist scientist in his account of his hosts treats them to *nihil nisi bonum* because it is felt, that being the anglophile he was, put blinkers on him. The account also gives the opportunity to explore the outcome of the interplay or conflict in character of some of those involved over the twenty years or so following the visit of Pictet and Rumford to Beechwood, the home of Sir John Sebright. LETTER XII is written from London, 17th September, 1801. The Sebright extract from it follows.

We arrived before nightfall at Beechwood whither Sir John had preceded us. Here a sight different from what we had seen on our previous visit awaited us and no less pleasing than anything we had seen at Woburn.[1] It was that of Lady Sebright, the loving mother of her family, surrounded by her children.

There is an essential something wanting in the house in which a woman is not there to do the honours. But that is not the case at Beechwood so that I shall remember the two days I spent in that house as among the most pleasant of my life.[2]

To his love of the country life and his passion for agriculture Sir John adds a great love of sport and especially of falconry. He is one of a small number of country gentlemen who have complete establishments for this type of sport and he had prepared a party for us for the next day. For Count Von Rumford but more especially for myself it was an event indeed.

We spent a most pleasant evening and next day we dined *en famille*. Sir John, as we were not due to take to our horses for our outing before eleven o'clock, utilised the time to show us a few things he knew would be of interest to us, and it will, no doubt surprise you to learn that one of these, if not indeed the most interesting, was his dovecote.

I had no idea of the varieties to be found as to form, colour, natural behaviour in the birds coming under the name of 'pigeon'. The rarity of the birds

---

[1] Pictet and Von Rumford had just left Woburn, the seat of Francis, fifth Duke of Bedford (1765-1802) whose establishment was that of a bachelor.

[2] The true state of affairs at Beechwood was not one of domestic felicity: whatever of his wife, his children lived in terror of Sir John (see biographical note on him in the appendix).

kept by Sir John is their chief value: one we saw actually cost ten guineas. One type in particular filled me with wonder by its singularity. A bird of this type can fill his crop with wind in an instant, just as he wishes, and in proportion as he pulls himself up in consequence he causes his neck to win out over his head; he gives thus the impression of moving it backwards until it finally appears to be in the middle of his back. If viewed from the front as he proudly struts along he gives every appearance of having no head. Our host showed us the homing variety. Beechwood is more than thirty miles from London. Sir John has made the experiment of conveying one of these birds from his dovecote to London in a basket covered with a cloth and releasing him in a street there. In a very short space of time the bird managed to reach home. It is difficult to comprehend the instinct which directs a homing pigeon.

We mounted our horses at eleven and joined by some neighbouring gentlemen we formed quite a cavalcade. The falconer had gone on ahead of us with five falcons and a goshawk. It is really essential for this sport to have a very bare stretch of countryside and there was no such piece of countryside within a league of Beechwood.

We passed on our way a very stony field which Sir John had chosen as considered unworkable for the plough – the subject of a wager of fifty guineas between himself and Mr Cook,[3] who doubts whether the Norfolk plough which Mr Cook proposes to employ can work in that ground. At any rate the wager has been announced in the newspapers and the trial will likely be made next month.

But to return to the hawking – we had two spaniels for raising the partridges. A beginning was made by hawking crows and whenever one was observed sitting in a field, a falconer mounted and the bird on his fist

---

[3]   Coke, Thos. W. (later) Earl of Leicester and Holkham (1754–1842).

made the circuit needed to get above the wind. Using wonderful dexterity he removed the cowl from the bird the moment the crows rose from the ground. The bird shot forth like a released arrow and if the crow was not by that time close to a place of safety she was not likely to reach it, there was no escape for her.

All the sportsmen put their horses to the gallop the very moment the bird was released by the falconer and they followed up hill and down dale at full gallop. My horse, knowing more about this sport than his rider, made the spurt he deemed necessary whilst I, commending myself to Providence and not knowing very well where I was bound, came up with the bird just as he was giving up his prey and doing so with good grace to the falconer. He then took up his perch again on the fist and had the cowl placed on him once more.

There is, in my view, something remarkable in the faculty these birds display for emerging from the state of darkness under the cowl and instantly in the brightness of daylight picking out their prey which at times may be a considerable distance off.

The hawking of the partridge is even more strange. Once it is known that there is a covey in a particular patch of stubble the dogs are sent in. When it is felt by the commotion of the dogs that a partridge is about to be raised the hawk is released. He seems to realise that he is part of the business (even the horses give the impression of being involved). Off goes the hawk, back he flies and passing overhead he is seen to stretch his neck in anticipation of picking out a partridge about to be raised by the dogs. The unhappy things are at length forced into flight by the dogs. Selecting one the hawk swoops down on her. He may stun without killing, but stun or kill he swoops on to another bird in the same flight. But there is no escape for the partridge; she may reach the apparent safety of a hedge whither the hawk, for fear of damaging his wings, will not follow and so escape his claws, but the dogs are

soon caught up with her and sooner than risk the fierce
claws of the hawk she will allow herself to be taken by
them.

I spare you any further details of the hunt. We took
a crow and six partridges and did not return to
Beechwood until half past seven in the evening when,
for me at least, the sense of tiredness had begun to
blunt the edge of enjoyment.

In the morning we said goodbye to our gracious and
excellent hosts. Their house is for me the exemplar of
complete domestic felicity. May the members of that
household be preserved in its enjoyment *ad multos
annos*.

Professor Pictet finishes off LETTER XII and so his book with a short
account of a round he made in the poorer suburbs of London with a
vaccinating surgeon, Mr Ring.[4]

I came to know a Mr Ring, a surgeon of high repute
and very zealous promoter of vaccination who is about
to publish a two-volume work on the observations he
has made in that disease in which the researches of our
friend Professor Odier hold a distinguished place.
Mr Ring invited me to accompany him on a round of
vaccinations. He prepares that preventative and
vaccinates a complete street free of charge in the areas
of the poor. "I do not," he told me, "go seeking them.
I do not press them. I make it a point to find out some
free-talking mother in the street who consents to the
trial; she is sure to make known the success of my
ministration and then I will have all the practice I can
desire." His two fine horses carried us for three hours
at a fast trot in different areas and I witnessed many
moving scenes of the deep recognition of mothers of
that man whom they considered the saviour of their
children. The genuine expression of those sentiments is
the only recompense that worthy man has.

---

[4]   John Ring (1752–1821). Pioneer in vaccination for smallpox: began practising,
London 1799.

Good-bye, my friends: I set out forthwith and I shall not write to you before I reach Paris – where I am not likely to make a long stay.

PART THREE

Biographical

Richard Chevenix, Pictet's Travelling Companion

Richard Chenevix (1774–1830) the apparently modest, unobtrusive companion of Professor Marc-Auguste Pictet in his travels in England. Scotland and Ireland was the only son of Lt. Col. Daniel Chenevix of Ballycommon in what was then known as King's County (Offaly). In 1801 he was twenty-seven and was thus twenty-two years younger than Pictet, a fact which may account for his somewhat seen–not-heard part in Pictet's letters, though Pictet's egotistical record of the journey has possibly more to do with it. It is to his credit that on the few times that Pictet records his remarks they are not lacking in wisdom, as for example when in Armagh (LETTER VII) he warned his companion not to criticise the horses to the coachman. One of the abiding traits of Chenevix's character was a strong fundamentalist Calvinism, often belied by his talk, wit and literary performance but revealed in its entirety in his posthumously published *Essay on National Character*. Certainly he loved the company of men of science and it must have been something of a privilege for him at his age to be the travelling companion of Pictet who had an established reputation in the scientific academic and publishing world; but Pictet's association with Geneva must also have drawn him to the older man.

He was of Huguenot extraction carrying a deep and lasting memory of the sufferings of his forebears in France. A grand-nephew of another Richard Chenevix, Anglican bishop of Waterford and Lismore, he was accordingly a descendant of Rev. Philippe Chenevix, pastor of Lismay near Nantes, who when his brother, a president of the Parlement of Metz had been murdered, settled in England.

There was apparently a strong literary strain in the Chenevix family. His second cousin was Melesina Chenevix–Trench whose journal and letters published after her death by her son under the curious title of *The Remains* is a minor classic and 'a brief chronicle of the times'. Both her sons, one the Anglican Archbishop of Dublin at the time of the Disestablishment, were also very literary and, like their mother, spiritual. Richard Chenevix, Pictet's travelling companion is today practically unknown and Professor Pictet, catering for an audience to whom he was well known, tells us nothing of importance about him until he reveals his surprise at discovering in Coleraine the two pieces of dramatic poetry *Leonora* and *Etha and Aidallo* by Chenevix. This and the discovery that their author had been imprisoned in Paris come as startling intelligence. Further evidence of literary accomplishment is revealed with the reading by Chenevix and his sister, Mrs Sarah Tuite, of a play by Coleman the Younger.

It has not been possible to procure copies of Chenevix's drama or poetry but fortunately the *Edinburgh Review* in 1812 deals with two of his plays, *Mantuan Revels* and *Henry the Seventh* at length and quotes sufficiently from them to give a fair sample of their style. In relation to Chenevix's poetic language there is a strange affinity between what Pictet and the *Edinburgh Review* both say of it. Pictet: 'The language is that which would have been spoken in that heroic age: all the time noble, sometimes sublime': the *Edinburgh Review*: '...the work of a person of no ordinary accomplishments and intellectual activity – possessed of considerable taste and fancy... There is something delicious, however, even in the faintest echoes of those enchanting strains which were born in the golden days of our poetry'. Pictet is, of course referring to a mythical heroic age; the *Edinburgh Review* to the Shakespearean age for the plays are in blank verse in what may be called imitation Shakespeare. Chenevix seems to have become most adept at writing in this style which, like imitation Gothic, lacked inspiration and life. Here is an example given of the range of Mr Chenevix's powers of imitation... addressed to a weeping Damsel.

> Let them flow!
> The tears of woe oft are as dews, that fall
> Upon some sad and sun-distempered seeds
> The heedless winds had from their bosom scatter'd;
> Which now, conceiving by the pregnant drops,
> Load all the vagrant air with sweets, – the sweeter,
> That once we knew but anguish in the shower.

Of the two plays this is said:

The two plays contained in this volume may be regarded, we think, as the boldest, the most elaborate, and, upon the whole, the most successful imitation of the general style, taste and dictation of our older dramatists, that has appeared in the present times.

But later:

...he is never, by any accident, direct or natural for a single instant – and though his conceptions are often striking, and still oftener ingenious, there is such an appearance of artifice in the whole structure of the style, that the reader is at last both wearied and disappointed... The perpetual recurrence of metaphor, and the attempt to copy the boldness and originality of the metaphors employed by Shakespeare, render him very often obscure, and, to say the truth, not unfrequently altogether unintelligible to our weak faculties.

Without gainsaying this criticism, it can with truth be said also that Shakespeare has given a living to a good number of experts making him intelligible to 'our weak faculties'.

Whatever may have been Richard Chenevix's ideas on the importance of literature in the scheme of things prior to 1812, by the late 1820's he comes to have a rationalist utilitarian opinion on the subject.

The state of literature, of science, of the fine arts, is generally considered as the most direct standard by which intellect can be measured, and in cultivated individuals this may be held as sufficiently correct, but large bodies of men must be examined in more complicated points of view, and the relations in which the members of a community stand towards each other, are juster measures of the understanding of nations... *Paradise Lost* has been read, perhaps, by one five-hundredth part of the British nation, and in that five-hundredth part how few can form a proper judgement upon it? But the meanest individual uses some artificial texture to cover his limbs – the dullest helps to raise the shed which protects his body. If anything, then, can be held as a universal characteristic, comprising at once the mind of the first and the last of the highest and the lowest without compact or premeditation, it is industry.

Essay on National Character

But whatever may have been his place in literature in 1812 there can be no mistake about it in science. The reviewer of his plays in the *Edinburgh Review* introduces him: 'Mr Chenevix has long been known as a learned chemist and mineralogist...'

The following references to his place in science are all taken from reviews in the *Edinburgh Review*.

> *A System of Chemistry in Four Volumes* by Thomas Thompson, MD, etc. Lecturer in Chemistry in Edinburgh '...Dr Thomas has, in general, adopted Mr Chenevix's nomenclature...' (1804)

> It is a fact too well known... that the mineralogists of Europe at least are divided into two contending sects, the follower of the French and of the German professors... in our opinion mineralogical knowledge will be found commensurate exactly with the distance to which it leaves the unintelligible jargon of the oryctognosie of Freyburg. Much has been lately effected by the exertions of our own professors; and, more by the wholesome exposition of the celebrated Chenevix, who, acquired an indisputable title to pass judgement on the plan of instruction adopted by Werner by having himself attended during his whole course of lectures, published his renunciation of the German system and its utter inadequacy to the purposes of science.

> *The American Mineralogical Journal* for January, February, March 1810

Speaking in 1804 on his paper on palladium read to the Royal Society, the *Edinburgh Review* which was, as might be expected, unaware of a blunder Chenevix had made in that paper (but which was not apparent for some time) both praises and chides him. His paper was 'excellent' but he exposed 'himself to criticism both by the affection of his nomenclature and by the introduction of general reflections; a department in writing in which Mr Chenevix does not excel'.

He was obviously something of a polyglot though he would have had French and English from childhood and he must have picked up German on the way. But where did he learn his science? In *A Three Month Journey* we are told that he spent two years at Glasgow (LETTER VI). Mr James McGrath, Archivist at that University, confirms this. 'He is recorded as having matriculated in 1785 in the class of Logic under the supervision of George Jardin, MA (Professor of Logic): "Richard Chenevix, only son of Daniel, armour-bearer [sic] of Ballycommon, in King's Country [sic] in Ireland".'

His name appears again in 1787 among the list of attested students, in the following form:

> Glasgow College, 14th November, 1787. We the matriculated students of the University of Glasgow promise to attend the lectures of the several professors annexed to our names for the space of three months at least from this date... [a list follows on which is]:
> 'Richard Chenevix, Natural Philosophy, matriculated 1785.'

There is no record of his having graduated. If then he was two years at Glasgow he left there at thirteen. Though the records of Trinity College, Dublin, are silent about him, Taylor attributes an AB degree of Trinity to him.

How long Chenevix spent in Ireland or England at that time is not established but the next event recorded of him is mentioned both by Professor Pictet (LETTER VII) and Maria Edgeworth. He was fifteen months in prison and put his imprisonment to good use, laying, in fact, the foundations for his career as a chemist of standing. Writing in October 1800, from Edgeworthstown, Maria Edgeworth says:

Mr Chenevix, a famous chemist, was so good as to come here lately to see my father upon the faith of Mr Kirwan's assurance that he would 'like Mr Edgeworth'. I often wished for you, my dear Sophy, whilst this gentleman was here, because you would have been so much entertained with his conversation about bogs, mines, and airs and acids, etc., etc. His history of his imprisonment during the French Revolution in Paris, I found more to my taste. When he was thrown into prison he studied chemistry as pioneered by Jean Chaptal and Antoine Laurent de Lavoisier with all his might, and then represented himself as an English gentleman come over to study chemistry in France, and M. Chaptal got him released, and employed him, and he got acquainted with all the chemists and scientific men in France. Mr Chenevix had taken a house in Brook Street, in London, and turned the cellar into a laboratory; the people were much afraid to let it to him, they expected he would blow it up.

He must have remained in France until 1798 before crossing to England for his first scientific publication was made in France – in the *Annales de chimie* in that year. He was awarded the Copley Gold Medal in 1803 when he published the result of an analysis in Nicholson's journal and about this time he was beginning to contribute to the Royal Society. Up until 1811 he was a regular contributor to the *Annales de chimie*, the Royal Society and the *Journal de physique*.

His paper on palladium seriously injured his reputation as a chemist but from the account given of the discovery of this metal in the treatment of Chenevix by the *Dictionary of National Biography* one cannot be sure whether he or Wollaston was the discoverer. The facts which the *DNB* does not mention are strange and redound to the credit of neither party. As Chenevix states in his paper read to the Royal Society he learned on 19th April, 1803, from a Mr Knox, that a substance announced in an anonymous handbill as a new metal was for sale at a Mr Forster's in Gerrad Street. Chenevix bought some of the substance, thinking it to be a hoax. His tests on the substance baffled him so he purchased the entire quantity in Forster's possession to work further on it. The material was in a wafer-like state as if it had been put through a 'flatting mill'. Chenevix then described the series of experiments he performed on the substance and made the fighting unscientific declaration 'Palladium is not, as was shamefully announced, a new simple metal but an alloy of platina... and mercury'. He described how he had made the 'alloy'.

His paper was read by the Secretary to the Royal Society, Dr William Hyde Wollaston. Shortly after it was read a challenge was issued anonymously offering a reward to anyone who could make palladium by the method described by Chenevix. Later Wollaston signed a statement that it was he who had sold the substance through Forster in the first instance and who had issued the anonymous challenge. On 22nd June, 1804, he read to the Society his own paper on palladium in which he explained that palladium was in fact a simple metal and he suggested that perhaps Mr Chenevix had in his experiments released some palladium from the crude platina and was led into thinking that he had formed an alloy from the platina and the mercury.

Chenevix's mistake was attributable not so much to his want of skill as to a defect in his character, prejudice, the very same defect which led him into such lamentable arguments in his *Essay on National Character*. It might not be amiss here to make prejudice synonymous with lack of maturity which in turn might well be traced to his being spoiled as an only son by his elder sister Sarah (Mrs Tuite) (see biological note on Mrs Tuite). In his paper on palladium he warns against acting on a preconceived idea yet this was what he had done in preparing the paper. He began with the notion that the advertisement was a hoax and he set out to prove it was a hoax, most likely persuading himself that he had succeeded, but even the *Edinburgh Review* as we saw, which accepted his findings (this was before Wollaston's paper appeared) found his language out of taste.

The *Dictionary of Scientific Biography* speaks of him as leaving England in 1804, his scientific reputation damaged, to settle in France for the rest of his life. He did not, in fact, settle in France for many years after this and there is much evidence that his scientific reputation showed a surprising resilience. In 1805 he sent from Freyburg a paper on the same subject, on *The Action of Platina and Mercury on Each Other*, to the RSL. In it he speaks of his mortification that experiments on the lines he had suggested in his paper of 1803 'had been generally unsuccessful'. His opinion still was that Palladium was an alloy. Eminent French and German chemists were still puzzled. The *Edinburgh Review* never lost its opinion of him and in 1808 Humphry Davy in his Bakerean lecture on oxymuriatic gas cited Chenevix as having suggested the possible combination of oxymuriatic acid and oxygen which was to produce the gas. Moreover whilst Davies Gilbert gave him a very chilly obituary (quoted later) before the Royal Society in 1839 this owed nothing to his palladium paper and the *New Monthly* in its obituary could say of him, 'In Chemistry his name ranks as one of the highest who have cultivated the analytical branch of that Science'.

As for Wollaston's part in the affair, especially when it is remembered that it was he who read Chenevix's paper before the Society, he would appear to have behaved shabbily even though as Secretary it was his function to read papers whether he agreed with their contents or not. Reilly suggests that Wollaston tried to persuade Chenevix to withdraw the paper, but the subsequent challenge anonymously issued by Wollaston hardly accords with this suggestion. Reilly also states that Wollaston had invested what was for him a very considerable sum purchasing crude platinum, feeling he could refine it to sell at a profit, and when he had discovered the process for producing palladium he had to defer his findings until he could recoup himself which he tried to do by selling the palladium. It is also possible that he had set a trap for the pugnacious Chenevix.

The Chenevix who emerges from the letters of Maria Edgeworth is a young man with a fund of scandal and an incessant talker, not quite the unassuming young man of Pictet's *A Three Month Journey* and if one's first meeting with him is through Pictet one wonders what could possibly have led to the imprisonment of such a man. It was not the most difficult thing to find oneself in prison in the France of Robespierre and if Richard Chenevix held in 1792 the views he committed to paper before his death in 1830 the wonder is not that he was imprisoned but that his head remained on his shoulders.

> If something worse than the worst man that ever existed were conceived, and that being multiplied by the number of the conventionalists, and all their bad propensities increased by the mad audacity which

association gives to vice, it would present a feeble picture of this body; yet the laws which they enacted in about three years, amounted to eleven thousand two hundred and ten.

Essay on National Character

How much passion there is in this statement and how much straining after figurative effect it is hard to say. Still if he had said anything like it in 1792 the conventionalists would have wasted little time over semantics.

From 1800 to at least 1812 his life seems to have been taken up with scientific matters and writing, with endless movements from England to Ireland, to France, to Scotland, to Germany; though the renewal of the war in May, 1803, curtailed his trips to France. Indeed from a reference to him by Sir Charles Blagden in a letter to Sir Joseph Banks dated 29th September, 1803, he seems to have been fortunate to have got out of France without the fate of many others of having been interned – 'Mr Chenevix has at length got out of France'.

If Wollaston was his rival in one sphere Humphry Davy was so in another. In 1808 a vivacious and attractive young widow appeared on the stage on which the famous scientists, the Davys, the Von Rumfords, the Chenevixs, the writers, the Edgeworths and the churchmen wits, the Sydney Smiths, were to be seen. Mrs Jane Apreece, only daughter and heiress of an Antiguan merchant, a lady described by her great admirer Sydney Smith 'as brown as toast'. About 1810 she introduced herself on a grand tour to Irish society, calling unannounced on, among others, the Edgeworths. In 1812 we learn from Maria, 'She is in Edinburgh and charmed with the wits there... she already has enough philosophers at her feet, viz. Mr Davy and Mr Chenevix – one at each foot and it is doubted which will succeed'. (Did Chenevix have his literary work reviewed in the *Edinburgh Review* that year to strengthen his chances?) The reviewer was very surprised to learn that he was also a poet and a poet with reverence for the style and language of past times. If so it was in vain.

A knighthood awaited Humphry and he won the lady's hand.[1] The poet fled to France and, on the rebound, into the arms of an ageing countess for whom he had at first the worst possible opinion according to Sir John Sebright at whose house he had first met her. Sir John had indeed loudly blamed the same lady for the ruination of his own marriage. She was the Countess Rohault, referred to as Madame de Riou by Maria Edgeworth.

Chenevix's obituary spoken by Davies Gilbert at a meeting of the Royal Society of London, 30th August 1830, is a strange mixture of praise and rejection.

> Mr Chenevix was undoubtedly a man of considerable ability acquirement and industry. We have from him seven contributions to the *Philosophical Transactions*...
>
> In the latter years of his life, which could not have reached three score, he appears to have abandoned chemistry, and to have fallen on speculations, wholly unworthy of being noticed from this place.

These speculations were most likely contributed in articles to various journals but which are treated at length in his posthumous work the *Essay on National Character*, one of the more curious contributions to literature but important for the origins of the ideas expressed, the presentation and the light it shows on its author.

In this two-volume work published on his instructions after his death he examines the character of the French, the English and to some extent the Irish and the Scots in the light of 'self-approbation, environment of climate and soil'. He developed it with all the ruthless logic of a pet theory pursued relentlessly throughout the two volumes which often irritate, at times infuriate, but which never bore. Whatever about his poetry there is nothing ambiguous about his prose.

Self-approbation according to Chenevix is universal but can take two distinct forms, 'the one resulting from actions which, whatever other qualities they possess, must be intrinsically meritorious; the

---

[1] Of Davy's capture of the lady a punning wit wrote:
Too many men have seen
Their Talents underrated;
But Davy owns that
His have been Duly *Apreeciated*.

other from actions, which, whether meritorious or not must attract the eye of the world'. The most appropriate words to describe these two strains of self-approbation are 'pride' and 'vanity', both words used he expressly says without any reference to praise or blame. Yet, at this point he seems to slip into some form of mental limbo, for whilst he claims to eschew praise or blame in the use of these two words yet the actions associated with pride are meritorious and those with vanity are not. In the sphere of religion the cult of the Reformation provided it abjures show and ceremony, is the child of pride, that of imaginative (used in a pejorative sense) religion is of vanity.

Turning to soil and climate he says,

> The whole industry of the world, then, may be comprised in two general modifications – the industry of necessity, and the industry of luxury. The former is that to which the inhabitants of a poor soil, lying under no fertilising sun, are compelled to toil in order to procure the necessities of life. The latter is that to which the natives of more favoured regions are invited, by the hope of increasing the indulgence of which bounteous nature has spontaneously granted an ample provision. Necessary industry is the attribute of proud nations. Luxurious industry is the companion of vanity, and of all the modifications of character which are derived from easily obtained prosperity and splendour.

Behind the theory one detects the invisible influence of the former holder of the Chair of Moral Philosophy of Glasgow University, Adam Smith, in this field the pupil of Mandeville (*The Fable of the Bees*). Chenevix's 'vanity' is in essence that of Mandeville, with its own prejudiced nuance. With Mandeville production for the idle rich is the production of 'vanity'; with Chenevix it comes to be the easy fruits of good soil and climate, promoting the soft living of the vain nation. He thus divides nations into 'proud' and 'vain': in the first category the English and the Scots, in the second are the French and the Irish (at least the southern Irish).

But he is above all concerned with the comparative study of French and English character and he makes the analysis under the headings of Social Habits, Patriotism, Morality, Government, Intellect, Industry,

The Arts of War, and of course, Religion. Frivolity, showiness, loose living, the most bestial of cruelty, witness the persecution of the Huguenots and the foul deeds of the Revolution – the absence of a Shakespeare, the poor showing in advanced industry, the vain-glory of Napoleon in his campaigns, an 'imaginative religion' all these were the mark of the vain French not of the proud English.

The date at which Chenevix abandoned science for his other speculations must have been about the time of his marriage and he seems to have been for a long time feeding his spleen on an anti-French diet, though in fact he was more French than English. The *Essay* was published after his death in 1830. As early as 1820 when she made her second visit to Paris, Maria Edgeworth had to listen to his poor opinion of the French. Cane in hand, he was a constant caller on Maria and by no means always welcome, for he talked merely for the sake of talk. On a particularly lovely morning in May, 1820, when the Champs-Elysées and the Tuileries were at their best, the trees out in full leaf and the deep shade under them enchanting, he came in conversing 'delightfully but all the time holding a distorting magnifying glass over French character and showing horrible things where we thought everything was delightful'. Was Richard Chenevix, unhappily married, projecting his intense dislike for Mrs Chenevix on to the French people? Like Pictet's revered Count Von Rumford, Chenevix married a French widow for, apparently, social reasons and, like Rumford, he married unhappiness.

No matter what may be thought of his opinion of the French as expressed in it Chenevix must have been something of a pioneer in the *Essay on National Character* in using a mathematical symbol for an economic concept. He measures the standard of civilisation (by which we might understand the standard of living) in terms of quality and quantity of product in relation to price.

> The bent of civilisation is to make good things cheap; and, with this due restriction, if I represents quality[2] and n quantity and p price the algebraical expression of civilisation, deduced from industry is In ÷ p or quality multiplied by quantity and divided by price.

---

[2] How does one quantify quality?

In every instance in which this formula is applied to English civilisation as compared with that of France then English civilisation is superior.

The hardwares of England have been the first of the world; and the very excellent cutlery, saws, files, steels, which she manufactures in very great quantity, are little dearer than the indifferent productions of other countries; insomuch that the formula of civilisation, In ÷ p, never was more thoroughly satisfied than in this, the most important of all the metallurgic arts... the increase of general industry. In, bears more than a ten-fold ratio to its former value, in iron alone, while it has made the ratio of p diminish almost in the same proportion throughout every other branch.

Again, it is just possible that it was not what he had to say on national character, but an interest he developed in cryptology about the beginning of the 1820s which drew forth the terse and caustic remark from the President of the Royal Society in his obituary reference to Chenevix. At any rate there appears in *The Journal of Science, Literature and the Arts* (1821) 'On a New Method of Secret Writing' by Richard Chenevix, Esq., FR and ASMRIA, Communicated by the Author.

Cryptology suffered a great set-back in the Napoleonic wars. It is possible that the disaster to the French armies in 1812 was attributable, at least in part, to the fact that the Russians were able to decipher intercepted French messages. But apparently Chenevix felt that he had invented an unbeatable code. He began his paper:

A method of writing, so occult as to escape detection, has long been among the desiderata of governments, and of all whose occupations may make secret communication advantageous; and though, from the earliest times, attempts have been made in all countries to attain this object, no mode has yet been devised which fulfils the three conditions required by Lord Bacon: 1st, that it should not be laborious either to

read or write; 2nd, that it should be very difficult to be
deciphered; 3rd, that it should be void of suspicion.

He goes on to say how Bacon's own attempt had been 'remarkable for
nothing so much as for transgressing the very rules he had himself
established'. He then expounds his own method and giving a coded
message ends up with a challenge on eighteen ciphers he supplied in
his paper in these terms:

> The first person, in any country, who accomplishes
> them all, and makes known the result of his researches
> through the channel of this journal, or by a
> communication addressed to the author on or before
> the last day of December, 1822, shall immediately
> receive one hundred pounds; or should he do no more
> than decipher Nos. 17 and 18, he shall immediately
> receive fifty pounds.

In a later number of the same publication came a reply from the Rev.
Edward Hincks, AM, and formerly Fellow of Trinity College, Dublin,
in which the Rev. Hincks ably solves Mr Chenevix' eighteen ciphers
and takes the two ciphers which Chenevix had represented as the most
difficult numbers, 17 and 18, showing that he could not only read but
write in these by giving the substance of number 17 in the cipher of
number 18 and vice versa remarking 'I am not very sanguine in my
expectations of the reward offered for deciphering these specimens,
and yet I think the following sentences comply with all the conditions'
which might well imply that the Rev. Edward Hincks merely
interpreted Mr Chenevix's money challenge as a hyperbolical
statement which Mr Chenevix was not in honour bound to meet. There
is no record available as to how the matter ended.

Chenevix has a long list of publications in the *Annales de chimie*.
among them letters to Pictet and Vauqueline. A paper published in
vol. LXV on Mineralogical Systems and concerned with the Werner–
Hauy conflict on mineralogy was regarded by English geologists of the
period as of outstanding importance. It was translated into English by
a member of the Geological Society of London. Chenevix was a
member of the first council of that body: another member was the

Hon. C.F. Greville whom Pictet mentions in one of his letters (No. 1) as possessing a first class mineralogical collection.

Richard Chenevix must have had substantial wealth behind him to support his studies, his travels and experiments. He was, for example, in a position to buy up Wollaston's entire stock of palladium; he could issue a challenge on ciphers backed by sums of £100 or £50.

Pugnacious, self-opinionated, sharp-tongued as he was he could yet display sensitivity for a servant in sickness or for a coachman (with whom he could identify as a 'fellow countryman') whose horses Professor Pictet wished to ridicule. He had very many successes and only one, dismal as it was, failure in his researches in chemistry. A man of outstanding ability and in his time, with as high a reputation as Davy his name is little known today.

Fond of scandal he possibly paid dearly for this weakness in an unhappy marriage: before life soured him he was a pleasant companion, a man of great wit and charm – 'We have had a bevy of wits here – Mr Chenevix, Mr Henry Hamilton, Leslie Foster and his particular friend, Mr Fitzgerald' (Maria Edgeworth).

Chenevix, whom Pictet met in London, though he may have known him in Paris accompanied the older man on his travels from London to Dublin going by stage coach and horse-cab via York, Edinburgh, Glasgow, Portpatrick, Donaghadee, Belfast, Ahoghill, Portrush, Coleraine, Stewartstown, Armagh, Castleblaney, Delvin, Edgeworthstown, Mullingar. In Dublin they parted, Pictet travelling via Holyhead to London, Chenevix returning to his sister, Mrs Tuite, at Sonna for a pause in his apparently restless wanderings.

Sir Benjamin Thompson 1753–1814

(Count Von Rumford in Pictet's book; Graf Von Rumford by his Bavarian title)

Most of LETTERS IX and X are concerned with the biography of Von Rumford. Indeed these two letters provided the basic material for Rev. George Ellis for his biography on Von Rumford published in 1876. The material in them will be used in this biographical note but, in the light of other material available and in the absence of the constraint of friendship which Pictet felt for the man he obviously very much admired, Von Rumford will appear a somewhat different person from the Von Rumford of those two letters – which are not given here.

Count Von Rumford was born Benjamin Thompson. Married in 1772 in Concord to a woman nearly twice his age on the outbreak of the War of Independence, he deserted her conveniently to join the Royalists. Soldier of fortune, he later earned himself a name as a scientist. By 1801 when Pictet visited him the title of Sir Benjamin given by George III had been superseded by that of Count Von Rumford. In his biography, Ellis points out a few minor errors in the account of his life given by Rumford to Pictet but these are not very germane. He does though mention something which Pictet does not, most likely because Rumford chose to remain quiet about it, and that is the fact that Thompson was a very unpopular man in Concord at the time he left it. In fact he must have felt himself lucky, despite his apparent outwardly brave face, to get out when he did, and the circumstances of his getting out go a long way to explain why he never returned to his native place in later life despite very flattering American invitations to do so. Thompson was under suspicion, at the time the Americans were arming to defend themselves against the taxes being imposed by the mother country and, as it turned out, to win their independence, of being in communication against their interests with the Governor of Massachusetts and the military garrison in Boston; he was in fact taken before a committee to explain the part he had played in getting two Royalist deserters to return to their unit in Boston, two men who, skilled in arms, would have been of great use in drilling and in the use of firearms to potential insurgents apart from augmenting the numbers of Royalists defending the garrison. Thompson was too clever for the committee and throughout a long inquisition avoided incriminating himself by representing himself as anti-Royalist; yet suspicions persisted and he had to endure an unfriendly environment.

Ellis represents Thompson as a man greatly wronged and forced to go over to the English forces by the treatment he received from his neighbours and this, for the century and a half between 1775 and 1932, was the accepted version – reinforced by Pictet's account given in his *Voyage de trois mois*.

Pictet says nothing of the 'boycotting' (to use a word which came into the English language for that kind of treatment in the second half of the nineteenth century), he speaks of Thompson as going over to the English because of ties of friendship with the Governor. Thompson had indeed found favour with the Governor but he was the classical social climber delighting in acceptance in high circles as witness a letter he wrote to the Governor (Wentworth)[1] 13th December 1774, and which has only within recent years come to light. Describing to Wentworth the part he played in getting the two deserters to return, a part which differs very much from the one he made public, he goes on,

> Inclosed [sic] is a letter to General Gage, which I beg your Excellency would peruse, and if you think it proper, would seal it and send my servant with it to Boston – if not you will be pleased to dispose of it as you think proper. For I must humbly intreat your Excellency's direction in this difficult affair – as I have no other person to apply to for advice, on whose Judgement and friendship I can depend. And indeed I think it the greatest honour and happiness of my life that I am allowed to make known my difficulties to a person in such an exalted station, and one of your

---

[1] Wentworth, Sir John (1734–1820). Governor of New Hampshire, he dissolved the Assembly there in June 1774; partial to his favourites.

Excellency's known Wisdom, and Humanity. And you
may rely and depend upon it that it shall be the main
study of my future life to behave in some measure
worthy of the great kindness and distinction your
Excellency has been pleased to honour with me.
[Quoted by Allen French].

Professor Pictet gives a touching account of Count Von Rumford's
sorrow as he looked back from 1801 to the time in 1775 when he
parted with his wife and child to join the British forces. The incident
is characteristic of Pictet in one respect – his making judgements in
the light of his own preconceived notions. For Pictet, the intensely
family man, separation from wife and family must have appeared a
great sorrow. There seems little doubt that he disliked partings even
though he becomes a trifle tiresome at times as he moralises over
farewells, to this friend or that, as he proceeds on his travels.
Projecting himself into Thompson's position twenty-six years earlier
he concludes that Thompson must have felt keenly the break with his
family. The reader of Pictet's account of Rumford's pain in Brompton
Row as he recalls the event is likely to be suspicious that the Count is
moved by a different feeling other than recollected sorrow: he is
acutely embarrassed at the recollection of a very mean action – the
deliberate desertion of his wife and infant daughter.

In 1772 then the tall, handsome Benjamin Thompson married a
rich widow; he was something short of twenty, his bride was thirty-
three. His marriage to a lady well placed in local society gave him
position, the ability to pursue his studies, and above all an introduction
to the Governor of the Province and the military circle. When the
opportunity came to cleave to the Governor and his circle without
incurring reproach for leaving behind his, by eighteenth century
standards, middle-aged wife he took it.

Revolution was in the air. His father-in-law, the Rev. Walker, was
committed to the American side as were all his neighbours. Siding
with the British would willy-nilly bring about a separation from his
wife – so much the better if siding with the British was the thing most
desired as leading to advancement.

Thompson left home and except for one long letter to his father-in-
law, (which time has shown to have been deceitful in that it presented
himself as having to go over to the British by the suspicious and

intolerable behaviour of the Patriots whereas he was in fact a spy in the pay of the Crown) he made no attempt to get in touch with his family again. Even his sympathetic biographer, Ellis, finds it hard not to believe that Thompson had tired of his wife (by then the mother of their only child, Sarah).

> Whether we are to recognise in this disparity [i.e. of ages] of the parties one reason for the seeming indifference of the husband when in exile to the wife whom he had left at home must be referred to the judgement of the reader.

Seven years after leaving home Benjamin Thompson was a colonel in the British army in New York. Ellis is concerned that he still made no attempt to communicate with his family.

> It would be agreeable to be able to recognise here any effort by Colonel Thompson to communicate with his family... I cannot say that he did not make such an effort, but I have been unable to find any trace of it. The attempt would have been attended with difficulties, though these were by no means insurmountable. Constant intercourse was kept up across Long Island Sound between the British troops in New York, and neutrals, loyalist sympathisers, and time-servers in Connecticut, and contrivance and money would have effected the object had it been one of strong desire. I am forced to the conclusion that Thompson was either indifferent to or alienated from his family.

Mrs Thompson died 19th January 1792, aged fifty-two. There seems to be little reason to disagree with J.A. Thompson in his forthright conclusion that Benjamin Thompson deserted his wife. In the event he found solace in the arms of the countesses of Munich, one of whom, the Countess Von Baumgarten came to have a daughter with an unmistakable resemblance to Count Von Rumford.

Thompson had the art of singling out people who could help his advancement – his first wife, Governor Wentworth, General Gage,[2] Lord George Germain, the Electors of Bavaria, the Princes Charles Theodore[3] and Maximilian.[4] In a surprisingly short time from leaving home Thompson was successively Secretary for Georgia and Under Secretary of State for the Colonies in London owing the latter distinction to Lord George Germain. Lord George, made a scapegoat for the American debacle, fell from power to rise as Viscount Sackville, his protégé becoming lieutenant–colonel of an almost non-existent regiment, the King's American Dragoons, returned to America not, as even Pictet's eulogistic description cannot conceal, to any worthwhile military activity much less glory – a fact which did not deter him later in Europe from representing himself as a seasoned campaigner. Not only did he not earn military glory in the American war, but the people of Long Island were long to remember Lt.-Col. Thompson as something of a barbarian for desecrating a church and using tombstones to erect an oven to bake bread for the remnants of his dragoons.

Back in England in 1783 he retired from the army to set out on his European adventure which was to bring him a knighthood from George III; the Order of St Stanislas from the unfortunate Stanislas II of Poland; the title of Count of the Holy Roman Empire, and the self-important look so characteristic of his portraits.

The boat he crossed in for Europe set sail for Calais but was forced by strong winds to Boulogne. There were only three passengers. One of them was the historian, Edward Gibbon (1737–1794) who from the mock–serious way he refers to him would appear not to have shared Thompson's notion of his own importance. Gibbon's account of the crossing is given in a letter to Lord Sheffield (17th and 18th September, 1783). If Von Rumford's story, as relayed by Pictet (LETTER IX), of how he frightened Gibbon out of his wits by the manner which he drove his horses be true then the honours would

---

[2]   General Thos. Gage (1721–1787). In America 1763–1775. Resigned October 1775.
[3]   Charles Theodore (1724–1799). Elector-Palatine 1746–1777, when he also became Elector of Bavaria; an autocrat.
[4]   Maximilian Joseph (1752–1825). Nephew of Charles Theodore, to whom he introduced Rumford. Elector in 1799, he became king in 1805. Liberal and understanding, he ruled a happy people.

appear to have been even, for by Gibbon's account Thompson was no sailor.

> We start about one o'clock... The Triumvirate of that memorable embarkation will consist of the Grand Gibbon, Henry Laurens Esq.,[5] President of the Congress and Mr Secretary, Colonel, Admiral, Philosopher Benjamin Thompson, attended by three horses who are not the most agreeable fellow passengers... Instead of Calais the wind has driven us to Boulogne... I had not the least symptom of sea sickness while my companions were spewing around me.

At Strasbourg Thompson did his great stage act to attract the attention of Prince Maximilian and Rochambeau[6] the sharer of Washington's victory in 1781 at Yorktown. There can be few better examples of retrospective self-love and self-satisfaction than his own description of himself on that occasion to Pictet eighteen years later in Brompton Row. Seated in the saddle on his magnificent charger arrayed in his military best, the Lt. Col. observes from a respectable distance the manoeuvres and inevitably attracts the curiosity of the officers and the invitation to discuss military matters. Thompson is ready to give the others chapter and verse from his portfolio for which he sends. The discussion is long, animated and interesting, for who can restrain the military man from talking of his campaigns real and imaginary? The invitation to meet again is made and the introduction by letter to the Elector of Bavaria is given.

Both Thompson and Charles Theodore were eminently suited. Charles was a cultured, intellectual man with a taste for science, but autocratic: Thompson whose ideal was the absolute rule of the Chinese dynasty was his man. He was offered service under the Elector, but before accepting he first sought the approval of George III. The permission was granted and with it a knighthood. For some reason Pictet does not give the citation which accompanied the knighthood though he mentions it and speaks of its flattering terms. If one largely

---

5   Laurens, Henry (1724–1792). Revolutionary statesman of Huguenot extraction.
6   Rochambeau, Jean Baptiste (Comte de) (1725–1807). Commander of the French troops sent to the aid of the Americans.

supplies the terms oneself the adjective 'flattering' takes on a slightly bogus note. Research has shown that there were about twenty families of Thompsons in Massachusetts, all of them ancient in the sense that Adam was the common father of all. As for the coat of arms it is to be found among the exercises in engraving in which Thompson as a boy had considerable skill. Here is a copy of the citation as it is given by his namesake and biographer, James Alden Thompson:

> Whereas it appears by a Memorial recorded in the College of Arms, that Sir Benjamin Thompson of St James's, Westminster, Knight, Colonel of the King's American Regiment of Light Dragoons, and Fellow of the Royal Society of London, later Under-Secretary of State of the Province of Georgia, and Colonel of a Regiment of Militia in the Province of New Hampshire, in North American, Son of Benjamin Thompson, late of the Province of Massachusetts Bay, in New England, Gent., deceased, is one of the most ancient families in North America; that an Island which belonged to his Ancestors, at the entrance of Boston Harbour, near where the first New England Settlement was made, still bears his name; that his Ancestors have ever lived in reputable situations in that Country where he was born, and have hitherto used the Arms of the ancient and respectable family of Thompson of the County of York, from a constant tradition that they derived their descent from that source.
>
> Whereas, at a very early period of the late Troubles in North America the said Sir Benjamin Thompson having engaged warmly in support of the British Government in the Country, and in the course of the War been distinguished for his good Conduct and Bravery in the Line of his Profession, and recently received a very honourable Mark of His Majesty's Approbation and Favour...
>
> Know ye, therefore, that we do by these Presents grant and confirm to the said Sir Benjamin Thompson

in Testimony of his Merits and Services the Arms
distinguished as follows...

Thompson did signal service for Bavaria. First of all, he rid Munich
of beggars and Munich was, after Rome, the most beggar-plagued city
in Europe. By a law passed for the purpose Thompson on 1st January
1790, swept the beggars, all 2500 of them, off the streets into pre-
prepared workhouses and to prevent any new arrivals entering the city
he threw a cordon of military round it. Those in the workhouses he
put to work and added 10,000 florins a year to the state revenues by
their work: by the end of the year his work force of ex-beggars had
been reduced from 2500 to 1400. He was not the man to neglect the
opportunity for experimenting afforded by the presence of so many
inmates in the workhouses: feeding, heating and lighting them in the
most efficient and economical manner became a passion with him. He
was later to apply the principles and methods of heating, cooking and
lighting he evolved in the workhouse of Munich to the Foundling
Hospital in London; to the Heriot Hospital in Edinburgh; to his own
home in Brompton Row, London; to private houses and to other
institutions in England, Scotland and Ireland. Some wit had it that he
cooked his meals by directing the smoke from his neighbour's
chimney to his own use. He did not escape the genius of Gillray the
cartoonist and one of the funniest of the cartoons is that dated 12th
June, 1800, with the caption 'The Comfort of a Rumford Stove'. Nor
did he escape the attention of the rhyming satirist, Peter Pindar.

> Knight of the dish-clout whereso'er I walk
> I hear there Rumford, all the kitchen talk,
> Note of melodious cadence, on the ear,
> Loud echoes 'Rumford' here, 'Rumford' there.
> Lo every parlour, drawing room I see,
> Boasts of thy stoves and talks of nought but thee.

He earned from the Elector the supreme satisfaction for his vanity the
title of Count (Graf Von) of the Holy Roman Empire, which Charles
Theodore, as Vicar on the death of the Emperor Joseph, had it in his
power to confer. The other services he performed for the Elector are
fondly recounted by Pictet. They include the draining of swamps, the
planting of gardens, reform of the police, the preserving of the

neutrality and safety of the city in a menacing situation when the French and Austrian armies faced each other within shell-fire of it... But in all things he was the supreme administrator concerned with order for the sake of order. As the great French naturalist, Cuvier,[7] who had known him for ten years, said when he spoke Von Rumford's panegyric in 1814,

> Regarding as he did order as some kind of divinity regulating the affairs of this life he made himself its model in all points and in every conceivable connection. His needs, his pleasures, his work were all as planned as his experiments.

Ellis also quotes Cuvier:

> He thought it was not wise or good to entrust to men in the mass the care of their own well-being. The right, which seems so natural to them of judging whether they are wisely governed appeared to him to be a fictitious fallacy born of false notions of enlightenment.

He regarded the generality of men as simple machines and nations as best run on despotic lines.

But it was in connection with his high position in Bavaria that he came to earn the important place he holds (perhaps not entirely merited) in the history of the development of the theory of heat. Noticing the great heat generated in the boring of a cannon, he experimented to find that by dipping the cannon heated by the bore into a tank of cold water he could raise the temperature of the water to boiling point in the space of two and a half hours, he reflected on the nature of heat. He reasoned that since the only thing conveyed to the cannon by the bore was, as he said, 'motion', the existing theory of heat as a 'flow of caloric' was untenable. He published his observations in 1798 – *An Enquiry into the Source of Heat which is Generated by Friction*, (PTRS, 1798). Von Rumford said nothing about the internal behaviour of atoms but most of the scientific world

---

[7] Cuvier, Georges (Baron) (1769–1832). Author of works in comparative anatomy and palaeontology.

accepts him as the progenitor of the modern theory of heat. So in many ways he did well by his stay in Munich. This is not the place to argue his merits in the history of science. What is extremely noteworthy is the fact that Pictet's visit to Von Rumford and his stay at his home at Brompton, brought together the two men with whose names are associated such advances in the theory of heat as the discovery of radiant heat and the modern concept of thermodynamics, at least in embryo.

Thompson remained off and on fifteen years in Bavaria. A ten foot statute, erected in Munich during his lifetime, is still there but, this fact notwithstanding, it would appear that by 1798 he had outstayed his welcome. Pictet confirms this fact and he is merely relaying what Von Rumford told him, Von Rumford knowing at the time that it was so, welcomed the chance to leave the country as Bavarian Ambassador to London, if indeed he did not arrange the appointment himself. At any rate he reckoned without the stubborn inflexibility of George III, whose dull logic could not accept someone he regarded as one of his own subjects, as ambassador from a foreign country, even if that subject had been in all but name a foreign citizen for fifteen years. When Von Rumford arrived in London with his credentials from the Elector of Bavaria as his Ambassador he found he was not acceptable. The effect on his self-esteem may be left to the imagination.

Whatever the effect, he then began what has been described as his greatest work – the founding of the Royal Institution, a description of which takes up so much of Pictet's LETTER I and for which, according to one of his biographers, H. Bence Jones, a later secretary of the Institution, he did not get the credit he deserved.

Autocratic, paternalistic, despotic, whatever adjective may be chosen for him he was an improver and, as experience at the Royal Institution was to show, he was ahead of his times, paradoxically too radical for the country ruled over by the heavy reactionary George III. From the programme quoted at length by Pictet there is no doubt that Von Rumford intended the Institution to have functions like those of the Dublin Society, also undertaken to some extent at Glasgow University and in the Anderson's College, Glasgow in line with what he himself had done in Munich. It was, too, his intention that research done at the Institution should be fed out into industry and agriculture. Mechanics were to come from all over England to be perfected in their work and then act as a leven throughout the country, something in the line of the polytechniques being established in France.

At the time the Institution was projected, Von Rumford heard of a young Orkney man, Thomas Webster,[8] who began life as a draughtsman and architectural student and was at that time giving scientific lectures to building mechanics. He engaged Webster as clerk of works but also with the intention that he should later undertake the lectures to the mechanics whom Von Rumford saw as having a central place in the scheme. Both he and Webster had a clear understanding of how he saw the Institution developing. Here were Von Rumford's instructions to the younger man: 'Go there. Live in the house and think for us. You know our objects generally, but we leave you to work out the details. Make plans for the house.' This on Webster's authority who goes on:

My first attention was to instruct bricklayers, joiners, trimmers, iron-plate workers, as these were the trades most connected with our improvements at that time. In a large room on the ground floor, we built up for practising the men, chimneys and types of fireplaces of all kinds in a slight manner and pulled them down again and built others. We fitted improved models of fireplaces in old-fashioned cottages, also boilers of various kinds and showed how smoky chimneys might be cured; models of various cullinery [sic] vessels were made and put in the model rooms... In designing the Lecture Room of an institution so peculiar, my object was to adapt it to different ranks in society, for any attempt to destroy any distinction must be absurd. I constructed a gallery intended for those who either wished not to be observed or who, for obvious reasons, would not wish to sit down by their employers, it was also to receive such inquiring mechanics as had gained a title to be there. To this gallery a separate stone stair led from the street – the whole was built – but this project for improving mechanics which had already

---

[8] Webster, Thomas (1773–1842). Orkney-born, he became, following his spell with the Royal Institution, an outstanding geologist, ending as professor of geology, University College, London.

gained for the Institution such golden opinions, was doomed to be crushed by the timidity of a few; I was asked rudely what I meant by instructing the lower classes in science. I was told likewise that it was resolved upon that the plan must be dropped as quickly as possible, it was thought to have a political tendency; if I persisted I would become a marked man. It was in vain to argue... Count Rumford left England at about the same time, the management of the Institution fell into other hands, and my mechanics' stone staircase was pulled down at considerable expense. All the cullinery [sic] and other contrivances which the Count and I had taken such trouble to fit up in the kitchen as an exhibition (and many of these were good things) were put away.

Yet there must have been against Von Rumford at the time a great deal of dislike if not suspicion: colonials were expected to know their places whilst this particular colonial had submerged an English knighthood (which he possibly obtained through favouritism in the first place) beneath the title of Count of the Holy Roman Empire. But there was more to it than that. As the young Benjamin Thompson he had left his native Concord under suspicion of being a spy, a suspicion which as we saw research in the twentieth century was to confirm. History was to repeat itself. Here it is necessary to return to Thompson's relationship with Lord George Germain.

Soon after his arrival from America he was on the most intimate terms with Lord George, Lady Germain and her daughters. He lived with the family for some time, accompanying her Ladyship and daughters to balls, acting as dancing partner when no one else came forward to ask the privilege. Later when he moved into accommodation of his own he still had his meals with the family.

It was through Lord George's patronage that Thompson became (absentee) Secretary of Georgia. His salary was £100 per year, but on top of this he had a further unspecified salary for acting as secretary in Lord George's office. His earnings are reckoned to have been, shortly after his arrival in England, nothing short of £7,000 per year. No wonder he could live in style, donate prizes to the Royal Society and other bodies as well as keep fine chargers.

In 1781 he had to quit his post for being inefficient and corrupt. The charge of being inefficient appears much out of character. What is more likely is that, whilst he was performing his heat experiments with the guns of the navy which involved sailing with the ships, he was writing to Lord George the most inordinate criticism of the conduct of the fleet by Keppel and Hardy and as a consequence gave so much offence that he had to resign. More seriously there is a suggestion that he was selling naval information to the French and that Lord George prevented his prosecution for doing so. Perhaps he was an exception to the disclaimer that the sciences were never at war, though the notion persists that he was the exception that proved the rule: in other words that he was no scientist. Thus Wright and Evans writing in 1965 say of him, 'It is hardly necessary to state that Count Rumford was one of the most remarkable pretenders to science of his time'. Prejudices die hard. Certainly Lord George's biographer does not hold that opinion; he refers to Von Rumford's 'genuine talent for the sciences'.

His letters of the period to Lord George make unpleasant reading. They recall something of the tone of his earlier letters to Wentworth but one should allow for the accepted patronage-seeking language of the age.

In 1801 there must have been a great weight of personal animosity towards Von Rumford in London, and, in the light of the real state of affairs at the time Pictet visited the Royal Institution when the disagreement recorded by Webster must have been at its worst, Von Rumford's account of the unity of purpose of the managers makes ironic reading. It is possible that Von Rumford was unaware of the plot to thwart him, but after his experience in Munich he could hardly have been unaware of the opposition which new ideas can generate.

On the domestic side, his daughter, Sarah, joined him from America in 1796. It was their first meeting since he had deserted her as an infant with her mother, twenty-one years before. Shortly after her arrival in London, Von Rumford brought his daughter to an Italian grand opera but the poor provincial girl was bored and confessed later that the performance was not to be compared with that of Black Prince, an old fiddler back in Concord. For his part her father was often to wish he had left her in Concord. To his great displeasure, he once found her curtseying to the maids. She accompanied him to Munich and marvelled much at the grandeur of his appointments though she was for a while saddened to find out that she had a half-sister – even that half-sister was young, beautiful and had a Countess for her mother. In Munich, Sarah had the attentions of an Italian Count, whose address was both genuine and sincere, but her father prevented the match – as he was to do later again in London when a man many years her senior, Sir Charles Blagden,[9] asked for her hand. Sarah returned to America in 1799. She and her father carried on an uninterrupted correspondence until 1811 when she returned to Europe to be with him in Paris after his second disastrous marriage (to be mentioned). In the house in Paris there was a somewhat mysterious lady who attended the flowers in the garden. To satisfy her curiosity about this lady, Sarah asked a few questions from the domestics. For her reward she was given a rest in Switzerland. The mysterious lady became the mother of a half-brother of Sarah and of the young Bavarian Countess. He grew up, never married and was killed at Sevastopol.

Pictet's last letter depicts himself and the Count setting out – by special concession for France, Pictet to return to Geneva where, as was seen in the account given of his life, high employment awaited him, Von Rumford to return to Munich where disappointment awaited him. On his passage through Paris Von Rumford met the widow of the great chemist Lavoisier.[10] Lavoisier and she had been a devoted couple though she was considerably his junior. As a young wife she had copied his notes for him. Now after his execution during the Terror she revered his memory. Whether for personal charm or reflected glory she impressed Count Von Rumford.

He went on to Munich to find it changed. The Elector, Charles Theodore his old patron was dead, his place taken by his nephew, Maximilian, the man who had first introduced Thompson, as he was then, to Charles Theodore. Maximilian, affected by the spirit of the French Revolution, did not believe, like his uncle, Charles Theodore, in autocratic rule. Machiavelli had lost his Prince: there was no place now in Munich for a man with the Count's bias towards despotic rule. By 1802 he was back in England but it must have been only to settle

---

[9]   Blagden, Charles (1740–1820). Medical doctor and scientist, he was long the chief medical officer to the British Army. Intimate friend of Von Rumford.
[10]   Lavoisier, Antoine Laurent de (1743–1794). One of the founders of modern chemistry.

his domestic affairs for in the same year he was dining with a new Cesare Borgia, the First Consul, the man often depicted back in England as Lucifer incarnate, but by then Count Von Rumford was a true cosmopolitan. He spoke French, German, Italian and Spanish as naturally as he spoke English.

In Paris he kept up his acquaintance with Mme Lavoisier. In 1805 the six foot, well-figured Graf Von Rumford with an international reputation as scientist, statesman, soldier, was married to the widow of Lavoisier, the founder of modern chemistry. He was fifty-two, she in her mid-thirties. The wedding had an inauspicious start. The name Von Rumford was not good enough for the widow of Lavoisier, whose name she insisted on retaining, but in any event it turned out to be a disastrous union. The ill-matched pair bickered and squabbled over the slightest trifles, but then Count Von Rumford did not recognise trifles. They parted by mutual agreement in 1809.

Von Rumford died at Auteil in 1814. He is buried there. His daughter, Sarah, was in Paris when he died. Later she returned to Concord to live as a spinster, known as Countess Rumford. By almost any standard, the life of Benjamin Thompson, the young colonial from Concord, was an amazing one.

Others of Note

Sir James Hall (1761–1832)

Sir James Hall, who gave so much of his time to Professor Pictet and Richard Chenevix when they visited Edinburgh in the summer of 1801 and who received them in his home at Dunglass, occupies an important place in the history of the development of geological science: he was one of the pioneers in experimental work on rock synthesis. He performed for his time, astounding experiments on rocks employing the furnaces of an iron foundry. By experiment he was able to show that if basaltic rock is melted and allowed to cool quickly it becomes a mass of glass, whereas if it is cooled slowly it assumes its original crystalline form. The most significant of his experiments were those performed on limestone. By heating powdered chalk in a gastight gun-barrel he converted the substance into a crystalline mass so giving physical support to Hutton's contention that marble was derived from limestone by the application of heat and pressure.

The other great interest of Sir James as we learn from Pictet's LETTER III, was Gothic architecture, an interest which came to him as a consequence of his travels in France and Italy in 1785. It became his great aim to awaken others in an age which for the most part looked on Gothic as barbaric, and this is much to his credit, to 'appreciate its [Gothic] merits, and to show the high estimation to which it is entitled in point of both beauty and utility'.

He was seeking the unifying principle of the Gothic, examples of which he had taken from such churches as St Mary's Beverley, Holyrood House, York Minister, St Mary's, Isle of Galloway when one day travelling in France he became convinced he had found the principle in the realm of natural vegetation.

> It happened that the peasants of the country through which I was travelling were then employed in collecting and carrying home the long rods or poles

which they make use of to support their vines, or to split into hoops; and these were to be seen, in every village, standing in bundles, or waving, partly loose upon carts. It occurred to me that a rustic building might be constructed of such rods, bearing a resemblance to works of Gothic architecture, and from which the peculiar forms of that style might have been derived.

There followed an investigation carried on over fifteen years and he was able with the aid of 'some friends both in the collection of materials, and in the solution of difficulties to reduce the most intricate forms of this elaborate style to the same simple origin'.

He goes on to describe how he was able to imitate with long poles and rods of willow that striking feature of the Gothic church the...

...double row of clustered pillars, composed of an assemblage of long and slender shafts, which reaching from the ground nearly to the summit, there separate and spread in all directions, forming the ribs of groins (as they are called) of a vaulted roof. In the meeting of these groins, and in the windows of the sides and ends, we see the form of the pointed arch, the principal characteristic of Gothic architecture.

Such buildings have I conceived, been executed in imitation of a rustic dwelling...

It is a dangerous conjecture to read too much out of shapes –

Hamlet:	Do you see yonder cloud that's almost in shape of a camel?
Polonius:	By the mass, and 'tis like a camel, indeed.
Hamlet:	Methinks, it is like a weasel.
Polonius:	It is backed like a weasel.
Hamlet:	Or, like a whale.
Polonius:	Very like a whale.

Hamlet
Act III, Scene ii

But what follows is of interest to the reader of Professor Pictet's *Journey*.

Sir James constructed his model Gothic church in his garden from poles, rods and wickerwork but as is the way with willow rods they struck and supplied him with a further development of his theory and caused, incidentally, some ambiguity in Pictet's description of the church. The sprouts on the rods which had struck and the bark curling on those which had not presented the imagination of Sir James with a strong resemblance to the embellishments, the crockets and so on, of Gothic architecture: he had probed the mystery!

One gets the impression from reading Pictet's description of the little imitation church that he imagined it was fashioned entirely from living trees or bushes. But it was early in the morning when Pictet saw it, a wet morning at that, and the morning after a hard day of scrambling up and down the goat paths of St Abb's Head and over the Scottish moors in downpours and mists. Sir James in his enthusiasm for things geological was not one to spare his guests.

Sir James's wife, Lady Helen, was the second daughter of Dunbar Douglas, 4th Earl of Selkirk. They were married in November, 1786. She survived Sir James by five years from his death in 1832. They had six children, three sons and three daughters.

Pictet shows Sir James as a very extensive landlord whose tenants were prosperous and progressive. Elsewhere we learn that some of these tenants paid the amazing rent of 2000 pounds sterling attesting indeed to the agricultural monopoly of the times driving prices up on the new working classes flocking into the new industrial towns. His hospitality was Scottish and that in Pictet's terms was praise indeed.

Rev. William Richardson, DD (1740–1820)

Richardson was a graduate and fellow of Trinity College, Dublin. He was for long Rector of the Parish of Clonfecle, Moy, Co. Tyrone. He ministered at a time when settled ideas on creation based on a literal interpretation of the Old Testament were being challenged. He was a challenger of the challengers. An ardent Neptunist for whom all rocks were the result of deposition – likely from the flood – the theories of the Vulcanists, which saw volcanic rocks as the result of internal fires of the earth, were dangerous heresy. He felt he had the evidence in

Portrush to show the Vulcanists in the wrong. Convinced that Pictet would accept his view he looked to being able to quote his 'friend Professor Pictet', which he later did, in corroboration of his belief. But Pictet's later writing on the subject showed that whatever else he was he was no Neptunist.

The great argument of the Vulcanists was the absence of fossils in volcanic rocks.

Then Richardson 'found' the answer to the Vulcanist objection. He sent to Kirwan in Dublin a sample of a 'basaltic' rock with fossils. This was the rock that he rushed Pictet out to see practically the moment he and Chenevix arrived in Portrush, and apparently before they had anything to eat. The rock contained ammonites and its particularly hard nature gave it the appearance of being basalt. Moreover, it seemed to be part of a system which was without doubt basalt; but, to quote from the late Professor Charlesworth,

> ...the Portrush rock consists of two rocks, namely, a sill of olivine-dolerite[1] which becomes fine-grained along its roof and has been intruded into Lias shale. This blue porcellanite, on account of the baking it has suffered, breaks with pronounced shell-like fracture and is so brittle that it is virtually impossible to extract the ammonites.

The original sedimentary Lias had thus become so hard and intimately bound with the igneous rock that it is easy to see how Richardson was mistaken in thinking that he had found a volcanic rock with fossils and so had disproved the theories of the Vulcanists.

Dr Richardson was a deeply religious man but of fundamentalist outlook. He saw religion as being assailed by rationalists like Voltaire and Desmarest, 'the Antichristian Conspirators' who would use their theories as,

> ...instruments to support infidelity, concealed under the mask of mere physical opinions, whose object was... to shew that a much longer space of time is required for the formation of the universe, than the history of the

---

[1]   A basaltic rock.

Creation, as delineated by Moses, leaves us room to suppose.

Considerable classical scholar that he was, he relied on the ancients, then on Francis Bacon, then on French writers like Abbé Barruel[2] and other French Jesuits as well as on 'facts' as he saw them to counter the false doctrines, especially...

...advising those, who admit the necessity of repelling these frequent attacks upon revelation, carefully to ascertain the facts, before they suffer themselves to be led into the mazes of theory, and puzzled by speculations *a priori*.

Pictet's help was enlisted in a way that gives an interesting explanation to the riddle of why Pictet, the friend of Dolomieu,[3] the pioneering Plutonist, Pictet who had found the Plutonist theories of Sir James Hall very acceptable, came to publish the opposing theories of Richardson.

Conversing once on this subject [the basaltic rocks of Sicily] with my friend, Professor Pictet, of Geneva, he requested me to put my sentiments on paper, that he might communicate them to his friend Mr Dolomieu: I did so, and aware that I was exposing myself to a charge of presumption, for discussing the construction and productions of a country I had never seen, I limited myself to the facts stated, the admissions made by Mr Dolomieu himself; but before my observations could reach him, he was no more. Professor Pictet has since published them, in his *Bibliothèque britannique*.

---

[2] Barruel, Abbé Augustin de (1741-1820). French Jesuit and scientist; in his book *Les helviennes* he opposed the theories which were changing utterly man's concepts of the origins of his physical environment.
[3] Dolomieu, Deodat de Gratet de (1750-1801). Outstanding mineralogist. Gave his name to the Dolomites. Ruined in health by imprisonment under harsh conditions by the Neopolitans. He died soon after his release and before Pictet's book was published. Pictet knew him personally.

They form the substance of Richardson's two letters published by Pictet in his *Voyage de trois mois*.

Perhaps his search for facts explains why he gives the impression in his writings of not being able to see the wood for the trees: few people before or after him, certainly before him, could have had, whatever his opinions on their origin, the detailed knowledge Richardson had of the rocks of Antrim and Derry, as revealed for example, in a letter from him to Sir Humphry Davy, and read before the Royal Society of London, 17th March, 1808. As he had done for Pictet and many others he acted as guide to Davy in the area.

In 1801, when Pictet met him he had already been Rector of Clonfecle for thirty years and he had been going to Portrush in the summer of each year during most of that time, a fact which led Pictet wrongly to describe him as '*Ecclésiastique etabli depuis plus de trente ans, dans la petite paroisse de Portrush*' which gives the impression that Pictet regarded him as the Rector of Portrush. Mr H.A. Boyd, MA, MLitt, Ballycastle, an authority on Church of Ireland history, has pointed out that Dr Richardson could not have been Rector of Portrush in 1801 as Portrush was not at that time a separate Parish of the Church of Ireland; otherwise it might have been imagined that Richardson had the living of both Clonfecle and Portrush.

It was easy for Pictet to regard Richardson as in fact the Rector of Portrush, for one can be sure that the good man's head was so full of the wars of the Neptunists and the Vulcanists, of Plutonists, and the implications for his concept of Revelation, that he had no time to comment on trifles such as who was or was not the local incumbent. Moreover, as Mr Boyd states, Dr Richardson's house in Portrush, Craigintemple – Gaelic for 'rock of the church', from its situation – was right beside the church; and indeed, in the absence of a local clergyman, one can be sure that Dr Richardson frequently took the service during the summer months, ensuring, no doubt, that 'the history of creation as delineated by Moses' was properly expounded.

The Richardson family remained long associated with Portrush. It was a granddaughter of Dr Richardson's, back in the dark ages of woman's enslavement who drove the first electric tram in the world when the tramway from Portrush to the Giant's Causeway was inaugurated in 1883, a right her grandfather had surely earned for her by his many journeys on horseback in all kinds of weather over the same route. Most likely when he made the journey on horseback on that rainswept morning in July 1801, to allow his guests ride in a carriage, he had had little sleep the night before, for no matter where the family of the Doctor put up, the guests, though they came at an awkward time, were given the best beds in the house.

Richardson's letters, concerned only with defending his own views on geology, have no general interest and under the weight of the very many authorities he calls to his aid are boring in the extreme. Though published in Pictet's book (in French) they are not given here.

He had though a facility for expression and communication that many writers on scientific subjects today might envy and this facility seems to have had its part in the spell he cast on Pictet. But then one must not overlook the interest both men had in common in religion nor Richardson's enthusiasm, nor his hospitality. Pictet does not mention the common interest in religion but the other traits are revealed in the Professor's account of his visit to Portrush.

This extract from a letter to the *Newry Magazine* will illustrate Dr Richardson's facility in communication and indeed his descriptive powers:

> Before we took a boat at Balintoy, we examined on our left, a Whyn Dyke,[4] cutting down through a limestone facade vertically: the only instance I know of on our coast, where Dyke and limestone meet... here though the line of demarcation be as correct, as if drawn by a pencil, yet the limestone and basalt pass without interrupting the solidity or continuity of the materials, into each other.

And his description of the famous rope bridge of Carrick-a-rede as viewed from a boat:

> We set out among limestone facades; the material of the coast is changed at Carrick-a-rede, the great precipice near 250 feet high is pure basalt, and from this emerges at right angles, the great Carrick-a-rede mass, or island, now separated from the main by a

---

[4]   A whyn dyke – a phenomenon formed by the intrusion of basalt into another rock – at Ballintoy into chalk. Professor Pictet in his account of his geological outings in Edinburgh seems to have fallen in love with the word whin.

tremendous chasm, the sides perpendicular and 80 feet from the water; across this a bridge of ropes is thrown, affording a frightful passage into the island, and I was more terrified than amused, by seeing from the boat the fishermen passing the swinging bridge, at such an enormous height above me.

His other great scientific interest was agriculture and he campaigned with his usual zeal for the adoption of fiorin grass especially for high ground, arguing that by its adoption much greater numbers of stock could be supported.

His obituary in the *Belfast News Letter* refers to his various interests:

> To his labours, Geology, an interesting branch of literature, and the art of agriculture, are deeply indebted, for some important late discoveries. His ideas possessed the rare merit of originality, and were supported by a clear, nervous and argumentative series and style of reasoning altogether peculiar to himself; and he was seldom, if ever, overthrown in any of those controversial discussions into which he was frequently led by the boldness and singularity of some of his speculations. He was, indeed, an amusing, instructive, perspicuous and ready writer, whose prime object was to benefit the human race and, in support of this noble design, he was at all times ready to contend *totis viribus*.

He himself amusingly though unconsciously attests to his being an untiring controversialist in this letter to the *Newry Magazine*: 'Several years ago I had determined to prepare a particular account of our magnificent basaltic coast, from Magilligan to Glenarm; and had proceeded a good way, when partly deterred by the magnitude to which it was growing, and partly interrupted by calls that came on me for particular parts especially in controversy...' One is reminded of another eighteenth-century vicar, this time of fiction, who was ready at the drop of a hat to defend his particular brand of monogamy.

However Dr Richardson may have fought his distant opponents in the two letters published by Pictet, he did not, in the eyes of a writer in the *Edinburgh Review* make much of a show when he once met a party of Huttonian geologists in Scotland. The incident is recorded in a review of a book *Geology and Mineralogy Considered with Reference to Natural Theology* by the Rev. Wm. Buckland, Canon of Christchurch and Reader in Geology and Mineralogy in the University of Oxford:

> As a specimen of the reasoning by which the Huttonian theory was assailed by its enemies we may mention a circumstance which occurred in our person. Dr Richardson of Portrush who, we believe, had signalised himself by a violent attack upon the Huttonian theory came to Scotland on the subject of his fiorin grass. He was introduced to Sir James Hall, who requested Dr Hope and the writer of this note to meet him. It was arranged that the party should go to Salisbury Craggs to show the Doctor a junction of sandstone with trap[5] which was regarded as an instructive example of that class of facts. After reaching the spot, Sir James pointed out the great disturbance which had taken place at the junction and particularly called the attention of the Doctor to a piece of sandstone which had been whirled up during the convulsion and enclosed in the trap. When Sir James had finished his lecture, the Doctor did not attempt to explain the facts before him on any principles of his own; nor did he recur to the shallow evasion of regarding the enclosed sandstone as contemporaneous with the trap; but he burst out into the strongest expressions of contemptuous surprise that a theory of the earth should be founded on such trivial appearances! 'He had been accustomed,' he said, 'to look at nature in her grandest aspects, and to trace her hand in the gigantic cliffs of the Irish Coast; and he could not conceive how opinions thus formed could be

---

[5] An igneous rock.

shaken by such minute irregularities as those which had been shown him.'

The two Huttonian philosophers were confounded; and if we recollect rightly the weight of an acre of fiorin and the number of bullocks it would feed formed the remaining subjects of conversation.

But perhaps Richardson, the unsoundness of his geology notwithstanding, was wiser than Sir James and his companions reckoned. Those beetling cliffs and enormous stacks of the Antrim coast, with the waves of the North Atlantic crashing at their feet, are not entirely to be explained by the clear evidence of lava flows over vast geological periods running into millions of years. Sight of them has silenced more than one person into reflecting on their mystical significance, as the epiphany-like magnificence of the chasm beneath Pleskin moved Professor Pictet when he visited the Causeway with Richardson.

Mrs Sarah E. Tuite (1768–18?)

'The peeps', to use a phrase of Dr Richardson, we get in Pictet's *Journey* of Mrs Tuite, Richard Chenevix's sister, are appealing. There is first of all the undemonstrative meeting with her brother on his return to Sonna after a long absence. She and her husband, according to Pictet, radiate happiness yet they are living in a house whose owner, her husband's brother, is eccentric and unsociable. There is moreover the memory of the brutal murder in that house of her husband's half-brother (see the biographical note on Hugh Tuite).

In 1801 her four children had all been born. Her husband was fifty-four, she thirty-three. Married nine years, she had been twenty-four and he forty-five at the time of their marriage.

Her own family, Huguenot in origin, had suffered persecution under a Catholic monarch in France in her great grandmother's time, yet now she and her husband were giving asylum to a Catholic Priest, a refugee from the French Revolution. Not only do they give him asylum but they entrust their children's education to him whilst her governess corrects the faulty English grammar of his sermons to be delivered to good effect in the nearby Sonna 'chapel'.

What her feelings were towards the mutinous peasants who flocked to that place of worship we are not told, though the description of the still fortified windows through which the besieged family had in 1798, three years before, looked out at the Rebel camp on the hill indicates a continuing sense of unease. This is in keeping with an account written less than three weeks after Pictet's visit to Sonna by a returning absentee Wexford landlord, her own second cousin and friend, Melesina Chenevix–Trench:

August 11th, 1801

Arrived at Mr Alcock's, Wilton, near Enniscorthy, an uncle of mine by marriage, and a worthy, valuable man. I find the Rebellion is the prominent object in the minds of his family, as it is, more or less, to most who have passed through it. It is their principal epoch, and seems to have divided time into two grand divisions, unmarked by any lesser periods; before and after, the Rebellion. The first of these seems to resemble Paradise before the Fall. They had then good servants, fine flowers, fine fruit, fine horses, good beer, and plenty of barm – that indispensable requisite of rural economy. Since that period of perfect felicity, the servants have been unmanageable, the horses restive, the beer sour, the barm uncome-at-able, and all things scarce and dear. Great part of the evils complained of are undoubtedly felt; some are imaginary, and some arise from causes which are not so important or so pleasant to put forward as the word Rebellion.

Mrs Melesina Chenevix-Trench

Pictet is at his most pompous state of rectitude when he lectures Mrs Tuite on her manner of entertaining her guests. He did sugar the pill by saying how much he would have preferred to spend the evening in the engaging company of the family alone, but his two enthusiastic excursions within twenty four hours to Edgeworthstown might have caused Mrs Tuite to suspect the compliment. His criticism of the Irish landlords hiding themselves in wine, tea, coffee and over-eating in a starving country rings true in the light of the appraisal of them attributed to Grattan – 'fit only to carry claret to a chamber pot'. Most of the guests at Sonna the evening Pictet was there were no doubt poor company for a man who wanted to talk of science, of educational reforms and agriculture. But his hostess had invited them to honour the distinguished visiting scientist and among them was Edmund Malone, a man as eminent at least in literary circles as was Pictet in the scientific world. Then there was his hostess' brother, Richard Chenevix, his travelling companion, who has left behind him a name for being a pleasant, entertaining and witty member of any company at this stage of his life. Pictet's own behaviour must have been very off-putting, walking from one room of guests to the next and sizing them up as ready copy for *Bibliothèque britannique*. Moreover it was 1801; England and France were at war; Pictet was a French citizen and no émigré. There may well have been guests who would have been gayer in other company. In all, the criticism of the class was true and merited; but the choice of the occasion and of the person to whom it was delivered made it ungracious. But concern here is with Mrs Tuite: the rebuke did not make her forget her manners towards her guest, she returns no harsh word, but one suspects a white lie when she agrees with Pictet.

Mrs Tuite figures both in the letters of Melesina Chenevix–Trench and in those of Maria Edgeworth.

In the year 1790, as Miss Chenevix, she accompanies the inconsolable, widowed Mrs St George (as Melesina then was) on a recuperative trip to England. Later there are two letters from Melesina in December, 1816, thanking Sarah Elizabeth for condolence on the death of a daughter. Sarah Elizabeth had lost her own eldest son five years previously when he was seventeen. It is not difficult to guess at the tone of the letter by that of the reply:

Bursledon Lodge, 20 December, 1816

I thank you for the sympathy you express in my deep affliction, and am aware (for I am practised in sorrow), of the effects of time and religion. Truly does Wallenstein say, under deplorable calamity:

'I know I shall wear down this sorrow;
What sorrow does not man wear down?'

Mrs Melesina Chenevix-Trench

The writer of a letter to a friend reflects in it something of the writer and the friend:

London, February, 1818

We have taken a house in Gloucester Place. It has in my eyes but one fault, being too well furnished, filled too much with that knick-knackery I should banish were it mine, and dislike guarding for another. Then I unfortunately saw the lady who possesses it, or rather, is possessed by it; and she gave me so many directions about covering it, dusting some chairs under the covers, and scarcely sitting upon others, and watching over the extremities of unrobed ladies who hold the lights, and not suffering the housemaid to touch their projections, and not using leather to the gilding, nor aught save the breezes from the feather-brush, that I was really quite sick of internal decoration, which, like many other species of wealth, is often a plague to the possessor.

I saw your friend, Lady H. today. She is just going to bring her daughter into the world. This second birth is sometimes as painful as the first; and when circumstances are not favourable to the wishes of the mother, it is quite a protracted labour.

Mrs Melesina Chenevix–Trench

Sarah Elizabeth's own daughter, Penelope Melesina, was married two years later at the age of twenty-one; it is to be hoped that Mrs Tuite's second childbirth was not so protracted. At any rate, judged by the type of letter she obviously appreciated, she was no prude and had a sense of humour. Perhaps after all she was not too much hurt by Pictet's lecture.

She is revealed by Maria Edgeworth in a letter to Miss Ruxton, August 1st, 1802, as very close to her brother and as a warm hostess:

> Mr Chenevix and his sister, Mrs Tuite, and with them Mrs Jephson spent a day here [Edgeworthstown] last week: She is clever and agreeable.

It is to be noted Mrs Tuite visits with her brother, not her husband. Again to Miss Ruxton, December 1809:

> I have spent five delightful days at Sonna and Pakenham Hall. Mrs Tuite's kindness and Mr Chenevix's anecdotes, French and Spanish, delighted us at Sonna...

There is a rather singular remark in a letter from Maria Edgeworth to her stepmother dated 12th February, 1822, which whilst being a commentary on scientific rivalry also illustrates further the very close ties between Sarah Elizabeth and her brother. (In the biographical note on Chenevix the rivalry between Wollaston and Chenevix in their work on palladium has been noted.) Here Maria Edgeworth is anxious to protect a scientific secret on behalf of its author, the American, Perkins, who had just discovered a revolutionary fact about the compressibility of water by submerging a cylinder of water in the sea, a discovery which was to have profound effect on geological thinking:

> Wollaston... has verified and warrants the truth of these experiments. They have not yet been published and the author of course wishes to have the producing them to the public, therefore, my dear mother, you will not send them through Mrs Tuite to Mr Chenevix.

Mrs Tuite seems to have acted as a sort of librarian to an informal book club in Edgeworthstown: 'I believe I told you I found much instruction and interest in Paris [on a] Life of Sir H. Davy, I wish Mrs Tuite would bespeak for me for the Society the Octavo Edition.' (Letter from Maria to Honora Edgeworth, April, 1831).
Finally one more quotation from Maria Edgeworth:

Mrs Tuite is a very clever woman with a great deal of conversation, literary and anecdotal, but not philosophical or logical... Mrs Smithe I should prefer as a friend, Mrs Tuite as a companion – Mrs Smithe's manners are gentle, conciliating and such as to inspire affection and confidence, Mrs Tuite's more brilliant and captivating.

The Tuites of Sonna

The family was descended from the Norman, Sir Richard de Tuite, Knt., who accompanied the Earl of Pembroke (Strongbow) to Ireland in 1172. The seat was at Sonna in Co. Westmeath and about seven miles west of Mullingar. Concern here is with those members of the family who were at Sonna and with two of their forbears whose lives had influenced the circumstances Pictet found when he called on 19th July, 1801.

Hugh Tuite (1747–1843), the brother-in-law of Richard Chenevix, was the younger son by the second marriage of Sir Henry Tuite. Hugh's full brother, Sir Henry, the misanthropic recluse and ex-navy man mentioned by Pictet, had inherited the title on the death of a half-brother, Sir George, by whose will, again, Hugh was to inherit Sonna on his brother Sir Henry's death in 1805.

According to John Charles Lyons, writing in 1855, tragedy had accompanied both the birth and the death of Sir George. On her way to Dublin for her confinement and while the horses were being changed at Kinnegad, Lady Tuite, the mother-to-be of the future Sir George, had been very upset at the sight of a beggar with two thumbs on one hand. She became obsessed with the idea that her death was near; she felt that she would die at midnight when the child had been delivered. The Dean of St Patrick's, Jonathan Swift, visited her to reassure her and used all the persuasion, of which he was the undoubted master, to rid Lady Tuite of her morbid fancy. The child safely delivered the mother asked to see it. There was no concealing from her searching eye that a second thumb had been surgically removed from one hand but the Dean drew her attention to the hour, the clock had just struck one, the fatal hour of midnight was already well behind. She smiled gratefully at the knowledge of a pious deception – and died. The clock had been put forward one hour. That was in the month of September, 1728.

In the month of February, 1783, as recounted by Dr Horgan, Sir George and his favourite spaniel were found cruelly beaten to death in the study. The murderer was never discovered but the motive was centred in 'domestic treason'. At the time of the murder of Sir George, Hugh must have been at Gibraltar. Was the subsequent strangeness of the heir to the title, Sir Henry, in any way connected with it?

Pictet says nothing of the physique of Hugh but he was a tall and powerful man. According to Edmund F. Dease he founded the Sonna Harriers in 1802. He was 'a sportsman of the true old type. Pea-green coat, with black collar, buff facings and vest, was the hunt uniform, and the hunt button was only presented to a select band of followers'.

An anecdote by Lyons is of interest both in relation to the character of Captain Tuite and the other character – a very historical one – involved. Lyons was a son-in-law of Captain Tuite. Obviously the family took what to many today will appear as childish pride in things military, illustrating the tyranny over human minds in the vanity of matters they were expected to regard as important. The anecdote refers to Dublin society in the 1790s. After the Siege of Gibraltar, Captain Tuite retired from the army but continued to wear the queue as a military symbol. He spent his winters in Dublin, often frequenting the 'salons' of the Countess of Ormonde – and you had to be somebody to get an invitation there – where on an occasion he was engaged in a game of cards. Captain Wellesley, the future Duke of Wellington, was a guest. He was an aide-de-camp to the Lord Lieutenant, Lord Westmoreland. Captain Tuite seated at his cards became conscious of some mischief going on behind his back. He turned sharply to surprise the future Duke playing with his queue to the amusement of the other young officers present. He stood up in his towering height. He lifted the luckless aide-de-camp off the floor by the neck, shook him and dropped him. He resumed his game expecting at its end to receive an invitation to the notorious Fifteen Acres, the duelling site in the Phoenix Park. Instead, up came a very agitated Captain Wellesley accompanied by another aide-de-camp to apologise for the unwarrantable liberty he had taken with the queue. The offended Captain, drawing himself up to his full height replied, "As the apology is as public as the offence I forget it, Sir," and he bowed.

Judged by Lyons' account of the incident Captain Tuite gloried in having participated in the Siege of Gibraltar: any doubt on this point will disappear when we find Professor Pictet being told of it when he calls at Sonna in July, 1801 which leads to another reflection. Perhaps the criticism made elsewhere in the biographical notes in this book of the Professor's censorious remarks of his hosts at Sonna was not entirely unmerited.

Captain Tuite lived an exceptionally long life and his neighbour Maria Edgeworth, in a letter to Miss Ruxton in March, 1843, records his death:

'Mr Tuite, that dear good old gentleman, died a few days ago at Sonna in his ninety-seventh year; his good son, in his note to my mother, announcing the event says, "It is a comfort to think that to the very last he had all the comfort, spiritual and earthly, that he could need or desire".'

The Tuite Children

Pictet in his letter describing the arrival of himself and Chenevix at the great house of Sonna with its serpentine drives, tree-dotted lawns and ornamental pond tells of how the children of the house ran out to fling themselves on their Uncle Chenevix's neck on that sun-drenched Sunday afternoon of 19th July, 1801. Hugh and Sarah Elizabeth Tuite's family consisted of four children.

Henry, the eldest was born in 1794 and died in 1811.

Hugh Morgan, (1795–1868), after his father became the owner of Sonna. His picture, given in the *Complete History of the Westmeath Hunt* (Dease) contrasts with that of his father, also given, the son having more introspective appearance than the father. The father founds the Sonna hounds: the son keeps them going efficiently and well but, one suspects, out of a sense of tradition and duty as well as from a desire to keep up an employment-providing establishment. It would be unlikely that he would not have read his Uncle Chenevix's posthumous *Essay on National Character* which developed in its own special way (*inter alia*) Mandeville's thesis that the spending of the wealthy on luxuries provided employment for the poor. According to Dr Horgan:

The late owner of the property, H.M. Tuite, was a good landlord, and did all in his power to promote the prosperity of his tenants. He was no absentee, and it was a favourite saying in the locality 'always at home like Tuite of Sonna'. He was the first candidate in Westmeath to contest the County on liberal principles, which he did in 1829. He was a good employer and benevolent to his labourers, and the break up of the establishment was a great loss to the poor of the vicinity.

He was twice MP for Westmeath for a total of nine years. His neighbour Maria Edgeworth, who herself did so much to aid distress during the famine of 1847 tells, in a letter dated 8th May, 1847, to Lady Beaufort of his concern:

I cannot answer your Admiral's question as to the number of deaths caused by the famine. I believe that no one can form a just estimate. In different districts the estimate and assertions are widely different, and the priests keep no registry. Mr Tuite, who was here yesterday, told us that in the House of Commons the contradictory statements of the Irish members astonished and grieved him, as he knew the bad effect it would have in diminishing their credit with the English. Two hundred and fifty thousand is the report of the Police up to April. Mr Tuite thought a third more deaths than usual had been in his neighbourhood.

George Gustavus (1796–1849) served in the navy and army ending up a Lieutenant Colonel.

Penelope Melesina (1799–?) called, no doubt, after her mother's friend, the diarist, Melesina Chenevix-Trench, married in 1820 John Charles Lyons of Ledestown who later compiled biographical material on his wife's family.

Sonna House

The word Sonna is the Gaelic ('*sonnach*') for a palisade. In all likelihood there was a prehistoric garrison on the site long before the Norman Tuites arrived there. By Pictet's account of the siege in 1798 the house really earned its name anew. Later it was to be less impregnable. Today little remains of Sonna House itself – a casualty of the troubled twenties in Ireland. It appears to have been badly damaged, late in the last century or early in this, by a fire started through negligence, but then restored... Of the extensive outhouses an enclosing wall of red brick, ivy-coloured in places and generally in ruins, is all that remains. Westmeath bullocks graze on what were the vast tree-covered lawns of 1801 as noted by Pictet. The ornamental pond, long since silted in, has left behind a trace like that of a river which has shifted its course.

A pleasant old-fashioned chapel which in the summer of 1975 had still eluded the modernisers has, according to the parish priest, Rev. Michael Kilmartin, replaced the one in which the refugee French priest, the Abbé Nicolas Cabley, ministered in 1801. The Abbé's name was discovered in a curious manner by Rev. Michael Smith,[1] Bishop's House, Mullingar in a privately published work in (1942) by Rev. John Brady entitled *A History of the Parishes of the Diocese of Meath*. In this work is a list of chalices belonging to the parish of Ballynacargy of which Sonna is now a part and on one in silver is the inscription '*Ex dono admodum Honorabilis Henrici Tuite, Baron, Reverendo Nicolao Cabley Sacerdoti Gallia exultanti 1802.*'

This strange gift of the ex-navy man and traveller turned recluse can only add to his mystery.[2]

---

[1] Now Bishop Smith.
[2] Though it is just possible that the gift was made by Captain Hugh Tuite, and his wife Sarah, in the name of the head of the house, Sir Henry.

The Edgeworths

Richard Lovell Edgeworth (1744-1817)

It would be unfair to him simply to identify Richard Lovell Edgeworth as the father of Maria Edgeworth, the writer, which he was, but this would be to say that his place in the scheme of things was to have sired a novelist. To have been the father of Maria Edgeworth was no mean achievement: indeed Richard Lovell can be given the credit for setting his daughter on her way as a writer by his encouragement; but in his own right he was, by almost any standards, a very remarkable man.

His ebullient personality bursts out from Professor Pictet's account of his two visits to the family on the Monday and Tuesday 20th and 21st July, 1801, (LETTER VII). Early in life he developed a delight in science and Pictet recorded that all his family had come to share in that delight, more or less.

In life Richard Lovell Edgeworth overshadowed his children, even Maria. Mrs Colvin quoting Isaac D'Israeli tells how Maria 'in her father's lifetime when she came up to London... was like a sealed fountain, but now... she pours down like the Falls of Niagara'. This statement gives a clue which a perusal of Pictet's account of Richard Lovell would conceal, perhaps; he was not a popular man. According to Mrs Colvin,[1]

> ...he was not a popular man either in Ireland or in London society; in Ireland he was too educated and too unconvivial for his neighbours and, while participating in local and national politics rejected their notorious

---

[1] Mrs Colvin, *née* Butler, a descendent through Harriet, Edgeworth's daughter by his fourth wife, Frances, *née* Beaufort, Harriet having married an Irish antiquary, Rev. Richard Butler, Rector of Trim.

venality; he was looked on as crazed in the County of Longford: in London he was thought by many to be an egotistical bore.

Mrs Colvin goes on to say that his offence in London seemed to have consisted in talking down self-opinionated wits. Be this as it may, it is of interest to learn that he shared Pictet's strictures on the social habits of the local ascendancy or was he in reality Pictet's monitor, the latter on his return to Sonna merely echoing what he knew to be the thinking of Richard Lovell and Maria?

The fact that Professor Pictet and Richard Lovell Edgeworth were men of science did give them a feeling of affinity and, bore or no bore, Richard Lovell Edgeworth was a warm-hearted and intellectually vivacious man. He had a dynamic compelling capacity for friendship, a perfect illustration of which was his need to accompany Pictet part of the way back to Sonna, but then this 'going a piece of the way' with a visitor was a characteristic of past generations. The story is told of two old friends from Ballynakelly in County Tyrone. One was visiting the other. It came time for the visitor to leave for home. "Wait, I'll leave you a piece of the way," said his friend. He did – right to the other's door.

"Look, you've come the whole way, I'll leave you back a piece." It is not recorded how the vicious (if such a word can be applied to such sociality) circle was broken that night. But it all happened a century ago before television robbed visitors of the attention of their hosts.

There are several threads connecting people mentioned in different places in Pictet's *Journey*: to mention only one, Dr Beddoes (LETTER II) was a son-in-law of Richard Lovell Edgeworth, having married in 1794 Anna Edgeworth, Richard's daughter, whom he met when the Edgeworth's were staying at Clifton.

Though very likely not on visiting terms with his neighbours at Sonna (he was not of one of the party Mrs Tuite entertained on the occasion of Pictet's visit) Richard Lovell had a common ancestry with the Tuites, a Francis Edgeworth having married a noted beauty Lady Jane Tuite of Sonna who on her husband's refusal to seek satisfaction for a trifling or imagined slight shown her by a neighbour left him to live in France. Later she returned to Ireland and founded an abbey in Dublin.

Edgeworth was an inventor. In 1768 he obtained a silver medal from the Society of Arts for a land-measuring device known as a 'perambulator'. He also invented a turnip cutter and a one-wheeled chaise. He was one of the earliest to experiment with the telegraph and was interesting the Government in a scheme to link Dublin with Galway at the time of the 1798 Rebellion, but the collapse of the rebels brought the proposed scheme to a close.[2] He may well have been the first person to fashion a pre-fabricated structure, an iron spire placed on the existing spire of the parish church in Edgeworthstown. This 'spire' had to be removed a few years ago as it had become unsafe.

Professor Pictet lists some of his inventions to be found in the house at Edgeworthstown: a device which wound up a clock each time a door was opened; a double door which ensured an absence of draughts; sashes fitting wedge-wise into the lower part of the window frame and which, incidentally, can still be seen in the surviving original part of the building (now a nursing home having been rescued some years ago from near ruin). The renovations needed to rescue the structure and fit it for its present purpose revealed in the process something of the restless mind of its one-time owner Richard Lovell Edgeworth; in an unexpected cavity there was discovered a chimney and chimney piece complete. The eastern facade of the house, as it was when Pictet visited it, can still be recognised from early pictures but the main entrance from the peristyle where the Professor first saw his host has been built up. The chapel in the nursing-home is most likely the living room where Maria wrote undisturbed by the lively activities of the large family of brothers, sisters, half-brothers and half-sisters from the four unions of her ebullient father, a family full of life and harmonious companionship. In the hall were paintings of the three deceased wives and the fourth who was to survive her husband.

Always interested in education, as witness his collaboration with his daughter, Maria in *Practical Education*, and his own publications, *Poetry Explained for Young People*, 1802; *Professional Education*, 1808; *Readings in Poetry*, 1816; he was a disciple of Rousseau. While

---

[2] A Frenchman, Claude Chappé, had in 1792 been the first person to use a mechanical semaphore in signalling and also to use the word telegraph for the transmission of messages by signalling. Chappé installed twenty-two semaphore stations between Lille and Paris.

in Paris in 1771 he proudly showed one of his boys to Rousseau explaining that the boy had been schooled on the philosopher's principles. Education began in the home. Domestic animals at a house will give a clue to their treatment by members of the household; an easily frightened, fearful cat betrays rough treatment by someone about that house. At least Pictet is right in general on this matter but one suspects that his enthusiasm for the Edgeworths carries him a little bit too far when he claims that even the birds in Richard Lovell's garden showed unusual lack of concern on the approach of himself and the others strolling through the garden. Both the Edgeworths, father and daughter, had by the beginning of the nineteenth century an international reputation as educationalists and when a board inquiring into Irish education was established in 1806 Edgeworth was one of the members and remained so until 1811.

He was an enterprising landlord. He also tried out schemes for the reclamation of bogs and for the improvements of roads but in all his schemes for improvement, and this applied to his many alterations to his house, he always worked within his means. He employed no middlemen (often the curse of Irish landlordism) and he always allowed the rent of one year to lie. But he did not encourage idleness.

He was just, so that there was an oft-quoted statement in the district, 'Go before Mr Edgeworth and you will get justice'.

A member of the last Irish Parliament he voted against the Union though he felt it would be good for Ireland: he was disgusted with the means to achieve it. He spurned offers of personal reward from his public life.

Maria Edgeworth (1767–1849)

It is a further example of the coincidences and interconnections in which Professor Pictet's account of his journey abounds that his travelling companion, Richard Chenevix, should be on his way to visit his sister, at Sonna, the home of the Tuites, only a two-hour drive from Edgeworthstown House where Maria lived with her father, his fourth wife and her numerous step-brothers and sisters. The opportunity of visiting the writer and her father was one of the strongest inducements for Pictet to extend his journey to Ireland: he was already one of the most ardent admirers of Maria and her father. He had published in the *Bibliothèque britannique* two of the stories from Maria's *Parent's Assistant* as well as parts of the joint work of her and her father – *Practical Education*. He had also published two extracts from *Belinda* and was unsparing in his praise. 'We must welcome this agreeable and moral work and hope that she will continue to employ her great talents for the instruction and amusement of her readers.' His excitement on his approach to Edgeworthstown House is evident, in his recorded account of it (LETTER VII). She was absent when he called the first time and had to content himself with her father's company, return to Sonna for the night and come back to Edgeworthstown the next day. Then after all the excitement of waiting to see her she turned out to be not quite what he expected:

> I had persuaded myself that the author of the work on education and of many other useful and readable works must surely be singled out by some very distinguishing outward feature; but I was wrong. Of small stature with eyes nearly always down-cast, of profoundly modest and reserved appearance; little expression in the features when she is not speaking; this was the sum of my first observation. But when she spoke, something which for my liking happened too seldom – nothing more thoughtful, and well-said though always timidly expressed, than that which fell from her lips.

Maria was usually silent when she and her father were in company together but on this occasion though Professor Pictet did not know it – and it might have spoiled the effect he wished to create in his description of her had he known it – there was a very feminine reason why Maria spoke so little. She had been enjoying herself at Castle Sanderson thirty miles away and obedient as she was to her father's every wish she had dutifully returned, with the messenger her father sent to fetch her, to meet Pictet. Thirty miles were thirty miles in the year 1801 and it was asking something to fly from pleasant company to meet someone who had just dropped in, even if that someone was a scientist of international standing and who had been publishing her works in Geneva. Later she was to find that she owed more to Pictet than she realised as she discovered when she visited the Continent two years later:

234

'Since we came to France we have found M. Pictet's account[3] very useful, for at every public library, and in every *Ecole centrale*, the *Journal* [sic] *britannique* is taken, and we have consequently received many civilities', she was to write from France. Though when she was to meet him in Paris for the first time since his Edgeworthstown visit she still bore a grudge for the 'down-cast eyes' description. 'Tell my Aunt Mary that I am grown as fond of her favourite as her heart could wish and have forgiven him for *les yeux baissés* and for bringing me home from Castle Sanderson.'

Maria Edgeworth began her career as a writer by composing stories for her young brothers and sisters. Later she was encouraged by her father to translate Madame de Genlis'[4] *Adele et Théodore*. Her apprenticeship in education was served by teaching her little brother Henry. In 1795 came her defence of female education, *Letters to Literary Ladies*. By the time Professor Pictet visited this shy, diminutive lady so much overshadowed in company by her flamboyant but generous father, she had to her credit in addition to the works mentioned – *Patronage*, *Parent's Assistant*, *Practical Education* (jointly with her father), *Castle Rack Rent*, *Belinda* and several children's stories with a practical educational purpose.

She had from her father an interest in science. Under his influence she also became a competent bookkeeper and estate manager. Her competence as an estate manager was put to good account for half a century, pulling the estate on at least one occasion out of the mess her brother, Lovell, was to get it into after he inherited it. Her contact with the people of the countryside gave her the knowledge of their speech and habits which she portrayed in her novels.

'I could not but be charmed with him, because I saw that he thoroughly appreciated my father,' Maria was able to say this of the Protestant Archbishop of Armagh, William Stuart, fifth son of the 3rd Earl of Bute. There must have been many occasions when she was very unhappy on her father's account because of his unpopularity: the statement is a measure of her reverence for him. His influence on her was enormous. Timorous about riding she yet rode long distances with him over the estate and elsewhere just to be in his company, and her

---

[3]   i.e. of his visit to Edgeworthstown published in *Bibliothèque britannique*.
[4]   Genlis (Stéphanie Félicité de Crest de Saint-Aubin, comtesse de) (1746–1830). Governess of the children of Philippe Egalite, Duke of Orleans, authoress of educational works, mother of Pamela, wife of Lord Edward FitzGerald.

reserve when they were in company together lasted as long as he lived. His death in 1817 emancipated her from her reserve. Up until then Maria Edgeworth in company – and that was almost invariably with her father – whether in Ireland, in English drawing rooms or in Parisian salons, remained substantially the person described by Pictet in 1801; notwithstanding that by 1801 she had already established herself as a writer of international standing. In a letter to James Ballantyne, Scott said of her, 'if I could but hit Miss Edgeworth's wonderful power of vivifying all her persons, and making them live as beings in your mind I should not be afraid'. It was *Castle Rack Rent* which induced him to attempt depicting Scottish national character.

It would be many years yet – not until 1823 – before she was to visit Scott at Edinburgh and in Abbotsfield where he received her with a hospitality that did nothing to belie that which Pictet and Chenevix had at the hand of the Scots they met in 1801. Later Scott went to visit Maria at Edgeworthstown and they visited Killarney together.

In fact, Maria Edgeworth met most of the literary and scientific people of her time – Byron, Macaulay, Sydney Smith, Davy, Wollaston, Chenevix, Mme de Genlis, Herschel (Jnr), Moore, to mention some. Though she never met Jane Austen, the author of *Emma* sent her a copy on the first appearance of that book.

She delighted in Sydney Smith but did not share his opinion of Macaulay.

> We had a very pleasant evening, I need hardly say [at Dr Holland's, Sydney's son-in-law] but to Boswell Sydney Smith would out–Boswell Boswell and is past my powers. Sydney had not his merry andrew jacket on,... over his canonicals tho' now and then it peeped from underneath unbecomingly... Sydney to my astonishment declares he acquits Macaulay of all vanity. Thinks he only pours out talk and listens to no other mortal man or woman only because he cannot help pouring out. Did you ever see a beer barrel burst Miss E...? Well Macaulay bursts like a beer barrel and it comes all over you and he can't help it. He really has no wish to show off. I had a great mind to ask whether he ever bursts in private – in his own room alone. Why burst always in public?... Sydney was

exceedingly good-natured and absolutely kind to me.
[3rd December, 1843]

But though she was much travelled and saw much of people in the
'great world' it was at home at Edgeworthstown that she spent most of
her long and mostly happy life cherishing her many brothers and
sisters, managing the estate and writing long letters which tell so much
of her times and her wide circles. Her long unbroken friendship with
her father's fourth wife, Mrs Frances Anne Edgeworth (née Beaufort),
two years her junior, filled both their lives with happiness. Happy
though she was she lived through two of the most terrible events in the
history of the country she made her own: the Rebellion of 1798,
traumatic for her class, and the famine of 1846/47, harrowing for all
who were alive in the country then. In the former event she had to flee
from home with her family for fear of the rebels only to find her
father suspected of being in league with them. As it was, it was the
kindness shown at an earlier date by the Edgeworth's housekeeper,
Mrs Billamore, to the wife of one of the insurgents which possibly
saved the house from occupation and perhaps destruction.

During the famine it was at the request of Mr Powell, the local
vicar, that she began begging for the poor around her, her begging
being all the more meritorious because she found it distasteful.

> Mr Powell instigated me to beg some relief for the
> poor from the Quaker Association in Dublin – so,
> much against the grain, I penned a letter to
> Mr Harvey, the only person whose name I know on the
> committee, and prayed some assistance for Mr Powell,
> our vicar, to get us over the next two months...

Eighty years old as she was she began relying on her own efforts to
earn money by writing *Orlandino*. She preferred to see the poor
working and she welcomed the cheque she received for *Orlandino* in
these words... 'and so are numbers working and eating; for
Mrs Edgeworth's principle is to excite the people to work for good
wages, and not, by gratis feeding, to make beggars of them and
ungrateful beggars as the case might be.'

But even good rules and principles can be carried too far,
'Mr Hinds (presumably her land steward) has laid down a good rule

not to give seed to any tenants but those who can produce the receipt for the last half-year's rent.' (February, 1847).

It may be that this refusal was based on the conviction that the man who had paid his rent would make the best use of the seed for the general welfare but the blight that spread through the land was not the making of the man who had not paid his rent and if the refusal were not a system of rationing seed to the best possible use it was harsh. In this and in other references to her tenants Maria Edgeworth leaves little doubt of her ascendancy, though benevolent ascendancy, attitude to them, which is not to gainsay the great efforts made at the age of eighty for a starving people.

She, like her father, would have had her tenants prosperous and contented so that the order of things that she considered correct would continue with her and her class in their rightful place. She might delight her readers with the speech of a Thady but it was the speech of an inferior people,

> ...saw abundance of comedy. There were three Miss
> ...s, from the County of Tipperary, three degrees of
> comparison – the positive, the comparative, and the
> superlative; excellent figures with white feathers as
> long as my two arms joined together, stuck in the front
> of what were meant for Spanish hats. How they
> towered above their sex, divinely vulgar, with brogues
> of true Milesian race. [Description of a ball in Castle
> Pollard, January, 1809].

In a well-run landlord system she saw the prosperity of landlord and tenant but she had no doubt as to where power should lie and who should govern, and the importance of the Union.

In some respects she was the precursor of another member of the landlord class and a Unionist too, a man who began his life some seven years after she had ended hers, Horace Plunkett. Like Maria he felt that the good of Ireland lay in maintaining the Union but he looked back on landlordism, as it came to an end, with pain at the thought of the injuries the system had inflicted on the tenants and, not least, on the effect it had had on the landlords themselves and he set about with the help of some of his fellow landlords through the Co-operative Movement to make up for the centuries of neglect by their predecessors. One of his colleagues in the movement, Lord Monteagle, publicly declared that the ending of landlordism was for him emancipation.

In some respects Maria Edgeworth's relations with Ireland were like those she had with her father. Only too conscious of the fact that her father was not popular and regarded as eccentric she was ever concerned for his popularity as revealed in her remark already quoted about Archbishop Stuart: she could have said of him something like what she wrote of Ireland in 1849:

> Ireland, with all thy faults, thy follies too,
> I love thee still: still with a candid eye must view
> Thy wit, too quick, still blundering into sense
> Thy reckless humour: sad improvidence.
> And even what sober judges follies call,
> I, looking at the Heart, forget them all.

She had her own share of paradox, small in stature she was big in reputation. She was so small indeed that she tried stretching herself literally by the neck when she was a young girl, thereby nearly doing herself permanent damage. (Her lack of inches did not prevent her from getting an offer of marriage. It happened in Paris in 1803. The suitor was a Swede called Edelcrantz. She turned him down; but remembered him all her life.) It is noted elsewhere how her father's company subdued her in public. Nowhere is this better shown than in the contrast between her published works and her private letters. In the former she is constrained by his classical regard for style: in the latter she is herself. Her novels, largely neglected, are unlikely to be much read: her letters living, vivacious, racy, perspicacious things full of the spontaneity which creates its own style in which the dash is of more importance that the stop deserve to be read and most likely will be.

How full of perspicacity, how communicative of a battle of wits is surely revealed in the letter to Harriet Butler, 3rd December, 1843, telling of her difference with Sydney Smith on Macaulay:

> Sydney Smith has a very high opinion of his talents and
> of his style of writing essays and reviews – but no
> converser no no. 'Flashes of silence agreeable' you

recollect Harriet and so did I and low down said and
Sydney heard and smiled – Asked if I had ever seen or
heard. Yes once and but once when first he came out...

She is more likely to live by her letters than by her other works and
she would have been upset to think that the letters would ever be
published. These letters are of immeasurable value as a chronicle of
the times in which she lived, not least owing to the width of the scene
depicted in them and of the great number of public figures their writer
knew and met, from the workers on her estate to the scientists, writers
and public figures of London and Paris. They certainly give added
dimension to Pictet's description of the world he visited in England,
Scotland and Ireland in 1801. They depict real, living people. On the
other hand, Scott's admiration for her ability to portray local character
in her novels and Pictet's verification of the authenticity of Thady
notwithstanding, the characters in her novels suffer from the same
defect as Shakespeare's Captain MacMorris in Henry V; they are
stage Irish and are not convincing which is the inevitable consequence
of viewing character from a position of superiority.

Her publications amount to about thirty-five.

Other Members of the Edgeworth Family

Without taking into account aunts or in-laws the other members of the
family present when Pictet called in 1801 most likely were – the
fourth Mrs Edgeworth, Frances Anne (*née* Beaufort), children (like
Maria) of the first marriage (with Anna Maria Elers) Emmeline and
Anna Maria; offspring of the second marriage (with Honora Sneyd)
Lovell; children of the third marriage (with Elizabeth Sneyd)
Charlotte, Henry, Charles Sneyd, Honora, William; and of the fourth
marriage – Francis Maria and Sophia, with Harriet in the offing about
to be born. Children to be born in future years were Lucy Jane,
Francis Beaufort, and Michael Pakenham. Two children of the first
marriage, one of the second and four of the fourth were already dead.
In all there were twenty children, forty-eight years separating the first
birth (1764) from the last (1812). The last member of the family to die
was Lucy Jane, in 1897. In every year between 1764 and 1897, a
period of one hundred and thirty-three years, there was at least one
offspring of Richard Lovell Edgeworth alive.

Mrs Frances Anne Edgeworth, (1769–1865) was a daughter of the Rev. D.A. Beaufort who, as Pictet records, was responsible for the then most up-to-date map of Ireland. Pictet also correctly records that she was a lady with her own share of talent. Before her marriage she had provided illustrations for *The Parent's Assistant*, one of Maria's works and after her marriage she learned mechanical drawing to be of assistance to Richard Lovell. Her letters reveal an intelligent mind, a keen observer, a great deal of common sense and a sense of irony and humour. She certainly took the inhaling of oxide gas less seriously than Marc-Auguste Pictet:

> A young man, a Mr Davy at Dr Beddoes, who has applied himself much to chemistry, has made some discoveries of importance, and enthusiastically expects wonders will be performed by the use of certain gases, which inebriate in the most delightful manner, having the oblivious effects of Lethe, and at the same time giving the rapturous sensations of the Nectar of the Gods. Pleasure even to madness is the consequence of this draught. But faith, great faith, is I believe necessary to produce any effect upon the drinkers and I have seen some of the adventurous philosophers who sought in vain for satisfaction in the bag of Gaseous Oxide, and found nothing but a sick stomach and giddy head.
>
> Letter to Mrs Ruxton, 26th May, 1799

The friendship between her and Maria stretching well over half a century was of rare quality; it would possibly be no exaggeration to refer to it as one of the great friendships of history.

Emmeline Edgeworth (1770–1847). She married a Dr King of Swiss origin who was an assistant to Dr Beddoes. Her father referred to her as 'an agreeable animal'. But she was not stupid.

Anna Maria Edgeworth (1773–1824). She married Dr Beddoes by whom she had four children, one of them the future poet Thomas Lovell Beddoes. Flighty by nature she all the same had considerable charm as revealed by her letters.

Lovell Edgeworth (1775–1842), was the eldest surviving son in 1801 but it would appear that Pictet was wrong in saying that he had been to Edinburgh for it was his half-brother, Henry, who had been there. Perhaps Lovell was not at home when Pictet called so that Henry was the eldest son present. Lovell started an interdenominational school at Edgeworthstown following the family interest in education and revealed himself to be a very talented teacher. However, war as it had done to many a man before and since wrecked his life. From 1803 to 1814 he was interned in France and as a result became a drunkard. He eventually succeeded to the family estate but proved himself incapable and having the drunkard's deceit, he was a great worry to the family. Maria had to take over the running of the estate and to settle debts, the true state of which he kept concealing.

Charlotte Edgeworth (1783–1807). She was eighteen in 1801 not sixteen as stated by Pictet; but in all else said about her he was correct: she was the family beauty. He described her 'lovely, fresh as a rose whose eyes beaming with intelligence show that without desiring to put in a word of her own in the conversation she does not lose any of that which circulates around her and she knows how to listen, a quality rare enough in the young'.

Henry Edgeworth (1782–1813). Educated at Edinburgh University, he became a doctor. He died in 1813 at the age of thirty-one after a long illness which seems to have affected his mind.

Charles Sneyd Edgeworth (1786–1864). Educated at Trinity College, Dublin, he became a lawyer and married Henricia Broadhurst. Husband and wife were valetudinarian. After his father's death he ceased the practice of the law. He wrote a biography of the Abbé Edgeworth.

Honora Edgeworth (1791–1858). She married, in 1838, Francis Beaufort, later Sir Francis (1774–1857). Retiring, she lacked the Edgeworth liveliness but she was very reliable and was the 'ear' of the family for confidences. She helped Maria with her children's' books of the 1820s, copying, editing and correcting.

William Edgeworth (1794–1829). This was the little boy his father said had a head on his shoulders, the one who correctly drew the demarcating line on the seat of the stool missing a leg. His father was a true prophet. He was very intelligent. He became a rail and road engineer. One of his achievements was the scenic road from Killarney to Glengariff. But he was lethargic.

Frances Maria Edgeworth (1799-1839). Maria's favourite, Fanny, married in 1829 a Lestock Peach Wilson. She had the family interest in politics and science but her health was poor.

Henrietta Edgeworth (1801-1889). Harriet to her family, is included in these short biographical notes of the family who were alive in July, 1801, for though she had not yet appeared on the scene she was expected in a matter of months as Pictet noted. Lively, vigorous and impetuous, Scott described her as 'Kind-natured, clever Harriet'. She married the Rev. Richard Butler, Vicar of Trim in 1826. Butler was an Irish antiquary. It was from this marriage that the editor of Maria Edgeworth *Letters from England*, Mrs Christina Colvin (*née* Butler) is descended.

Rev. Dr Daniel Augustus Beaufort (1739-1821). Father of Frances Anne, fourth wife of Richard Lovell Edgeworth was the son of a Calvinist minister who had taken Anglican orders. The family had left France in the seventeenth century and after a series of peregrinations had come to Ireland. Daniel Auguste, popularly known as DAB from his initials, was born in London and educated in Dublin, graduating BA in 1759 and LLD (HonC) in 1789. He was Rector of Navan 1765-1818, and Vicar of Collon, County Louth, 1789-1821.

His nickname seemed to have been specially minted for him – small, enthusiastic, energetic he had many interests but did not concentrate on any one of them long enough to become the master he had it in his capacity to become. He had insatiable curiosity: he could not pass a site where building was going on without finding out all about it, its design, progress and merit. He was for ever calling at farms to see what work was in progress and especially to discover if there were any new machinery or new methods.

He was at once a clergyman, a cartographer, an architect, a traveller and a diarist though it is unfortunate for possible comment on Pictet that his diary is blank for the period end of 1798 till the end of 1801.

His great work is referred to by Pictet, his six inch to the mile map *Ireland, Civil and Ecclesiastical, accompanied by a Memorial Map of Ireland, illustrating the Topography of that Kingdom and containing a short Account of its present State, civil and ecclesiastical with a complete Index to the map*. It came out in 1792 having cost its author £1,000. It was a complete success; 2,000 copies were sold in eighteen months.

He was responsible for the church in Collon, County Louth, which he conceived as a reproduction of Kings College Chapel, Cambridge. The building of the church made severe inroads on his own purse which was always in a state which might have worried a less resilient character than DAB. The story is possibly apocryphal but in keeping with the man. It is said that during the building of the church at Collon DAB asked the joiner working there to go into the pulpit and say a few words so that DAB from the back of the building could assess the acoustics. When 'preacher' and 'congregation' had taken their places the 'sermon' came out loud and clear: "When are you going to pay me?"

The name Beaufort lives on in the Beaufort Scale, that scale with graduations from 0 to 17 for denoting wind strengths (a wind of force 12 being one that 'no canvas could withstand') devised by Rear Admiral Sir Francis Beaufort (1774–1857), a son of the Rev. Dr Daniel Augustus Beaufort, and who married Richard Lovell's daughter by his third marriage, Honora Edgeworth.

Sir John Sebright

Sebright, Sir John Saunders, (1767–1846) was the 7th baronet of Besford, Worcestershire, and Beechwood, Hertfordshire. He was a politician and agriculturalist. Forty-one when Pictet stopped with him (LETTER XII), in 1801 he had been married for eight years to the former Miss Harriet Crofts, an heiress from Norfolk. She died in 1826 leaving him with seven daughters and a son. None of the children who with their mother, Lady Sebright, formed the family circle which charmed Marc-Auguste Pictet could have been more than seven years old in August, 1801.

In 1801 Sir John was elected to parliament for Hertfordshire. As an MP he strongly advocated economy in administration and reform of the gaming and usury laws. Very anti-monopolist he was also opposed to unnecessary offices. He disliked indirect taxation. He was against allotments any larger than kitchen gardens – but willing to see larger ones tried out. A supporter of Reform he seconded Lord John Russell's first Reform Bill, 1st March, 1831. In December 1832 he headed the poll for Hertfordshire for the first Reformed Parliament but he retired at its close.

His keen interest in agriculture is very apparent from Pictet's account of his discussions with him and it is also evident that he was very knowledgeable in its art and practice. He had the eighteenth century love of the wager to support his opinion on a particular matter. But over and above this Sir John was very fond of his own opinions.

The picture which emerges from Pictet's account is one of a forceful, life-enjoying squire, enthusiastic about his estate and the advancement of agriculture and traditional sports, living in a lovely home in something like domestic bliss blest with a happy domesticated wife and no less happy children. About the beauty of the home there would appear to be no doubt but one lady, Maria Edgeworth, who knew Sebright over a longer period than Marc-Auguste Pictet, shows him in a more complete light:

Beechwood Park, Wednesday 16th January, 1822

...After a pleasant drive on a sun shining day arrived here yesterday just in good time for dressing for dinner. Sir John Sebright who had galloped past us as we left St Albans and who had taken a good stare into the carriage, met us with the most gracious countenance that his eyebrows would permit. A very fine park it is with magnificently large beech trees which well deserve to give their names to the place. The house is a fine looking house – was a convent in the days of Edward VI – part of the building of that time is still in being but all so modernised that this is only to say. The library, with books on all sides on open shelves, is very comfortable – 40 feet long opening from a carpeted hall and seeing into a little snuggery at the farthest end in which there was a blazing fire formed a goodly view on a cold day to travellers on their first entrance.

Letter from Maria Edgeworth to Mrs Edgeworth

Sir John might have pleased Professor Pictet with his fund of knowledge but there was a limit to what Maria Edgeworth could take from him.

We sat round the breakfast table and lingering round the fire in the breakfast room this morning till after one o'clock – Dr Wollaston[1] – Mrs Marcet – Sir John Sebright – Mrs and Dr Somerville conversing most agreeably. Sir John Sebright is certainly a clever man and entertaining when he does not talk all. Mrs Marcet says he is afraid of me and that this keeps him

---

[1]   Chenevix's scientific rival, pursued by Miss Sebright as a potential husband, but in vain.

agreeable. I am glad of it. He has not yet got talking above 2/3ds. His eyebrows are prodigious natural curiosities – color [sic] – size and projection...

Mardoaks, 19th January, 1822

...Sir John Sebright is one of the most entertaining characters I ever saw. He is very clever – very vain – very odd – full of fancies and paradoxes and with abilities to defend them all. He has not as much natural wit as Admiral Pakenham but he has a much greater variety and range of acquirement in literature and science – an excellent chemist – mineralogist – horseman – huntsman – breeder of horses dogs and pigeons. An essay on teaching of dogs, which he published in his huntsman's name and gave to me yesterday is as philosophical an essay as Bentham with Dumont's help could have written on rewards and punishments[2] and a lecture he gave me at breakfast on breaking horses and throwing a horse on his haunches was worthy of the first lecture in Christendom. His maxim is that no violence should ever be used to animals – that all we need to do is teach by gentle degrees the language of signs which tells them what we want them to do. 'Now suppose' turning to Fanny 'you were my horse – I want you to do so and so.' Half the company, including 2 of his daughters, were sneering and suppressing smiles while he was lecturing with great ability upon horsemanship. But alas notwithstanding his philosophical tenderness, principles about dogs and horses I am afraid he has been violent with his children. He has treated his daughters like dogs perhaps and his dogs like children. Certainly they all look under abject awe of him and scarcely speak above their breath when he is within hearing. They have all dogs' faces – dogs' mouths. I think the Pophar[3] would be struck with horror if he were set

---

[2] Refers to a treatise by Jeremy Bentham on a work by a French author, E. Dumont.
[3] Maria Edgeworth's spaniel.

down in the midst of these girls. Miss Sebright is the least disagreeable. There does not seem to be any communication between the sisters. They do not seem to live happily together and in the midst of luxuries and fine house and park this perception chills their guests...

Sir John however amused me incessantly. He is quite a new character strong head and warm heart and oddity enough for ten. He explained to me what is meant by being in the fancy – pigeon fanciers – rabbit fanciers &c. He showed us his pigeons – one which he would not sell for a hundred guineas. He took it up in his hand as he spoke and shewed me its pretty little white head but I could not see the difference between it and one not worth 10 shillings. The pouting pigeons who have goitres as Mrs Marcet said are frightful. They put their heads behind these bags of wind and strut about as if proud of deformity...

Whatever his relations with his family in 1801, the years which elapsed between that year and 1822 showed him a better breeder of pigeons and horses than a dispenser of family happiness, as Maria Edgeworth tells in her letters. At dinner on the night of her visit Sir John at the top of his voice went through all his matrimonial woes. His wife had left him and he attributed her going to the influence of that 'Infamous Madame de Riou (The Countess Rohault[4])'. Sir John had 'misguidedly invited her to Beechwood and who finished up by turning me out of my own house'. It was at Beechwood that Richard Chenevix had met her and although according to Sir John, Chenevix 'spoke of her in the grossest terms in the end he was possessed. I don't know how the devil it happened'.

Other people apparently could have told him. He was a household tyrant and in many ways a bore with his dogs, horses and pigeons and perhaps the entertainment Maria Edgeworth got from his company would not have outlived too big a sample of it.

According to the *DNB* Sir John built and endowed a school at Cheverell's Green, and a row of almshouses for sixteen paupers in the parish of Flamstead, Hertfordshire, where some of the family property

---

[4]   The future Mrs Richard Chenevix.

lay – a testimony to the warm heart Maria Edgeworth perceived in him.

His publications:

A letter to Sir Joseph Banks on *The Art of Improving the Breeds of Domestic Animals*! (1809): *Observations on Hawking, Describing the Mode of Breaking and Managing Several Kinds of Hawks Used in Falconry*, (1826); *Observations upon the Instinct of Animals*! (1836).

Bibliography

BOOKS

Austen, Jane, *Northanger Abbey*, Anne Ephrenpreis [ed.], Harmonsworth, Penguin, 1979

Belloc, Hillaire, *The Hills and the Sea* ('A Family of the Fens' therein), Vintage Books, 1943

Bence Jones, H., *The Royal Institution: its Founders and its First Professors*, London, Longmans Green and Co., 1871

——, H., *Biographie universelle, ancienne et moderne redigé par une societe de gens de lettres et de savants*, Paris, Firmin Didot frères, 1813

Berry, H.F., *A History of the Royal Dublin Society*, London, Longmans, Green & Co., 1915

Biggar, F.J., *The Ulster Land War of 1770 (The Hearts of Steel)*, Dublin, Sealy, Bryers & Walker, 1910

Boatner, M.M., *Cassell's Biographical Dictionary of the American War of Independence, 1763-1783*, 1973

Borgeaud, Charles, *Histoire de l'Université de Geneve*, vols I and II, Geneva, 1900-1959

Brady, Rev. J., *History of the Parishes of the Diocese of Meath*, Meath Chronicle, Mullingar, 1942

British Museum Catalogue of Printed Books

Burke, B., *A Genealogical and Heraldic History of the Landed Gentry of Ireland*, Dublin, Harrison & Sons, 1899

——, B. and Burke, A.P., *A Genealogical and Heraldic History of the Peerage and Baronetage*, Dublin, Harrison & Sons, 1915

Burtchaell, Geo. and Sadleir, Thos. Ulick, [eds] *Alumni Dublinenses, 1593-1846*, Dublin, 1924

Campbell, R.H., *The Carron Company*, Edinburgh, 1961

Caroe, A.D., *The House of the Royal Institution*, London, The Royal Institution of G.B., 1963

Cates, W.L.R., *Dictionary of General Biography*, London, 1881

Chambers' Encyclopaedia, 1959 ed. with 1964 suppl.

Charlesworth, J.K., *The Geology of Ireland*, Edinburgh, Oliver & Boyd, 1935

Chenevix, Richard, *Essay Upon National Character, Being an Inquiry etc.*, London, James Duncan Paternoster Row, 1832

Colchester, Lord Charles, [ed.] *The Diary and Correspondence of Charles Abbot, Lord Colchester*, London, 1861

Colvin, Christina, [ed.] *Maria Edgeworth, Letters from England*, Oxford, Clarendon Press, 1971

Compendium of Irish Biography, Dublin, Webb, 1878

Concise Dictionary of Irish Biography, Dublin, Crone, 1928

Coote, Sir Charles, *Statistical Survey of the County of Armagh etc.*, 1804; reissue, Ballynahinch, Davidson Books, 1984

Dean of Westminster, *The Remains of Mrs Richard Trench, Being Selections from her Journals, Letters & Other Papers*, London, Parker Son & Bourn, 1862

De Beer, Sir Gavin, *The Sciences Were Never At War*, London, 1960

De Mare, E., *The Canals of England*, London, Alan Sutton, 1987

Dictionaire Historique et Biographique, Genève, 1930

Dictionary of American Biography, New York, Scribner, 1928

Dictionary of National Biography, London, OUP, 1992

Dictionary of Scientific Biography, New York, Charles Scribners' Sons

Edgeworth, Maria, *Castle Rack Rent*, London, 1800

Edgeworth, R.L., *Professional Education*, London, J. Johnson, 1808

Edgeworth, R.L., *Readings in Poetry*, London, R. Hunter, 1816

Edgeworth, R.L. and M., *Memoirs of R.L. Edgeworth*, Shannon, Irish University Press, 1969

Ellis, George Edward, *Memoir of Sir Benjamin Thompson, Count Rumford*, Published in connection with and edition of Rumford's complete works by the American Academy of Arts and Sciences, Boston, Estes & Lauriat, 1871

French, Allen, *General Gage's Informers*, New York, Greenwood Press, 1968

Geike, Sir A., *Ancient Volcanoes of Great Britain and Ireland*, London, Macmillan, 1897

Geike, Sir A., *The Founders of Geology*, London, 1897

General Biographical Dictionary, London, Alex. Chambers, 1816

George, Mary D., LittD, *British Museum Catalogue of Political and Personal Satires*, vols VII and VIII

Grand Larousse encyclopédique, en dix volumes, Paris, Libraire Larousse, 1964

Griffith, Richard, *Geological and Mining Surveys of the Coal Districts of the Counties of Tyrone and Antrim*, Dublin, R. Graisberry, Printer to the RDS, 1829

Hadfield, Charles, *The Canals of South West England*, Newton Abbot, 1967

Hall, Sir James, *Essay on the Origin and Principles of Gothic Architecture*, Edinburgh, 1813

Hamilton, Rev. Wm. BD, MRIA, *Letters Concerning the Northern Coast of the County of Antrim, Containing Observations on the Antiquities, Manners and Customs of the County etc.*, Belfast, Simms, 1822

Handley, J.E., *Scottish Farming in the Eighteenth Century*, London

Hare, Augustus J.C., [ed.] *Life and Letters of Maria Edgeworth*, London, Arnold, 1894

Hartnell, Phyllis, *The Concise Oxford Companion to the Theatre*, Oxford, 1972

House and Story, [eds.] *The Letters of Charles Dickens*, vol. I, 1820–1839, Oxford, 1865

Hunt, Harold Capper, *A Retired Habitation*, London, H.K. Lewis & Co., 1932

Hurst, Michael, *Maria Edgeworth & the Public Scene*, London, Macmillan, 1969

Inglis-Jones, Elizabeth, *The Great Maria*, London, Faber & Faber, 1959

Lease, Edmund F., *A Complete History of the Westmeath Hunt*, Dublin, Browne & Nolan, 1898

Leckey, W.E.H., *Ireland in the Eighteenth Century*, London, Longmans, Green & Co., 1892

Le petit Larousse (illustré), Paris

Lyons, John Charles, *Grand Juries of Westmeath*, Ledestown, Ledestown Press, 1890

Mackie, J.D., *The University of Glasgow, (1451–1951)*, Glasgow, 1956

McCutcheon, William Allan, *The Canals of the North of Ireland*, Devon, David and Charles, 1965

McDonagh, Michael, *The Viceroy's Postbag*, London, 1904
Nicholas, R.H., and Wray, F.A., *The History of the Foundling Hospital*, Oxford, 1935
Nouvelle biographie générale, Paris, Firmin Didot frères, 1846–1859
Pictet, Marc-Auguste, *Voyage de trois mois* etc., De l'Impr. de la Bibliotheque Britannique, 1802
Post Office Directory, 1801
Prothero, Rowland E., [ed.] *The Letters Of Edward Gibbon*, Vol. II, London, 1896
Readers' Digest Book of British Birds, London, Readers' Digest, 1969
Smith, Adam, *The Wealth of Nations*, Dent, 1977
Stanhope, Sita and Gooch, G.P., *The life of Charles 3rd Earl of Stanhope*, London, 1914
Taylor, W.B.S., *History of Dublin University*, Dublin, 1845
Thompson, James Alden, *Count Rumford of Massachusetts*, New York, Farrar & Rinehart, 1935
Valentine, Alan, *Lord George Germain*, Oxford, 1962
Von Zittle, Karl A., *History of Geology and Palaeontology*, London, 1907
White, G.H., *The Complete Peerage*, London, 1949
Woodgate M.V., *The Abbé Edgeworth (1745–1807)*, Dublin, Browne & Nolan, 1945
Woods, Jas., *The Annals of Westmeath*, Dublin, Sealy, Bryers & Walker, 1907
Woodward, H.B., *History of the Geological Society of London*, London, 1901
Wright, T. and Evans, R.H., *Historical and Descriptive account of the Caricatures of James Gillray*, (nos. 459 and 520), New York/London, 1965

MISCELLANEA

Journals, Reports, Articles, Transactions, Original Material

Edinburgh Review:
    (a) Pictet, Marc-Auguste, '*Voyage de trois mois*', 1802, vol. III;
    (b) Chenevix, Richard FRSA, MRIA, 'Enquiries concerning the Nature of a Metallic Substance', 1803, vol. IV;
    (c) Thompson, Thomas, 'A System of Chemistry', 1805, vol. IV;

(d) *'American Mineralogical Jnl'*, Jan.-Mar. 1810, vol. XVII;

(e) Davy, Humphry, 'Researches on Oxymuriatic Acid etc.', 1810, vol. XVII;

(f) Chenevix, Richard, FRS & ES, MRIA, 'Two Plays: *Mantuan Revels* and *Henry the Seventh*', 1812, vol. XX;

(g) Buckland, Rev. Wm, 'Geology and Mineralogy Considered with Reference to Natural Theology', 1837, vol. LXV

Chenevix, R., contributions to *'Annales de chimie'* (references: volumes and pages)

vol. XL, p.166;
vol. XLI, p.188;
vol. XLIII, p.326;
vol. XLVI, p.221;
vol. XLIV, p.316;
vol. XLVI, p.274;
vol. XLVI, p.333;
vol. XLVII, p.151;
vol. L, p.173;
vol. LII, p.307;
vol. LIV, p.200;
vol. LIV, p.207;
vol. LXV, pp.5, 113, 225;
vol. LXVI, p 82;
vol. LXIX, p.5

Philosophical Transactions:

(a) Von Rumford; contributions as listed by Pictet. Volumes only: 1781, part I; 1786, part II; 1787, part I; 1787, part II; 1792, part I; 1795, part I (2 contributions); 1795, part II; 1796, part ?; 1797, part ?; 1798, part ?; 1799, part II;

(b) Mills, A., 'Some Account of the Volcanic Appearances in the North of Ireland and Western Islands of Scotland', 1787, vol. XXX;

(c) Mills, A., 'Mineralogical Account of Native Gold discovered in Ireland', 1796, vol. LXXXVI;

(d) Chenevix, Richard, FRSA, FRIA, 'Enquiries Concerning the Nature of... Palladium', 1803, vol. XCIII;

(e) Hyde Wollaston, Wm., MD, FRS, 'On a New Metal Found in Crude Platina', 1804, vol. XCIV;

(f) Chenevix, Richard, FRS, FRIA, 'On the Action of Platina and Mercury on Each Other', 1805, vol. XCV;

(g) Richardson, Rev. Wm, DD, 'Alterations Which Have Taken Place in the Structure of Rocks...', 1808, vol. XCVIII

Journal of Science, Literature and the Arts:

(a) Chenevix, Richard, 'On a New Method of Secret Writing', 1821, vol. X;

(b) Hincks, Rev. Edward A.M., 'On Secret Writing, in Reply to Mr Chenevix's Challenge', 1822, vol. XXII

Transactions of the Royal Irish Academy:

(a) Knox, George, MRIA, LLD, 'Observations on Calp', 1801, vol. III;

(b) Richardson, Rev. Wm, DD, 'Arrangements of the Strata and other Phenomena of the Basaltic Coast of Antrim', 1803, vol. IX;

(c) Richardson, Rev. Wm, DD, 'A Letter to the Bishop of Dromore etc.', 1803, vol. IX

Transactions of the Dublin Society:

(a) Introduction, 1801, vol. I;

(b) Kirolan, R., Esq., 'Report of the Gold Mines of the County of Wicklow with Observations by Mm. Mills, King and Waever', 1801, vol. I;

(c) Higgins, Wm, 'Essay on the Sulphuret or Lime as a Substitute for Potash or a New Method of Bleaching', 1801, vol. I

Clarke, Ernest, 'Agriculture and the House of Russell', *The Journal of the Agricultural Society of England*, Third Series, vol. II, p.123

Ellison, Canon C.C., 'Remembering Dr Beaufort', *Quarterly Bulletin of the Irish Georgian Society*, 1975, vol. XVIII, no.1

Gagnebin, B., 'Les relations entre Genève et l'Angleterre', *Atlantis Magazine*, Zurich, April 1946

Gillray, James, 'Scientific Researches – New Discoveries in Pneumatics – An Experimental Lecture on the Powers of Air', British Museum of Political & Personal Satires, no.9923

McNeill, D.B., *Coastal Passenger Steamers and Inland Navigation in the North of Ireland*, No.3 Handbook, Belfast Museum and Art Gallery, 1960

Reilly, Desmond, 'Richard Chenevix, 1774–1839 [sic], and the Discovery of Palladium', *Journal of Chemical Education*, 1955, vol. XXXII

Richardson, Rev. Wm., DD, 'A Description of the Basaltic Coast from Magilligan to Glenarm', *Newry Magazine*, 1817, Vol. III, no.13

Thompson, G.B., *Drawings of an Irish Wheel Car*, Ulster Museum

Vaucher, J.P., 'Marc-Auguste Pictet', *Bibliothèque universelle*, Geveva, tome XXIX, p.65

'Address of the President, Davies Gilbert', *Proceedings of the Royal Society of London*, 30th Nov. 1830, vol. III, 1830–1837

A Family of the Fens: Hilaire Belloc in Hills and the Sea, Vintage Books, 1941

'Biographical Particulars of the celebrated... M. Chenevix,' *New Monthly Magazine*, 1830, part III, p.40

'Looking Back', *Northern Constitution, Coleraine*, 1968

'Minutes of the Heriot Hospital 17th November, 1800', by courtesy of Mr D. Morris, BL, Solicitors' Clerk & Secretary

Obituary of the Rev. Wm Richardson, DD, *Belfast News Letter*, 1820

'Prospectus 1914–1915', Anderson College of Medicine, Glasgow

'Report of a Meeting of the Managers, 25th May 1801', *Journals of the Royal Institution of Great Britain*, 1801, vol. I

The Lord Mayors of Dublin 1795, National Library, Dublin

Exhibition of Drawings and Water Colours by Cornelius Varley Colnaghi and Co., London, 1973

Information by Mr James McGrath and Mrs Elspeth Simpson, Archivists, Glasgow University

Information on Brompton Row from Mr Melvyn Barnes, DMA, ALA, Borough Librarian and Arts Officer, Central Library, Royal Borough of Kensington & Chelsea.

Information on Ballynacargy (Sonna) Parish from the Very Rev. M. Kilmartin, PP, Ballynacargy; Rev. M. Smyth, Bishop's Secretary, Mullingar, Co. Westmeath

Senior Assistant Archivist, GLC Records Office, County Hall, London